After Jews

After Jews

Essays on Political Theology, Shoah and the End of Man

Piotr Nowak

ANTHEM PRESS

Anthem Press
An imprint of Wimbledon Publishing Company
www.anthempress.com

This edition first published in UK and USA 2026
by ANTHEM PRESS
75–76 Blackfriars Road, London SE1 8HA, UK
or PO Box 9779, London SW19 7ZG, UK
and
244 Madison Ave #116, New York, NY 10016, USA

First published in the UK and USA by Anthem Press in 2022

Copyright © Piotr Nowak 2026

This text is translated into English by Renata Senktas.

The author asserts the moral right to be identified as the author of this work.

All rights reserved. Without limiting the rights under copyright reserved above, no part of this publication may be reproduced, stored or introduced into a retrieval system, or transmitted, in any form or by any means (electronic, mechanical, photocopying, recording or otherwise), without the prior written permission of both the copyright owner and the above publisher of this book.

©Adam Mickiewicz Institute, Warsaw, 2022
This publication has been produced with the financial support of the Polish Ministry of Culture and National Heritage.

Ministry of
Culture
and National
Heritage of
the Republic
of Poland.

British Library Cataloguing-in-Publication Data
A catalogue record for this book is available from the British Library.

Library of Congress Control Number: 2025938725

ISBN-13: 978-1-83999-650-4 (Pbk)
ISBN-10: 1-83999-650-1 (Pbk)

Cover image: "The Tree", by Laura Makabresku

This title is also available as an eBook.

CONTENTS

Preface vii

1. The Chosen Ones (St. Paul) 1
2. The Secret of the Scapegoat (René Girard) 17
3. Making a Jew into a Christian (William Shakespeare) 25
4. There Should Be Time No Longer (D. H. Lawrence) 37
5. To Look Upon His Face and Yet Not Die (Jacob Taubes) 63
6. *Ex oriente lux?* (Joseph Roth, Primo Levi) 81
7. Pilloried by Necessity (Jean Améry) 99
8. German Rubble (W. G. Sebald) 109
9. Long Live! (K. K. Baczyński) 123
10. The Living against the Dead (Czesław Miłosz) 133
11. The Child of War (Friedrich Nietzsche, Krzysztof Michalski) 143
12. Plenty Coups and the End of the World (Jonathan Lear) 165
13. They Refugees (Hannah Arendt) 173
14. The Remainder of Christianity (Vasily Rozanov, Giorgio Agamben, Martin Heidegger) 191

Bibliography 207
Index of Persons 217

PREFACE

Prefaces are always written *ex post* and placed at the beginning, though it is not clear why, since you rarely start with them anyway, and even more rarely end with them. Therefore, prefaces might just as well be put as an extra chapter randomly in the book or abandoned at all. Sometimes, however—such is the case this time—the preface serves the author himself when it allows him to understand what kind of book he wrote and why he did it. That would be the first and by no means the most important reason for its creation. The second reason arises from the demand for such a preface as expressed by internal reviewers, who appreciated my book, yet they independently asked me to explain—to them and the readers—why it was written.

Well, some time ago I read *Journey to Poland*, a forgotten book by the eminent German novelist, author of *Berlin Alexanderplatz*, Alfred Döblin. Döblin, an assimilated Berlin Jew, for whom crossing the Oder and the Lusatian Neisse seemed like crossing some kind of Asian Rubicon, took me on a tour of my own country, albeit one changed by time. We started our journey around Poland a hundred years ago, in the fall of 1924.

First, we went to Warsaw, which was then home to 350,000 Jews occupying the northwestern district of the city. The Jews of Nalewki—I was born in Nalewki and lived most of my life there—seemed to Döblin unlike any human being he had ever met, dressed "in medieval garb, with their own language, religion, and culture."[1] They settled in Poland because Poland was an open country and welcomed the first Jews already in the eleventh century. Nearly a thousand years of growing together!

I walked with Döblin through the Jewish quarter, passing huge fruit stores, Jews who stood in the street as if sleeping, as if not fully awake. The magnificent synagogue in Tłomackie Street was filled to capacity, mostly by middle-class, enlightened, emancipated Jews. Döblin felt more comfortable among them. The upper seats were taken by women. There were far fewer women

---

1. Alfred Döblin, *Journey to Poland*, trans. Joachim Neugroschel (New York: Paragon House, 1991), xii.

than in Catholic churches, as if religious observance was a male occupation among Jews, as if God had nothing to say to women. In the synagogue, everyone—old and young, rich and poor—prays from books, because everyone can read, fertilizing their imagination with meaning, not with pictures that are simply absent from the walls. This is how, says Döblin, I always imagined the Middle Ages. "The liquidation of the Jewish Middle Ages in Eastern Europe commenced during the second half of the previous century. The modern era appeared at the small Jewish town with modern industry and capitalist economy. A chronic crisis began, demanding a readjustment, which was only partly feasible in this country. Emigration reached an enormous scale."[2] We sat down in an ice cream parlor in Leszno Street, where Döblin, taking notebook and pencil in hand, moved on to calculations and statistics. "How many Jews does Poland have?" he asked aloud to himself. "About three million. That's ten percent of the country's population. How many Jews are there in the whole world? Slightly less than fifteen million."[3]

It is puzzling that the Treaty of Versailles, signed a few years earlier, mentioned the Jewish religious minority but not the national identity of the Jews. Although their recognition as a political nation was advocated by most countries during the Paris Conference of 1919, Japan and Australia opposed it, following diplomatic disagreements.[4] It was yet another of the many interventions of the Western hemisphere in the affairs of old Europe, abolishing in fact the *ius publicum europaeum* that had been in force since the Congress of Vienna.[5]

Within the borders of the Republic of Poland, Jews were citizens of the Polish state, but at the same time they constituted its religiously heterogeneous and culturally unassimilated part. After all, there was a lack of unanimity on many fundamental issues within the Jewish community. Jews wanted state subsidies for Jewish schools, but could not decide whether the language of instruction should be Hebrew—the language of Zionists and Orthodox Jews—or Yiddish, spoken by the people, workers, laymen and socialists. They opposed the prohibition of trade on Sunday, disregarding the fact that, after all, they themselves closed their stores on the Sabbath. Döblin cites many similar

---

2. Ibid., 56.
3. Ibid., 57.
4. Carl Schmitt, "The *Großraum* Order of International Law with a Ban on Intervention for Spatially Foreign Powers: A Contribution to the Concept of Reich in International Law (1939–1941)," in *Writings on War*, trans. Timothy Nunan (Cambridge, MA: Polity, 2011), 98.
5. Carl Schmitt, *The Nomos of the Earth in the International Law of Jus Publicum Europaeum*, trans. G. L. Ulmen (New York: Telos Press, 2006), *passim*.

examples. Yet the most important obstacle to the reunion of Jews with the world of Gentiles was religion. It was an unbreakable barrier.

As I walked with him along Okopowa Street—the street where my grandparents lived after the war—I saw the "human river" rushing toward the Jewish cemetery.

That's where the big cemetery is located; it's surrounded by a low red wall; the iron gate is open. Inside, a forecourt with benches occupied by men, mostly in caftans and skullcaps or vizored caps; a few are smoking cigarettes. Along the wall, at the tree trunks, between the trees, men stand, alone or in groups, each man holding a book, murmuring, humming, rocking, shifting from foot to foot. Here, I already notice the grumbling noise that comes from my right, from the cemetery: individual cries, very loud, disjointed talking, also chanting. There must be a large crowd, a very large crowd here; I don't see it as yet. It's like being near a large assembly. Sometimes the singing, calling, the general confused din are so intense that the place sounds like a country fair. The human torrent veers right along the wall. The main current flows between the graves, a broad triumphal avenue. Rich monuments, marble plaques, black and white, loom up here, Hebrew and Polish inscriptions, many only Hebrew, long texts. One high plaque is covered with a scaffolding; the visitors surround the grave, reading, pointing: "Peretz, Peretz." I see another strange monument: a serpent twisting around a tree trunk, plus a broken wheel, a broken wagon shaft. Another gigantic plaque with a long Hebrew text; above it, the gold image of a crowned stag and a hand holding a knife. [...] everything in the cemetery is covered with green grass, with lovely, leveling grass, with rampant meadow flowers, white, red, blue—on the ground lies an elegantly dressed young woman next to an elderly one. The older woman, curled, clinging tight to the bottom of the headstone (I can't see her face, her head and shoulders are covered by a large black shawl), she screams, calls, calls, moans. She calls, in Yiddish: "Father, our beloved father, you were such a good man, you sat next to me in the room, all these years, in the shop. I've stayed here. I'm here. Help me to get the children to study so that they'll be well off. Life is hard. Life is so hard, Sarah is here. We're not well off. Why did you die, for us. I didn't do anything bad to you." Now and then, the younger woman sits up, blows her nose, wipes her eyes, lies down again. [...] They lie on the graves, weeping, lamenting, accusing themselves, calling, appeasing the dead. Many call in a simple tone of pain and lament. Many women use a liturgical singsong, similar to the chanting in temple. This is the place where they pray aloud; the divine service of the women is over the graves. The men with the prayer books stand upright, murmuring, bowing earnestly and solemnly; at their feet, the women and the girls huddle in the grass, lamenting, moaning, emitting the shrill singsong."[6]

Döblin could not have known that the Germans would murder this city, that they would crush it into dust. After all, he himself was German. Nor could he have known that he would be forced to emigrate. The first to burn down in 1943 was the Jewish quarter. A year later the rest of the city was destroyed. Those who survived the uprising were expelled. One million people were allowed to take as much as they could carry. Only the Jewish cemetery survived. Germans left it intact. No matzevot were used to strengthen trenches, no graves were plundered. Why it happened so—I do not know. And yet it happened. It remains a mystery to me.

For Jews, the cemetery was the center of their lives. In the cemetery, the dead interceded for the living, helped them, took care of them. Today, it is them—the dead—who must be helped. Little thought is given to what remained of them; they are consigned to oblivion. The dead who are not remembered by anyone die "the second death" (Rev. 21:8), disperse and perish forever. That is why we need to remember. When something remains of them, it is most powerfully deposited in individuals, even more powerfully than the "memory" contained in inherited objects or institutions established for its cultivation.

Jews had lived here for a thousand years. Then they were killed. In this book—or through it—I would like to restore something of their lives, to save those lives, to commemorate them somehow. I want to remind the reader what the idea of chosenness meant in the Jewish religion and what it still means. Following St. Paul, I point out the antinomies in it, later picked up by writers and thinkers such as Friedrich Nietzsche, D. H. Lawrence, Jacob Taubes or René Girard. In the chapters on William Shakespeare, Joseph Roth and Primo Levi, I explain the reasons why the Shoah could only happen under the conditions of late capitalism rather than in the atmosphere of primitive pogroms, the violent expulsion of Jews from their Anatevkas.

An important point of reference for my reflections is the postulates of the representatives of the Frankfurt School—I am thinking in particular of Max Horkheimer and Theodor W. Adorno's *Dialectic of Enlightenment*—who were the first to draw attention to the potentially criminal character of instrumental reason, disavowing at the same time the tradition of the *siècle des Lumières*, the approach that I am somehow inclined toward. Yet they looked for the causes of the Shoah not where these could be found, either in the "authoritarian

---

6. Döblin, *Journey to Poland*, 63–65.

personality" or in the difficulties of living, in the so-called social question. However, in order to understand what happened to the Jews in Central and Eastern Europe in the 1940s, one must resort to a language completely different from psychological, social, economic or police discourse. We must resort to the forgotten language—or better said, the language that is being forgotten—of theology, especially political theology. It is there, I claim, that one can find the right interpretative tools. It does not belong to the realm of superstition but is our last chance to understand what happened to the world yesterday and what is happening to it today. "It was the devil!" writes Alain Besançon, a witness of those times, "He was the one who communicated his inhuman personality to his subjects."[7] I do not know this for sure—maybe yes, maybe no. I do know, however, that it is good that a theological category—the concept of the devil, Antichrist—is returning to the philosophical and, more broadly, social and political discourse. The devil, Antichrist is not just a metaphor or a creature with a limp in the left leg and charred wings; it is rather the atmosphere we live in, manifesting itself in turning traditional values inside out, in replacing respect with tolerance, charity with dubious philanthropy, love with sex, family with any social organization, religion with science, freedom with safety, and so on. Examples abound.

In my book I renew the sense of such theological concepts as eternity, salvation—I have already mentioned the category of the chosen ones—apocalypse, hope. I give an account of contemporary social phenomena such as the immigrant crisis or the increasingly aggressive attitude of Western civilization toward people of strong faith, which may fill us with anxiety and make us think of the recurrence of the Shoah.

In the chapter on Krzysztof Kamil Baczyński, Polish poet of Jewish descent, I indicate the unobvious connections between Polishness and Jewishness, I reflect on the common fate of these two nations, and between the lines I ask why the good Lord God took us, Poles, to be the witnesses of the Shoah.

There are no more Jews in Poland. They had been murdered by the German Nazis, and those who survived were expelled by the Polish communists after the war. We live in a world "after Jews." Now we must tell ourselves what it means to us. It is important for them and for us. Important for the world.

---

7. Alain Besançon, *A Century of Horrors: Communism, Nazism, and the Uniqueness of the Shoah*, trans. Ralph H. Hancock and Nathaniel H. Hancock (Wilmington: ISI Books, 2007), 58.

The landlady was standing in my room, and was shooing away a swarm of birds from a tree that stood in the middle of my room. She clapped her hands, and the birds took to the air, and everything went dark…
(Thomas Bernhard, *Frost*)

Chapter 1

THE CHOSEN ONES (ST. PAUL)

And I will say to *them which were* not my people, Thou *art* my people.

(Hos 2:23)[1]

For though thy people Israel be as the sand of the sea, *yet* a remnant of them shall return.

(Isa. 10:22)

I

Whenever we deal with a significant philosophical or theological text, it is good to first establish both its author and its addressee. The author of the *Epistle to the Romans* (the possible date of origin being 57 or 58 years after Christ, the beginning of Nero's reign) is naturally Paul the Apostle, which is a historically proven authorship. Here is how an anonymous writer of the second century of the new era described him: "A man small in size, with meeting eyebrows and a rather large nose, bald-headed, bow-legged, strongly built, full of grace; for at times he looked like a man, and at times he had the face of an angel."[2] But whom did St. Paul address in his writings? Which Romans did he write to, if most of the paragraphs were addressed directly to the Jews? Well, St. Paul addressed his words to Christians (even though the term had not yet been known) as well as potential neophytes who inhabited Rome (it is in this sense that the term "Romans" is used here) and, therefore, to both Jews and Gentiles. Why to the inhabitants of that particular city and not any other? Because in those days Rome played a role similar to that of New York today, namely, a kind of center of the world, its most

---

1. All italicized emphases in quotes throughout the book are original, unless stated otherwise.
2. Tim Dowley (ed.), *Introduction to the History of Christianity* (Minneapolis, MN: Fortress Press, 2013), e-book.

blood-supplied part. It should be noted that the first Christian communities consisted almost entirely of Christianized Jews, and that Christianity was regarded as a result of tensions within the Mosaic religion, like a family quarrel of a strictly religious, Jewish character, and thus something regular at that time. Even when St. Paul traveled through the vast territories of Asia Minor, fulfilling his missionary service, he would stay primarily at the houses of Jews scattered all over the world. Despite the tension between the new and the old faith, he worshiped Christ within the walls of synagogues. This had not bothered anyone until it was discovered that what is inbred in Christianity (unlike in Judaism) is its proselytism, that is, winning others over, often violently, to the side of the new faith. But it was not Christian proselytism, or at least not just that, that was a bone of contention between Orthodox Jews and Christians. The gist of it boiled down to the question of whether Christ was the real messiah awaited by all religious Jews (which is a pleonasm, for there are no nonreligious Jews) or "the greatest sinner" (which is how the rabbinical tradition defines Him), a cheeky usurper, a juggler and miracle worker like many who rambled about the Roman Empire. Therefore, it was not a question of whether or not God exists, whether or not He fulfills the promise, whether He is the Creator of the visible world or has nothing to do with it. The dispute carried on, as it still does, about the divinity of the Crucified One and the political ("worldly") meaning of the Crucifixion and the Resurrection. Anyhow, the external tension between Jews and Christians was also reflected inside the Christian community that was divided into a "better" Jewish table and a "worse" Gentile table. "I'm not sure about this," writes Jacob Taubes, "but I don't think that Peter ever agreed to a common table fellowship. I can't imagine that from the point of view of Jerusalem, of the Jerusalem he came from."[3]

Out of Paul's rich epistolography (unluckily, he wrote 13 letters, although some argue it was 14), the *Epistle to the Romans* is the most expressive one, the richest in strictly theological and political themes, both essential to Christianity. It was written in Greek, the language used by the Jewish minority in Rome (only 1 percent of Jews spoke Hebrew and Aramaic). One can find in it some indications of the conditions that had to be met to deserve either condemnation or salvation. St. Paul emphasizes, for instance, that it is not ethnic but spiritual descent from Abraham that is necessary for salvation. Moreover, he discusses the problem of free will of God and man, sin, attitude to the flesh, and many other issues. Let us consider some of them.

---

3. Jacob Taubes, *The Political Theology of Paul*, trans. Dana Hollander (Stanford, CA: Stanford University Press, 2004), 19.

II

The *Epistle to the Romans* starts with the key question of salvation to which St. Paul would return many times throughout his letter. We read that the Jews will be saved first, then the Gentiles, that is, the Greeks. One must bear in mind that Paul is not building any hierarchical system here. He is not saying: we go first, and then you will follow, after us, to Heaven. He is saying something else: it is those whom God chose and made a covenant with (Jews) that will be saved first, then there will come a time for those who hate Jews and do not love God. Historians of antiquity point out that, contrary to popular belief, it was not the Romans but the Greeks who harbored an irreconcilable anger against Jews. "If our apostle was badly received in Athens," writes Emile Cioran,

> if he found there a society contemptuous of his lucubrations, it is because in Athens men were still *arguing*, because skepticism, far from abandoning, still defended its positions. In Athens, the Christian gibberish could get nowhere; on the other hand, it was to seduce Corinth, a vulgar city inimical to dialectic.[4]

St. Paul repays the Greeks. What primarily interests him are the Gentiles' corrupt customs that are the subject of his uncompromising, fundamental criticism in the early part of the *Epistle*. The Gentiles close the door on God, although they could easily know Him, if they wanted to, because God has revealed Himself to the world and in it. The Greeks, therefore, are stupid—they have stubborn heads and stony hearts. They seek *sacrum* in the guts of birds, tetrapods and amphibians. They are malicious and perfidious; their behavior stems from the perversity of dialectical reason. Covetous, wicked, disobedient to parents, calumnious, traitorous—these are just selected epithets addressed to them by St. Paul. And their gods are no different. Simply put, both deserve *death* (Rom. 1:32). In this case, however, God's righteous wrath is balanced by His mercy.

The question remains, what to do with those who live decent, pious lives while they do not know God? "For when the Gentiles, which have not the law, do by nature the things contained in the law, these, having not the law, are a law unto themselves"[5] (Rom. 2:14). What St. Paul refers to is the natural law, the innate ability to distinguish between good and evil, which is shared in by the righteous Gentiles who were included in the spiritual order long before the birth of the

---

4. Emil Cioran, *The Temptation to Exist*, trans. Richard Howard (New York: Arcade, 2012), 171.
5. All biblical quotations are after *The Holy Bible: Containing the Old and New Testaments* (Oxford: Oxford University Press, 1901).

Son of God. Therefore, it turns out that the act of salvation is retroactive and embraces those who, so to say, prepared the ground for Christianity, like Plato.

Let us proceed to the paradoxes embedded in the *Epistle to the Romans*. The first one is that God chose his own Son as an offering to Himself. Why He is sacrificing the Son to Himself, why this should be an expression of God's righteousness (Rom. 3:25), I do not know for sure, but I have a feeling that it might be regarded as an *act of highest self-denial*. For self-denial makes sense only when it is total, complete. In this act, God shows that He loves man to the extent that He does not hesitate a moment to sacrifice the one who is closest to Him in order to redeem human sins. "The Epistle to the Hebrews," notes Sergio Quinzio, "speaks of a perfect sacrifice in which the offering, the one who offers it and the one to whom it is offered are one and the same, one God."[6] That is all very well, but why is Christ to be given as prey to the Cross, the most degrading instrument of torture at that time? Because it is in Him and through Him that the body, the foundation of sin, must be destroyed. "Knowing this, that our old man is crucified with *him*, that the body of sin might be destroyed, that henceforth we should not serve sin. For he that is dead is freed from sin" (Rom. 6:6–7). In Christ, the human body, fortuitous and impermanent, is destroyed. The death of the body—physical, exposed to temptations—is to be a necessary but still an insufficient condition for salvation. What is a sufficient condition? In other words, what will suffice to be saved? "Only" faith, *sola fide*. "Therefore we conclude that a man is justified by faith without the deeds of the law" (Rom. 3:28). Can everyone believe? Is faith given to everyone? Probably not, that is, it is only given to those on whom the act of grace is conferred. Can one pray for grace or order it for someone else? A positive answer to this question would come from Pelagians. Generally, Pelagianism was such an optimistic, bright version of Christianity. Its creator, Pelagius, maintained that humans are good and can do good without God's help, even without divine grace, that they can certainly deserve divine grace by their good works or obtain it by good behavior and a virtuous life. God would never impose on man a burden beyond his strength (consequently, Pelagius also questioned the concept of original sin), otherwise He would seek man's punishment rather than man's salvation.[7] St. Jerome saw in Pelagius "that corpulent dog, weighed down with Scotch porridge,"[8] someone for whom Christianity is a technique of life and not a way—the only way—to salvation. But in fact it was St. Augustine who was filled with

---

6. Sergio Quinzio, *La sconfitta di Dio*, translated from the Polish edition: *Przegrana Boga* (Kraków: Homini, 2008), 60.
7. Paul Johnson, *A History of Christianity* (New York: Touchstone, 2014), e-book.
8. Ibid.

an intense aversion to his peer. He maintained (probably in the spirit of St. Paul's *Epistle*) that man was permanently corrupted by original sin and that only grace would help him reestablish his understanding of good and evil and make him capable of choosing between them at all. Can everyone be blessed with grace? Why, of course not! Only those predestined by God. The rest—the rest of the "animals" incapable of moral qualification—will be denied grace because the number of admissions to heaven is strictly limited: there will be as many saved as there are vacancies left by the fallen angels. Is that not at odds with God's mercy and justice, and especially with its earthly, "political" understanding? Well, we cannot say anything clear about it. Having no insight into God's thoughts, we do not know whether or not something is godly and just for Him, and—even worse—we do not know whether our concepts of godliness and ungodliness coincide with His understanding of these concepts. God is unfathomable; therefore, there is no point behaving like a top student before Him, doing one's best to please Him, as did Pelagius, because "God imputeth righteousness without works" (Rom. 4:6). We never really know upon whom God bestows His favor and what for, upon whom His all-seeing eye rests. "But Esaias is very bold, and saith," says St. Paul, "I was found of them that sought me not; I was made manifest unto them that asked not after me" (Rom. 10:20). In any case, if man—and only him—is granted the ability to distinguish between good and evil, then it is time to get up, wake up, sleep no more, abandon sluggishness and moral indifference, for "now *it is* high time to wake out of sleep" (Rom. 13:11). All right then, but how to choose good, if I do not choose it even when I want it but incline instead toward the evil that I do not want? (Rom. 7:19). And why do I incline toward evil? It turns out that it dwells in me; I have an excess of it (Rom. 7:21). This evil is ontological; it is not the result of my wrong decision or my wicked calculation. This evil is death. My whole existence gravitates toward it. It is death, being evil, which is that original sin inherited from the first man ("Adam"). Even if I did not deserve it, I still have no chance to resist its effect. Being a human, I live in "Adam"; enjoying God's grace, I live in Christ. Through the Cross (let me put it in a different way), thanks to the "consciousness" I have of my own death, I renew the relationship with myself. I also renew my relationship with God, since the consequences of original sin are eradicated on the Cross. "A result of the Cross," as René Girard puts it, "re-established the direct relationship between man and God, which has been interrupted by the original sin."[9] "For the wages of sin *is* death; but the gift of God *is* eternal life"

---

9. René Girard with Pierpaolo Antonello and João Cezar de Castro Rocha, *Evolution and Conversion: Dialogues on the Origins of Culture* (London: Bloomsbury, 2017), 148.

(Rom. 6:23). St. Paul refers to the provisions of Roman statute law, according to which slaves could receive payment for their work, a *peculium*, a necessary condition to purchase their freedom. Here, the condition of liberation—and yet another paradox of the *Epistle to the Romans*—is death, that "wages of sin" that the author speaks about.[10]

Evil entered man through the risk of death, through time that is the master of his body. The flesh, or more generally the corporality tangled up in a web of desires (Rom. 8:6), is sinful. "So then they that are in the flesh cannot please God," writes Paul (Rom. 8:8). Therefore, perhaps one should not particularly hasten the death of the body, nor there seems to be any point in hampering its decay (the motif is easily recognizable, for it is constantly present in Plato's *Phaedo*). Hence the postulates of asceticism: not to carouse, not to drink, to spare oneself in relations with women, to be free of quarrel and envy (Rom. 13:13); however, should it not be the other way round—the more one lives, the faster one wears out? Human sins will be accounted for individually, because they constitute the history of man, the "human comedy," at the same time they individualize him (Rom. 14:12). They are mine, just like my death is *mine* and not someone else's, like my body.

The body (*sarks*) is always on the move (also when it ages), that is, it "heads for" transfiguration, for resurrection, as shown by the torment and execution of Christ. The transfiguration of His body occurs in two steps. In the first, sin is destroyed through destroying the human flesh, through its "crucifixion" (Rom. 8:3). Christ is God, still He suffers like a human. In the second, however, Christ is reborn in a different body, in a different land, a reality transfigured by death and resurrection. Now it is man who "incarnates" in God, just like before God incarnated in man. The effects of that mystery, the effects of that "bodily" transformation are sometimes terrible and even traumatic. Let me remind you of Saul on his road to Damascus. When he saw Christ altered in form, the risen Christ, he experienced an ecstatic nystagmus (according to *The Acts of the Apostles*, he simply went blind)! This leads us to the conclusion that miracles are not to be watched; miracles are to be either attended or ignored. "In the human body that he gives himself—in this man, and woman, that he gives himself as a body—the creator doesn't reproduce his own image. The creator's strength comes from the original deconstruction of any recognizable image."[11] On the road to Damascus or later, especially under the fingers of the doubting Thomas, Christ revealed himself to the world in a

---

10. See Craig S. Keener, *Komentarz historyczno-kulturowy do Nowego Testamentu*, trans. into Polish by Zbigniew Kościuk (Warszawa: Vocatio, 2000), 323.
11. Jean-Luc Nancy, *Corpus*, trans. Richard A. Rand (New York: Fordham University Press, 2008), 63.

"deconstructed" body, devoid of any connection with corporality, that is, with its human dimension (which, again, is a paradox).

Man is a combination of two principles—dark and light, bodily and spiritual. He carries evil (Rom. 7:23), but he also embraces light. "But if the Spirit of him that raised up Jesus from the dead dwell in you, he that raised up Christ from the dead shall also quicken your mortal bodies by his Spirit that dwelleth in you" (Rom. 8:11). The spirit that is spoken about here is grace, God's seed sown in the sinful soul of man. The fact that these two principles both coexist and clash in man gave rise to Gnosticism.

"Being then made free from sin," writes St. Paul, "ye became the servants of righteousness. I speak after the manner of men because of the infirmity of your flesh: for as ye have yielded your members servants to uncleanness and to iniquity unto iniquity; even so now yield your members servants to righteousness unto holiness. For when ye were the servants of sin, ye were free from righteousness" (Rom. 6:18–20). We already know a little bit about what it means that man was made the servant of righteousness. As I mentioned earlier, one is delivered from sin through a kind of "payment" (*peculium*)—first through one's own death, then through the redemptive death of Christ. This is the meaning of the first sentence in the excerpt quoted above. On the other hand, to be a slave to righteousness is nothing but to submit to God's judgments that will be executed sooner (here on Earth? it seems unlikely) or later (at the Last Judgment). Does Paul appear to be a dialectician when he presents slavery as freedom and freedom as a state of slavery? Are we dealing with yet another paradox in which his writings abound? Well, not at all. The point here is that justice, if it is not an empty word, must be inevitable.

Another paradox, a kind of moral peculiarity that does not accord with our common perception of life, is to make a sacrifice for one's enemy. Surely each of us knows someone for whom we would give our life. The Jews allowed this form of sacrifice, though such a "substitution" did not seem anything worth boasting about at that time. Meanwhile, Christ dies (also) for the enemies, (also) for their glory (Rom. 5:6–7), because—as it was written—He is Lord both of life and death, the living and dead (Rom. 14:9). I wonder what it means that He is Lord of the dead? In what sense is He their Lord? Is He like the mythological Cerberus who lets some out to live while refusing this to others, the sinful ones? What power, then, would sacrifice have, or salvation, if its character were—as St. Augustine has it—selective from the outset? And of what living ones will Christ be Lord—those who inhabit heaven, or rather of all believers who stay alive for the time of His (still projected and awaited) Second Coming? More and more puzzles.

The next question, "how to believe?", is seemingly rhetorical. If there are so many unbelievers around us, it means that faith is not an easy thing.

"Happy *is* he that condemneth not himself in that thing which he alloweth," says St. Paul (Rom. 14:22). It turns out that one needs not only strong nerves but also a strong determination to be a Christian. Moreover, this resolution should be strengthened by ritual. One needs a kind of deafness or rather blindness: in other words, credit given to the new faith is a necessary condition if one wants to consider it one's own or at least something worthy of apologia. Beware, though: the point is not that one should believe in everything that can be believed, for such a stance would be little different from a complete lack of faith. The point is to believe Paul, to change your skeptical pagan consciousness that maintains that "it's impossible" into a religion of the heart, into genuine repentance and humility. But then you are already dead to the world, since a Christian no longer cares about his or her problems ("politics").

III

Let me now turn to the issue that kindles the imagination of all sorts of anti-Semites—the question of the chosen nation (Rom. 3:1).

It is worth knowing that the parents of St. Paul, or actually Saul of Tarsus, were educated Orthodox Jews who spoke to each other in Greek, Syrian and Hebrew. In his youth, Saul studied the Torah with Rabbi Gamaliel, the most distinguished rabbi in Jerusalem. Then for some time (strictly speaking, until his conversion) he was a zealous Pharisee persecuting Christians. Therefore, I am hardly surprised when that *Christian teaches the Jews* which one of them is a good, real Jew and which one is pretending to be a Jew (Rom. 2:28–29). It is commonly believed that Jewishness is determined by circumcision, which is regarded as the sign, the seal of covenant made with not just anybody but God Himself (Rom. 4:11). Paul does not question this. He argues, however, that it is not the actual circumcision but its spiritual dimension that seals the covenant.

The covenant, and thus a kind of bilateral contract, is binding upon both sides. God took a liking to the people of Israel, and His decision will remain inexplicable, just like love—we do not know why God loved the Jews, nor do we know what for. We only know that he had decided to keep his word (Rom. 4:21), as evidenced by the story of two old people—Abraham and Sarah—whose "dead bodies," as God had promised them, brought forth exceedingly numerous offspring (Abraham is considered to be the father of all Jews). In brief, Israel (in the person of Abraham) is a historically attested God's interference in history, in the sense of being an "empirical," tangible intervention of God in *historia profana*. In his fairy tale titled "The People of Israel, or the Consequences of Unselfishness," Leszek Kołakowski warns against this type of love:

Let us not rely on unselfish feelings. Rather, let us count on reciprocity, not kindness. Let us accept promises only when the maker of the promise knows that we can return the kindness. Dozens of philosophers, Thomas Hobbes in particular, have substantiated the validity of this rule of conduct—to say nothing of everyday life. Let us count solely on the fact that we shall receive only as much as we ourselves give.[12]

In the *Epistle* of Paul we are informed on Jews' extraordinary respect for the law. However, let me here refer to Jacob Taubes's doubts: "I'm not qualified (it's not so easy, I think) to sort out what Paul means when he says 'law.' Does he mean the Torah [the Pentateuch, but also Hebrew for 'teaching' or 'instruction'], does he mean the law of the universe, does he mean natural law?"[13] Anyway, when one agrees upon something with God, especially when one enters into a compact with Him, one must not depart from the arrangements but follow them to the letter. This is why the religious rite is performed in great detail and the Torah is read meticulously, for a slip of a single letter might have a lamentable effect on the whole world. One may say that it was only with the revelation of the Law and the strict observance of its principles that a Jew would become a Jew, and more generally—man, because it was the Law itself that enabled moral evaluation, the fundamental feature of human condition. This, I suggest, is how the sentence about sin that came with the Law might be interpreted (Rom. 7:9). Nietzsche, himself no doubt a Gentile, would probably add here—"for the law existed so that sins might be committed"[14]—that sin was invented by none other than the Jews, or that it is due to their influence that we are still afraid of "the politics of Yahweh" who, as seen from a human standpoint, can unjustifiably either elevate or throw one into the abyss of despair. The same conclusion—that God's reasons cannot be revealed, let alone translated into human reason—comes from Jacob Taubes who contemplates the question why God hated Esau and took a liking to Jacob already in their mother's womb. "So it can't be a matter of the deeds. It's already determined in the womb, that's election! [God's election] Dreadful things, one would ask in a modern vain: how can it be decided already in the womb, where is God's righteousness here?"[15] But Paul criticizes not only the Jewish Torah. He is equally passionate in his attack on the institutions

---

12. Leszek Kołakowski, *Tales from the Kingdom of Lailonia and the Key to Heaven*, trans. Salvator Attanasio (Chicago: University of Chicago Press, 1989), 97–98.
13. Taubes, *The Political Theology of Paul*, 24.
14. Friedrich Nietzsche, *Daybreak: Thoughts on the Prejudices of Morality* (§ 68), trans. R. J. Hollingdale (Cambridge: Cambridge University Press, 1997), 41.
15. Taubes, *The Political Theology of Paul*, 48.

of Roman law that he perceives as the devil's tools by means of which "the human province" is subdued. Perhaps Nietzsche was right when he claimed that Paul had not fitted into any of the normative systems in force at the time, that he could not comply with any of the laws known to him, be it sacred law or statute law. Had it been so, the figure of St. Paul may well pass as the archetype of a revolutionary unbinding the world from the shackles of first the old and then the new law.[16] For no revolutionary is satisfied with just destroying the state of affairs that they found themselves in. In the second step, they turn to what they have created—the flame of revolution engulfs everything and burns eternally. No wonder then that authors such as Alain Badiou or the aforementioned Jacob Taubes stressed the radically non-evangelical nature of the Pauline message, its separate logic, "revolutionary in spirit."

St. Paul loves his nation, yet revises the rules of belonging to it, and he does it in a significant way. Being aware of Jesus's Jewish roots (Rom. 9:5), he still emphasizes the universal nature of His teaching, His personality and His life. According to Paul, the true Jews are Christians, the orthodox heirs of the Jewish tradition. One does not become an Israeli citizen due to physical circumcision, blood ties, or because one particularly deserves it, but by God's disposition. Even a Greek can be a Jew if such is God's will. But how? How come? By requesting accession to the Christian community, a community that is open to all parts of the world and accepts everyone who believes that Christ is the Son of God, long awaited by Jews. "This is no blood kinship, but a kinship of the promise!"[17] "Because not all who descend from Israel are Israel. That is the key sentence. This means: this 'all' according to flesh is not identical to the 'all' according to the promise."[18] In this way, Jewish exclusivism, the conviction of one's own uniqueness coupled with closing doors on foreign religious trends and a strict observance of the Law, is transformed into Christian universalism, a religion available to everyone, like bread. "For there is no difference between the Jew and the Greek: for the same Lord over all is rich unto all that call upon him" (Rom. 10:12). Hence one more paradox of the *Epistle*: "God's state" is built by Christians so that they can become Jews (i.e., those elected by God, according to St. Paul). Therefore, "When a Jew becomes Christian, we have one more Christian, but we don't have one less Jew."[19] This is rather obvious,

---

16. See Alain Badiou, *Saint Paul: The Foundation of Universalism*, trans. Ray Brassier (Stanford: Stanford University Press, 2003).
17. Taubes, *The Political Theology of Paul*, 28.
18. Ibid., 48.
19. Franz König and Ernst Ludwig Ehrlich, Żydzi i chrześcijanie jedną mają przyszłość [Jews and Christians Share One Future], interview by Bernhard Moosbrugger (Kraków: Wydawnictwo Znak, 2001), 101–2.

since the conversion of all Jews to Christianity (i.e., those who only pretend to be Jews) is the condition for the world to be saved. "And so all Israel [those who believe that Christ is the Messiah; i.e. not the Synagogue, but the Church] shall be saved: as it is written"[20] (Rom. 11:26). This is the reason for Christian, especially Catholic, proselytism in the hopeless work of converting followers of the Mosaic Law into the New Law. Why this mission is without hope is explained by Constantin Noica during one of his long walks around Păltiniş:

> The people of Israel has a wall which it does *not* want, but still does nothing to pass beyond it. The wall of the people of Israel is a wall which limits against their will, a wailing wall which is in fact everywhere, in Cracow as much as in Jerusalem. The people of Israel does not want to move its being from where it is, along with the wall. This wall, experienced in its negative aspect, as a wall of tears, is not attempted in the sense of transcending it.[21]

The conversion of both the Gentiles and the Jews is a mystery, because it is not known how it is going to happen (Rom. 11:25). One thing, however, is certain: that "the conversion of the Jews is to ensue before the end of the world."[22] Jews are righteous, and the Gentiles are happy and wise, but only the Christians (i.e., Gentile converts and true "Jews") will be saved. And it was this hope that Paul clung to: "For Paul, the task at hand is the establishment and legitimation of a new people of God. This doesn't seem very dramatic to you, after two thousand years of Christianity. But it is the most dramatic imaginable in a Jewish soul."[23]

The story of St. Paul is that of liberating the free spirit from the closed, and in this sense the *limiting* Jewish tradition in a totally new, undefined direction—and therefore an uncertain one. Paul teaches that no form of tradition is forever settled, and if it is, it constitutes a form of oppression for those who try to rummage for some traces of life (God's life) under the surface of dogma

---

20. It seems that a living example of Jewish-Christian reconciliation "in the flesh" is Cardinal Jean-Marie Lustiger, the Archbishop of Paris, for whom Jews and Christians are guided by the same mission "to carry out their mission toward humankind, through vigilance and testimony." Jean-Marie Lustiger, *The Promise*, trans. Rebecca Howell Balinski, Msgr. Richard Malone and Jean Duchesne (Grand Rapids: William B. Eerdmans, 2007), 160.
21. Gabriel Liiceanu, *The Păltiniş Diary: A Paideic Model in Humanist Culture*, trans. James Christian Brown (Budapest: Central European University Press, 1999), 153.
22. Commentary on *The New Testament*, in *Pismo Święte Starego i Nowego Testamentu: Nowy Testament*, eds. Michał Peter and Marian Wolniewicz (Poznań: Księgarnia św. Wojciecha, 1975), 375.
23. Taubes, *The Political Theology of Paul*, 28.

and rituals. Seen from this perspective, Christianity is no longer the enemy of Judaism. Quite the reverse, it appears to be an originally Jewish response to the oppression of the official, dogma-oriented religion of the Pharisees and the Zealots. "I read the Epistle to the Romans," writes Taubes, "as a legitimation and formation of a new social union—covenant ([Ver]Bund), of the developing ecclesia against the Roman Empire, on the one hand, and, on the other hand, of the ethnic unity of the Jewish people"[24]—toward, let me add, universalism and utter openness to what is different or even hostile ("love your enemies"). It is only by creating a new religion, a new bond (from the Latin *religio*, "bond") that St. Paul could come closer to and also, in a way, be like his greatest political and religious competitor, no, not Jesus, but Moses. By going out into the wilderness, Moses starts a *new* People of God, whereas Paul wants to start his people *anew*. Obedient to the dead law, the "old Jews" mark time, do not move on, while the "new Jews," those who proclaim the divinity of Christ, represent a genuinely new opening. Let me illustrate it with a wonderful anecdote from Taubes's book:

> I have a very good friend—now he's a bishop in Stockholm, he used to be a professor at Harvard, where I knew him well—Krister Stendhal. And I remember (I'm telling you this as a personal story), he visited me once in New York and we were standing in front of a very large fireplace. And Krister—he's a real warrior type, you know, Goebbels would have envied him his figure—he says to me that his deepest worry is whether he belongs (we were speaking English) to the "commonwealth of Israel." So I said to myself, Krister, you super-Aryan from Sweden, at the end of the world, as viewed from the Mediterranean, other worries you don't have? No, he has no other worries! There I saw what Paul had done: that someone in the jungles of Sweden—as seen from where I'm standing—is worrying about whether he belongs to the "commonwealth of Israel," "that's something that's impossible without Paul."[25]

IV

"At bottom there was only one Christian, and he died on the cross,"[26] wrote Nietzsche. The Christian message, and especially St. Paul's epistolary legacy, is to him an area just as worth studying as it is vulnerable to the pamphleteer's gall. According to Nietzsche, it is a religion of slaves, an organization uniting

---

24. Ibid., 117.
25. Ibid., 41.
26. Friedrich Nietzsche, *The Antichrist*, trans. H. L. Mencken (Mineola: Dover, 2018), 38.

the sick-in-the-soul, the powerless, losers in this world, because it makes passivity a virtue, subordination to otherworldly forces—an imperative, and resentment—a flywheel of history, and lastly, derives eternal life from death. Who is responsible for this state of affairs? Who caused it? Christ, perhaps? No, not Him. Having incarnated in man, He proved that man is the highest value, namely, that the truth about life should be sought in this world, not a world made up by this or that apostle. "That God became man," says Nietzsche, "shows only that man is not to seek his bliss in eternity, but shall found his heaven on earth."[27] Nietzsche's understanding of the teaching of Christ is that it is but another technique of a good life, leading to its inner transformation, to the spiritualization of life. And so is the case with death. "'This bearer of glad tidings' died as he lived and *taught*—*not* to 'save mankind,' but to show mankind how to live."[28] Who, then, is responsible for the image of Christianity as we know it today, the image perpetuated with pitiful consistency for two thousand years? St. Paul, naturally. It was him, figuratively speaking, who nailed his Lord to the Cross, making the Crucifixion a truth about salvation that applies to all inhabitants of the Earth. It was him who added fuel to the flames of revolution that had lasted two thousand years. This does not mean, as Nietzsche further argues, that St. Paul falsified some truth communicated to people by Christ, the truth about the Beginning. Such a truth does not exist, he claims, because it never did.

> Christianity is not a process of lapsing from an initial truth which has been gradually lost along the way. Its life stems, rather, from very different roots, which from the time of first contact took over the alien root of Jesus in distorted form. [...] First of all, instead of the real Jesus, *the image of Jesus* was put forward: a fanatic, an aggressor fighting against priests and theologians; then, in Paul's interpretation, the figure of the savior, in which only death and resurrection remained important.[29]

The Christianity we know is therefore governed by its own logic and its own inertia. Its source is the "good news," that is, a distorted message about the death and activity of Jesus Christ. Against the background of Roman power, St. Paul leading the army of the first Christians, mostly Jewish converts and slaves, appears to be a weak figure—without actual political influence,

---

27. Friedrich Nietzsche, *Nietzsches Werke*, quoted after Karl Jaspers, *Nietzsche and Christianity*, trans. E. B. Ashton (Chicago: Henry Regnery, 1961), 9.
28. Nietzsche, *The Antichrist*, 35.
29. Nietzsche, *Nietzsches Werke*, quoted after Jaspers, *Nietzsche and Christianity*, 27–28.

"without tanks" (as "the Kremlin highlander" used to say). Weak, but not powerless. His strength, like the strength of every man of resentment, is the will to power pursued on the symbolic plane. Such a person will at best build glass houses or castles in the air, and at worst unleash revolution by creating a religion of universal scope and character. As Saul, he will persecute those who lay the foundations for the new faith; as Paul, he will provide his work with a firm foundation, falling victim to persecution by those who wish to thwart it.

V

To sum up: There are two types of faith—a "better" one and a "worse" one. The "better" faith is that which *trusts in God* rather than *believes in Him*.[30] At its best, this faith (which Martin Buber calls *emunah*) is driven by spontaneity—it is natural, just like some poems and all sunsets are natural. It is born out of the experience of an entire nation, not an individual human being (which is why it attaches importance to law and rituals). The other type of faith (*pistis*) is created outside the history of a nation—on its margins, so to say—and consists in the conversion of an individual human being toward a credo, most often an absurd one. His or her individual choice is thus made outside the community and is ahistorical. Jesus inclined to the first type of faith, whereas the second characterized St. Paul. Of course, one may ask why the first should always be better than the second, why prophecies (as the first ones) should prevail over the Apocalypse (as the second or rather the last one)—were it not for the fact that "the end" (as pointed out by Walter Benjamin) is governed by its own logic anyway.[31] I find this distinction sufficient along with the conclusion that *Christianity is primarily the result of the Apostle Paul's conversion* as well as the project of creating a political community out of the Jewish dissenters and the Gentiles. St. Paul would have undercut the roots of his own political mission if he had acknowledged Moses as his progenitor, if he had recognized the continuity of the Jewish tradition. Therefore, he is by himself. And thus he starts with himself and creates a new model of congregation beside the ethnic community and the Roman state, namely, the Christian community, the "Church." His Church—let me repeat it—is built

---

30. See Martin Buber, *Two Types of Faith*, trans. Norman P. Goldhawk (Syracuse: Syracuse University Press, 2003).
31. Taubes, *The Political Theology of Paul*, 6–7.

up from scratch. It is not yet an institution but a shared reality that is entirely new. This is the moment when the Cross is raised within us, just like it was previously raised outside of us. From now on, Christ will be dying in each of us, repeatedly, until the end of time, and we will be dying with him. "Always bearing about in the body the dying of the Lord Jesus, that the life also of Jesus might be made manifest in our body. For we which live are always delivered unto death for Jesus' sake" (2 Cor. 4:10–11).

Chapter 2

THE SECRET OF THE SCAPEGOAT (RENÉ GIRARD)

Where so little love exists that strife prevails,
There they will need some third person to hate
In order to come together—there, first, they wade in one blood,
There at least as they hew the cross and hammer the nails
Their quarrelsome natures must fatally unite.
Hence the continuous sacrifice and the Pascha on a plate.[1]

There is a mystery in a human being, and only religion can reveal this mystery to us. Up until now, especially in the nineteenth century, efforts were made to apprehend the essence of religion through science and philosophy, which led to the gradual impoverishment of religion on the one hand, and science and philosophy on the other. That was perfectly intuited by Martin Heidegger for whom religion was of great importance. He argued that in order to properly understand philosophy and science, one must first understand religion. René Girard followed in that vein, but using different means, different tricks and a completely different method.

Mimetic Crisis

Culture is a great mimetic mechanism where everyone imitates their neighbor, where they all counterfeit one another and change into mirror images of their fellow men. Having not the possibility of multiplying oneself *ad infinitum* in a row of mirrors, claims Girard, neither man nor culture could exist. People are not as diverse as it might seem at first glance; they are the same.

Mimetic behaviors, meaning when the same people pursue the same goals, contribute to the creation of a unified world, which, in turn, leads to social antagonism. This antagonism is the result of conflicting desires, but

---

1. Cyprian Kamil Norwid, "Pascha," in *Pisma wierszem i prozą* (Warszawa: Państwowy Instytut Wydawniczy, 1970). Trans. Christopher Reid and Renata Senktas.

the conflict is not about the fact that (take the example of children playing in the sandbox) Billy and George both like Laura and will soon find themselves fighting over her. It is not the object of desire (Laura) that is at stake in their game, but the desire itself.

> Doubling occurs as soon as the object has disappeared in the heat of the rivalry: the two rivals become more and more concerned with defeating the opponent for the sake of it, rather than obtaining the object, which eventually becomes irrelevant, as it only exists as an excuse for the escalation of the dispute.[2]

Therefore, Billy does not seek Laura's attention simply because he likes her. He does it because George did it first.

At first we deal with the chaos of antagonized individuals who collide with each other ("twins"). Girard refers to it as a mimetic crisis. This crisis can be obviated only by the presence of a victim, thanks to whom the entire community will then unite in the medium of hatred. The victim attracts the anger and violence of all members of the community (or "the mob," as Girard likes to say). By definition, the victim is incapable of defending himself or herself and does not provoke the impulse of revenge in anyone. The mystery that Girard shares with us is close to that of Freud (about the father being murdered by his sons), namely, the collective murder, the founding murder that gives rise to *human* community, is committed on a completely innocent and defenseless being.

> The most (or rather the only) effective form of reconciliation—that would stop this crisis, and save the community from total self-destruction—is the convergence of all collective anger and rage towards a random victim, a scapegoat, designated by mimetism itself, and unanimously adopted as such. In the frenzy of the mimetic violence of the mob, a focal point suddenly appears, in the shape of the "culprit" who is thought to be the cause of the disorder and the one who brought the crisis into the community. He is singled out and unanimously killed by the community. He isn't any guiltier than any other but the whole community strongly believes he is. The killing of the scapegoat ends the crisis, since the transference against it is unanimous. That is the importance of the scapegoat mechanism: it channels the collective violence against one arbitrarily chosen member of the community, and this

---

2. René Girard with Pierpaolo Antonello and João Cezar de Castro Rocha, *Evolution and Conversion: Dialogues on the Origins of Culture* (London: Bloomsbury, 2017), 42.

victim becomes the common enemy of the entire community, which is reconciled as a result.[3]

The victim is therefore identified with the evil that has been removed and is no longer posing a danger. But the victim is also identified with the good, because after all, in the aftermath of this removal (and in a way, *thanks to it*) the community regains its equilibrium. "The victim is responsible for the renewed calm in the community and for the disorder that preceded this return."[4] This is where its ambivalence lies. Girard illustrates his hypothesis of the mimetic crisis with the example of the Passion. Christ, understood as a victim living among other people, means death for the community, since it is impossible to accept either Jesus Christ the man or His teachings without overthrowing the present world, without an eschatological and social revolution. On the other hand, it is His death that can give life to a new community, a reborn community. "Christianity, in the figure of Jesus, denounced the scapegoat mechanism for what it actually is: the murder of an innocent victim, killed in order to pacify a riotous community. That's the moment in which the mimetic mechanism is fully revealed."[5]

Méconnaissance

"The lesson of the Bible is precisely that the culture born of violence must return to violence. [...] and that the culture founded on murder retains a thoroughly murderous character."[6] This can be recognized at the level of myth, "forgetting" or even obliterating fingerprints that we left on the victim's body. The murderer is very reluctant to think of himself or herself as a hideous monster. He or she clears himself or herself from their own deeds, even if these were utterly ugly. The murderer's inner hypocrisy, which Girard refers to as *"méconnaissance,"* comes in handy; it is the monster's defense mechanism.

The process of selection of the victim must be underlain by ignorance, or *méconnaissance*, which "allows one to have the illusion that one is justly accusing someone who is really guilty and, therefore, deserves to be punished."[7] The murderers are then well aware of committing murder; however, they consider their act to be completely *justified*. And the more murderers there are,

---

3. Ibid., 47.
4. René Girard, *Things Hidden since the Foundation of the World*, trans. Stephen Bann and Michael Metteer (London: Continuum, 2003), 27.
5. Girard et al., *Evolution and Conversion*, 61.
6. Girard, *Things Hidden since the Foundation of the World*, 148–49.
7. Girard et al., *Evolution and Conversion*, 62.

argues Girard, the stronger the mutual mimetism, the greater the ignorance and thus the greater the desire to murder. That shift in perspective is to some extent the result of the hypocrisy of the whole culture. After the murder has been committed, the victim is declared innocent, and the guilt and sin of the perpetrators (namely, ourselves) is condemned. Consequently, the victim is burdened with *our* sins in order to then redeem them. Here is the essence of Christian doctrine that is a great betrayal of the Gospel message. Christianity betrayed Christ, saying that He redeemed our sins, that He saved us from the fatal consequences of the original sin, while in fact He only released our mutual anger. Myth, therefore, "is a text that has been falsified by the belief of the executioners in the guiltiness of their victim" and also in that victim's divinity.[8]

The modern era questioned the sanctity a sacrifice. It ceased to be worshiped, and so all we have inherited from sacrificial ritual is naked violence in the circle of which we find ourselves today. We live in a world abandoned by what is sacred. "We remain capable, in other words, of hating our victims; we are no longer capable of worshipping them"[9] (though John Lennon may be an exception in this respect). "People do not understand that the very one of them who is untainted by any violence and has no form of complicity with violence is bound to become the victim. All of them say that the world is evil and violent. But we must see that there is no possible compromise between killing and being killed."[10]

Jesus Christ

We are of our father the devil, not God, as Girard seems to be saying. A culture that has forgotten its murderous origin ends up lying and gets stuck in violence.

> Satan's order had no origin other than murder and this murder is lie. Human beings are sons of Satan because they are sons of this murder. [...] It is an inexhaustible fund; a transcendent source of falsehood that infiltrates every domain and structures everything in its own image, with such success that the truth cannot get in, and Jesus' listeners cannot even hear his words.[11]

---

8. Girard, *Things Hidden since the Foundation of the World*, 148.
9. Ibid., 37.
10. Ibid., 210–11.
11. Ibid., 162–63.

Man disclaims the violence that he inflicts upon the victim, placing the blame for it on God, nature or society. He cannot do otherwise, since he is consumed by a lie. The passion of Christ, therefore, is not a sacrifice, neither a voluntary nor a substitutionary one. What we are dealing with here is a common homicide. This is why the traditional interpretation of the Crucifixion as an act of bringing people salvation is par excellence "bad news," which draws its power of persuasion from a "transcendent source of falsehood," that source being the history of the Christian religion, among other things, the history of developing a biased interpretation of God's Word. But Christ wants to make Himself known to people in his truth. This truth is unconditional reconciliation, meaning reconciliation that excludes the medium of the victim as well as the rejection of mimetic rivalry in favor of "good imitation," or imitation without competition. "Jesus saves all human beings because of his revelation of the scapegoat mechanism, which also deprives us more and more of sacrificial protection, therefore forcing us to abstain from violence if we want to survive."[12] Finally, this truth is the religion of love that advocates abandoning sacrificial way of thinking, *ergo*, culture. In other words, only the Kingdom of God and the abandonment of all forms of violence can free man from his own violence, that is, from himself. Man's idea of justice is deeply rooted in the theory of requital, according to which we respond to good with good and recompense evil with evil. Meanwhile, we should reject the right not only to repression but also to self-defense. This is what Christ preached turning the other cheek for another slap. "Since the violence is mimetic, and no one ever feels responsible for triggering it initially,"[13] its renouncement must be unconditional. This is a requirement of reason itself, because the curse that weighs on us originates with our failure to understand the Gospel, with *méconnaissance*.

But Christ, too, if only through the very fact of the incarnation, became entangled in the structure of *mimesis*. He does not, however, imitate his perpetrators and does not repay violence for violence. Instead, he imitates God the Father "who refrains from all forms of reprisal,"[14] the God of love, not the God of victims (if such has ever existed).

What is the conclusion then? Christianity, that is, the times *after Christ*, is a religion, theory, culture, mentality, you name it, of sacrificers, murderers who are looking around for victims, who repeat: "If we are two, then why don't we find the third one for a victim." Christ, however, could not be a victim because he was not guilty. *He did not voluntarily burden himself with man's evil in order to later redeem it. Christ took upon Himself the suffering and innocence of all victims and so,*

---

12. Girard et al., *Evolution and Conversion*, 49.
13. Girard, *Things Hidden since the Foundation of the World*, 198.
14. Ibid., 206.

naturally, He was not a victim. The conclusion is rather unpleasant, especially for Christianity, which is considered (not only by Nietzsche but also by Girard) as a religion of violence, blood and betrayal of evangelical values.

Girard's language is not too promising, certainly unsuitable for an average middle-class man hiding behind the curtains of his very own apartment. One might inquire what this patent office clerk of a somewhat sickly manner has to do with the demonic violence that Girard is talking about in his *Evolution and Conversion*. Why is he afraid to react against it? Why does he support social amnesia with his own self-bred amnesia? Why does he not dare to know? Because violence, the emanation of which today is the state, secures him peace and prosperity.[15] For only those who do not owe anything to violence can contest it—the uncultured ones, such as "Prince Myshkin," or simply the "idiot."

Scapegoat or Black Sheep?

René Girard, I suspect, must have had a hard time in his life even before he had become "a prophet in his own country." (What Frenchman leaves his homeland for America only to continue writing in French?) One might presume that his scapegoat theory was first hardened on personal, psychological, typically *resentful* grounds, only later acquiring the features of a scientific concept. But there is something else that bothers me about it; I mean its utter *outwardness*. Girard tends to emphasize the fact that he likes puzzles and secrets, or that he studies obliterated traces and explores forlorn paths. I do not think this is true. Girard is not at all interested in the human depths, the existential dilemmas of man torn between the "below" and "above"; he repeats that "one doesn't need to think in terms of transcendence."[16] In his view, all cultural phenomena can be explained by the empirical theory of the scapegoat and the mimetic impasse. The complexities of human nature are questioned, the puzzles of the inner life are solved, and everything is reduced to the "social phenomena," just like in today's theater. Seen through Girard's eyes, human beings are flat and one-dimensional, consisting only of words and behaviors that are easy to fathom. Therefore, they are predictable, cowardly (they act in groups), cruel and dangerous. Is this the truth about man? There is no other, says Girard.

Girard's *infantile* anthropology is capable of drawing into the orbit of its influence some emotionally underdeveloped people, hungry for

---

15. Ibid., 211. See also Girard et al., *Evolution and Conversion*, 160. As Thomas Hobbes put it, "obedience is more acceptable to God than sacrifice," in *Leviathan*, ed. Marshall Missner (New York: Routledge, 2016), e-book, 252.
16. Girard et al., *Evolution and Conversion*, 151.

comfortable or indisputable formulas and prone to reducing human complexity to parareligious simplifications. (Like any other prophet, Girard does not argue, but commands.) His theory should apply to the children's planet: assembly, scuffling over "Laura" for the first time, then the "serious" mimetic rivalry that does not result in selecting any scapegoat (nonsense), but a "black sheep," a born loser, the weaker one who then becomes subject to bullying. I am of the opinion that the scapegoat is not a religious concept (or at least that is not we have from Girard). It is an expression of herd reluctance inherent in preschoolers against another preschooler whom they somewhat dislike. We all remember from childhood that there would always be some galoot, some telltale, some pushover in the classroom or at a summer camp. It is them that Girard seems to deify in his own way; it is their "suffering" that he elevates and sanctifies. The "founding murder" intended to constitute a human community is in fact a "compulsive" treatment of the trauma acquired in the French "sandbox," and "we don't have to resort to theology to understand it."[17]

Girard's anthropology is like the letter from Edgar Allan Poe's short story: its secret lies on the table, in plain view. Hidden on the surface, it is revealed from the start and well known. Which seems to be the reason why so many sensible people eventually capitulate in the face of this "mystery."

---

17. Ibid., 152.

Chapter 3

MAKING A JEW INTO A CHRISTIAN (WILLIAM SHAKESPEARE)

Venice

Already in early Middle Ages this exotic melting pot—a multilingual, international center on Southern Europe's map—moved the imagination with its openness and color. Everything intermingled here: nationalities, denominations, languages, businesses. With the big money went a lack of any inhibitions. In Renaissance Venice, religious matters were a little looked down upon as it was believed they may have a negative impact on people's involvement in earthly affairs.

> It was believed that only by directing men's interests to something which could subordinate their religious attachments would it be possible to establish a way of life in which religious doctrines and their intransigence would not play the leading part. It was not thought possible to educate men to a tolerant view or to overcome the power of the established religions by refuting them; the only way was to substitute for the interest and concern of men's passions another object as powerfully attractive as religion.[1]

The pursuit of money, the effort to multiply it, became the substitute of religion, while the sphere of commerce—business, hustle, exchange—moved to the sphere of the sacred; "Men for whom money is the most important thing are unlikely to go off on Crusades."[2]

The Venice that Shakespeare has in mind is a place where the space available for values other than money has radically shrunk. Nobody manufactures anything here; the only thing made is the maniacally multiplied capital.

---

1. Allan Bloom and Harry V. Jaffa, *Shakespeare's Politics* (New York: Basic Books, 1964), 15–16.
2. Ibid., 16.

Money is no longer a convenient tool for the exchange of goods, rather it becomes an end in itself. A free coexistence of Jews and Gentiles is forced by the realities of early capitalism, which liquidates nonmaterial values, thus forcing tolerance for religious differences by making them of no importance. In such a place, time flows differently. Until then human life was entirely structured by natural time. Even if one year the harvest was bigger, and the next one smaller, the balance would in the end be even within one generation. If no wars were waged and no impressment or tribute was imposed, life in such an orderly world was relatively safe and comfortable. People expected the future to be much like the past. Capitalism changed it all. Time understood like this was replaced by the idea of progress, of linear development that in the further perspective was supposed to lead humanity to the longed-for Arcadia (in Shakespeare's play it is Belmont). At least these were the promises made at the time. Yet, in the nearer perspective, the future was uncertain, risky, full of danger.

> The merchant is constantly taking risks—if he is lucky, he may make a fortune, if he is unlucky he may lose everything. Since, in a mercantile society, social power is derived from money, the distribution of power within it is constantly changing, which has the effect of weakening reverence for the past; who one's distant ancestors were soon ceases to be of much social importance. The oath of lifelong loyalty is replaced by the contract which binds its signatories to fulfill certain specific promises by a certain specific future date, after which their commitment to each other is over.[3]

The scriptures—Leviticus, Deuteronomy—state clearly: "Thou shalt not lend upon usury" (Lev. 15:1–12). In the new reality—so detached from tradition—the prohibition, however, becomes meaningless. Only a business contract specifies to whom and on what conditions it is allowed to lend money. Who is one allowed to lend money to then? To anyone who asks. Shylock is a usurer, not a crook. He does not cheat people, but attempts to satisfy their needs at a price. He does not ask if they need money for pleasure or to multiply their capital. He does not care. So when Bassanio asks for three thousand ducats, Shylock does not ask questions. He is simply being cautious.

SHYLOCK
        Three thousand ducats—well.

---

3. W. H. Auden, *The Dyer's Hand and Other Essays* (London: Faber and Faber, 1963), 220.

BASSANIO
>   Ay, sir, for three months.

SHYLOCK
>   For three months, well.

BASSANIO
>   For the which, as I told you, Antonio shall be bound.

SHYLOCK
>   Antonio shall become bound, well.

BASSANIO
>   May you stead me? Will you pleasure me? Shall I know your answer?

SHYLOCK
>   Three thousand ducats for three months and Antonio bound.
>   (*The Merchant of Venice*, I.iii.1–10[4])

He wants to know how much and in what time his capital will grow and who will guarantee the loan. He does not care about anything else. This behavior may not be commendable, but it is not strange, unjust or, least of all, prohibited. Shylock does not break the law—he follows it blindly, like Moses.

Antonio—a Venetian merchant who with his capital creates a new reality—is an obscenely rich man, certainly richer than Shylock, whose fortune could not have been so big since his daughter managed to pack it into one small box. Back then the really rich people were not usurers but Jewish merchants. Their capital was fluid, indefinite, because it depended on the well-functioning net of mutual loans, which developed and flourished in the ghettos as early as the Middle Ages.[5] Christian merchants did not know this kind of system, so, when it was necessary, they turned to Jews.

---

4. William Shakespeare, *The Merchant of Venice* (1596), in *Complete Works*, ed. Jonathan Bate and Eric Rasmussen (London: Macmillan, 2007), 418–70.
5. Hannah Arendt, *The Jewish Writings* (New York: Schocken Books, 2007), 98. Under no circumstances should Shylock resemble a "wolf" of Wall Street, whose home is the stock exchange. But this is exactly how Peter Zadek saw him in his most famous staging of *The Merchant of Venice*, shown in Vienna's Burgtheater in December 1988. See Wilhelm Hortmann, *Shakespeare on the German Stage: the Twentieth Century* (Cambridge: Cambridge University Press, 1988), 259.

Antonio multiplies his money without enthusiasm; he just does what everyone else is doing. He does not spend the money on himself, but on his friends. He is well loved by them and knows how to reciprocate their feelings. When the money sinks, he realizes that without it he will no longer be able to exercise "the Roman virtue of honor" nor enjoy the Patrician melancholy his milieu is entitled to. What he shares with the Ancients is the awareness of how fragile life is, and that it is better to live it magnanimously, making others happy, than to choose isolation and become immune to empirical reality. As Auden rightly observes, "His hatred of Shylock is really a projection of his distaste for the whole society in which he lives, a distaste which makes him a melancholic."[6] Antonio hates the usurer for one more reason: Shylock negates the basic principles on which Antonio's world is built—the feelings of love and forgiveness. "Neither can regard the other as a human being in any significant sense because in all that is human they differ."[7] For Shylock, Antonio is not a human being since he does not respect the law. Shylock does not want to talk about justice and mercy. He sticks to the letter of the law. His guiding light in earthly matters is "the law gazette," and not some lofty values. He can see them, but they do not mean a thing. "I will buy with you, sell with you, talk with you, walk with you, and so following, but I will not eat with you, drink with you, nor pray with you" (I.iii.435–36), he says to Bassanio. In other words, when we are doing business, Shylock says, the differences and squabbles that appear are often an indispensable part of a broader spectrum and can be obliterated or resolved on the ground of the law. Yet when we start talking about values, the differences between us can be described, but they cannot be resolved peacefully. A Christian looks at it in a similar way. For him too, forgiveness, a duty we owe our neighbors, is an absolute, nonnegotiable value. If someone has really done nothing wrong or is not responsible for anything, forgiveness is in this case a meaningless act, a case of confusing values; it is in bad taste. Or even something unjust. But what happens if neither side wants war, but both stick to their values? In such a case, it is best for everyone to go home, to hung "the veil of ignorance" (Rawls) or, better still, make a stronger gesture and cut off the public sphere, the sphere of the law, from one's private axiology (Hobbes). This is exactly what Shylock does not do. And what does he do? He goes to dinner to a Gentile's house! And he does not himself understand what for (II.v.15–16). (His explanation that he is going there to eat away Christian money I reject as childish words uttered in anger.) Only once

---

6. W. H. Auden, "Two Sides to a Thorny Problem. Exploring Below Surface of Shakespeare's 'Merchant,'" in W. H. Auden, *Prose (1949–1955)*, vol. III., ed. Edward Mendelson (London: Faber and Faber, 2008), 357.
7. Bloom and Jaffa, *Shakespeare's Politics*, 19.

does Shylock compromise regarding values, namely, when he sits at the table with his enemies. This is exactly when he loses everything that he has and everything that he is. The merciful Christians take his money, his daughter and his hope for salvation. Brents Stirling is right when he writes that Shylock consistently stayed away from the affairs of the city and did not want to harm anyone with debt papers until he was not betrayed, humiliated, cheated.[8]

Lament

Lament expresses pain and grief; it uncovers man's helplessness in face of the forces of history and nature. In tears, in painful moaning we can feel without fail who is one of our own and who is not. Suffering brings us back to our community as the communal lot is made up of the history of suffering of the nation, generation, community—every community and every person suffers differently, in their own way, for a different reason.[9] "And all sorts of strange thoughts came to my mind: What did it mean to be a Jew, and what did it mean to be a non-Jew? And why did God create Jews and non-Jews, and why were they so set apart from one another, unable to get along, as if one had been created by God and the other not?"[10] Tevye the Dairyman wonders. Considerations on the meaning of the common lot invariably deepen the values cherished by the community.

> When God came to our great-great-grandfather Abraham and told him, *Get thee gone from thence, you must leave your native land*—did Abraham ask him, "Where to?" God said, *to the land of Arad*. We will go wherever our eyes take us, wherever all Jews go! [...] no matter how we keep from boasting about it, we must admit that we Jews are, after all, the best and the smartest people. As the Prophet says: *Who can be compared to Israel? How can a goy compare himself to a Jew?* A goy is a goy, and a Jew is a Jew, as you yourself say in your writings. You have to be born a Jew, *blessed be the Jew*. How lucky I was to be born a Jew and know the taste of exile and of always wandering, never sleeping where we spent the day.[11]

---

8. Brents Stirling, "Introduction," in William Shakespeare, *The Merchant of Venice*, ed. Brents Stirling (Baltimore, MD: Penguin, 1959), 16.
9. Martin Heidegger, *Being and Time*, trans. Joan Stambaugh (Albany: State University of New York Press, 1996), 230.
10. Sholem Aleichem, *Tevye the Dairyman and Motl the Cantor's Son*, trans. Aliza Shevrin (London: Penguin, 2009), e-book.
11. Ibid.

Uriel Acosta is a different case—he is an example of a premature rebellion against such a narrow view of Jewish tradition. His lament is of a different kind than Tevye's and is closer to Shylock's complaint.

Acosta was born in Portugal to parents who "were of the nobility, and originally descended from those *Jews* who were constrained to embrace the Christian religion in that kingdom."[12] He was himself the Jew who, emigrating to Amsterdam between 1612 and 1615 to do business, was also returning to the Jewish faith abandoned by his ancestors. Yet, being a man of reason, he could not accept those elements in the newly adopted religion that, in his view, defied common sense. His *Propostas contra a Tradição* (Propositions against the Tradition), which he had sent to the Jewish community in Venice—the community that in those days was considered the most authoritative—were rejected, condemned for their alleged atheism and epicureanism, and the author was excommunicated in 1618.[13]

> Then was read out of a little book my sentence, which was "that I must make my entrance into the synagogue dressed in a mourning vestment, holding a black wax taper in my hand, and there to read distinctly before the whole congregation a form of recantation penned by them in which they had described in black and odious colours, the great enormity of my crimes. Then I was to submit to be whipped in the same public manner, with a scourge made of leather thongs. After that to prostrate myself at the door of the synagogue, that they might all pass over me, and moreover to fast certain days."[14]

This is how he was treated by his brothers in faith even before he was rejected. When he finally was anathemized, Acosta sounded an enlightened lament, which made his adversaries even angrier and brought him—even though he rejected the idea of life after death—posthumous fame:

> Give me leave here to propose the following question: If these groundless fears which you instill into the minds of men [i.e., religion], are contrived on purpose to restrain that natural malignity which is inherent in them, and to keep within the bounds of their duty, those who would otherwise lead immoral lives; must not you at the same time reflect that yourselves are men of like passions with them, naturally averse to what is good, prone to evil, injurious, without compassion or mercy?

---

12. Uriel Acosta, *A Specimen of a Human Life* (New York: Bergman, 1967), 9.
13. Leszek Kołakowski, "Klęska i kariera Uriela da Costy" [The Defeat and Career of Uriel da Costa], in Uriel Acosta, *Wizerunek własny żywota / Exemplar Humanae Vitae* (Warszawa: Państwowy Instytut Wydawniczy, 1960), 9.
14. Acosta, *A Specimen of Human Life*, 19.

[...] What, are we not all pious, and merciful, and strict adherents to truth and justice? I answer, what you thus boastingly say of yourselves is notoriously false; your accusation of all other men is scandalously unjust (whose natural propensity to evil, you pretend to correct with your fictitious terrors). Impiously you reflect on the majesty and goodness of God, whom you represent as a tyrant and cruel destroyer; [...] lay aside those impositions, which are only fit to frighten children and simple folk; but if the disorder [i.e., evil] is incurable, then cease your vain delusive pretences, and no longer, like impudent quacks, promise men that health which you are not able to give them; [...] He who pretends to be neither of these and *only calls himself a man*, is far preferable to you; for if you will not believe him, you may stand upon your guard.[15]

In his final words Acosta refers—which is quite clear—to universal, humanist values or, more generally, to the universal reason that constitutes the common ground for those who want to think without respect for the tradition and religion of their ancestors. Yet Acosta himself was not consistent in his views. I do not mean here the recantation of his heresies he signed as an old man. I strongly believe that the rebellion Acosta started was Talmudic in its character; certainly, it was a strong rejection, yet it was directed against Jewish orthodoxy and not against Jewishness in its entirety. This is indicated by the last sentence in which he not only renounces the Jewish name he adopted in his youth but also decides to keep it.[16]

What can Shylock have in common with the Jews I mentioned above? They are connected by the same form of expression, the lament that makes us recognize the common fate. Apart from it, there is nothing that connects Shylock to Tevye, while the thing he has in common with Acosta is the search for a universally human, non-Jewish perspective in the perception and judgment of reality. It is revealed in the frighteningly clear Shylock's lamentation that constitutes a sort of requiem for Judaism:

I am a Jew. Hath not a Jew eyes? Hath not a Jew hands, organs, dimensions, senses, affections, passions? Fed with the same food, hurt with the same weapons, subject to the same diseases, heal'd by the same means, warm'd and cool'd by the same winter and summer, as a Christian is? If you prick us, do we not bleed? If you tickle us, do we not laugh? If you poison us, do we not die? And if you wrong us, do we not revenge? If we are like you in the rest, we will resemble you in that. (*The Merchant of Venice*, III.i.40–47)

---

15. Acosta, *A Specimen of a Human Life*, 39–40, 43.
16. Ibid., 45.

But here the universally human perspective seems a lie, an illusion. This is because it does not find support in a religious and corporal identity or, as in the case of the Greeks, in the universal partaking in the Logos, referring only to an animalistic corporeality both Jews and Christians are entangled in; it does not even reach for the natural laws, so dear to Acosta, but only cares about their trivial, biological equivalent. "Shylock justifies himself by an appeal to the universality of humanity," thus committing the error that is going to cost him everything, Allan Bloom observes.

> But, sadly, if one looks at the list of similar characteristics on which Shylock bases his claim to equality with his Christian tormentors, one sees that it includes only things which belong to the body; what he finds in common between Christian and Jew is essentially what all animals have in common. The only spiritual element in the list is revenge.[17]

With his convoluted history, with tradition inextricably woven with the law, with his ideas of justice, God and salvation, Shylock seems a perfect representative of Judaism. For him time passes irrevocably, moving in only one direction. By lending money Shylock opens up to the risk of loss. To the Christian "logic of the Cross," he opposes the Jewish sense of harm and the absurd. He is constantly torn between "having found" (the temptation of conformism) and "finding" (the fear of failure). His existence is marked by such contradictory passions as the feeling of expropriation, a radical uncertainty and an equally radical involvement on the side of history, finally: the equivalence of mutually contradictory interpretations.[18] One can say Shylock is—or at least can be—all of the above at the same time, with the exception of the narrowly understood animality. Why then does he choose to refer to it? Why does he make the mimetism, present in nature, or a dogmatically understood Cartesianism the starting point for his meditations on human nature? ("I am a thing that thinks, that is to say, that doubts, affirms, denies, that knows a few things, that is ignorant of many [that loves, that hates], that wills, that desires, that also imagines and perceives."[19]) Because Shylock wants to be like everyone else. His secret desire is to melt in the ocean of sameness, the blurring of differences, the fading away of all identity. "It seems to me," Antoni Słonimski writes, "that Jewishness

---

17. Bloom and Jaffa, *Shakespeare's Politics*, 23.
18. Sergio Quinzio, *Radici ebraiche del moderno*, translated from the Polish edition: *Hebrajskie korzenie nowożytności* (Kraków: Homini, 2005), 253.
19. René Descartes, "Meditations on First Philosophy," trans. Elizabeth S. Haldane, in *The Philosophical Works of Descartes* (Cambridge: Cambridge University Press, 1911), 167.

is grafted onto the character of Shylock quite randomly."[20] Whereas *a Jew needs to be different than everybody else, or he is not a Jew at all*. The same must be said about Poles, Russians or Germans. The choice Shylock is faced with is a simple either/or: "a hostile diversity on a high level or a common humanity grounded on an indifference to the opinion about the nature of the good."[21]

From the court verdict concerning the payment of debt in due time, we learn that Shylock—as an alien!—is guilty of an assault on the life of a Venetian citizen. Splendid! Therefore, Shylock's possessions are to be confiscated, and his life is in the hands of the Duke. The defendant is to kneel and beg for mercy. We do not know if he kneels. We do learn that his property is confiscated—half is given to Antonio, half to the city (IV.i.377–79). Then mercifully, a fine is adjudged for public purposes. Antonio is equally magnanimous—instead of taking Shylock's fortune, he only wants to manage it. In today's lingo—he is going to be the broker of a former usurer, satisfying himself with the interests from the capital. The capital itself must work all the time, be on the move—letting capital just lie idle would not be the Venetian way. Of course, Shylock has no say in the decisions concerning his money. He must make do with some spare change to survive. Fifteen hundred dollars a month. Yet there are two conditions: (1) after his death, all his money is to be inherited by his daughter who has already shown us how much it means to her when she exchanged a precious ring for a cheerful monkey ("Again, the first thing Jessica learns from her Gentile lover is conspicuous waste"[22]); (2) he must be baptized. On this condition depends the play's "happy ending." In his talk on *The Merchant of Venice*, W. H. Auden reminds us that Shakespeare's contemporaries did not perceive conversion as improper as they genuinely believed in the beneficial effects of baptism.[23] So only the verdict of the enlightened Duke endows the play with a happy ending without which it could not be called a "comical history."[24] (Now it can.) What may the verdict mean to Shylock? How does he feel about it? Already in the course of the trial he seems a broken man, stripped of dignity, money, the chance for salvation—in this world and in

---

20. Antoni Słonimski, *Gwałt na Melpomenie* [The Rape of Melpomene] (Warszawa: Wydawnictwa Artystyczne i Filmowe, 1982), 268.
21. Bloom and Jaffa, *Shakespeare's Politics*, 23. An equally perspicacious criticism of basing what is human on purely natural foundations one finds in the work of Hannah Arendt, in the chapter on "The Decline of the Nation-State and the End of the Rights of Man," in *The Origins of Totalitarianism* (New York: Harcourt Brace Jovanovich, 1973), 293–328.
22. Auden, "Two Sides to a Thorny Problem. Exploring below Surface of Shakespeare's 'Merchant,'" 357.
23. Ibid., 358.
24. Stirling, "Introduction," 15.

the other. Yes, he is still alive, but it feels as if he was dead already. He turned out to be a fool, a puppet, a cog in the big machine. He was even robbed of his right to revenge—the only value that was not connected to any financial calculation. One more question: what is the benefit of the sentence on the Jew for Christianity? Well, one more Christian. This is what Christian mercy consists in—"the softness and sweetness of rotting fruit" (Cioran)—in the formative period of capitalism: it is about making the debtor dependent on the creditor—Bassanio on Antonio, the Jew on the Christian; it is about the omnipresent, aggressive proselytism of modernity and also about the belief in an effective marriage of capital and divine mercy.

Belmont

A parallel reality in relation to Venice is Belmont. It is the land of sensuality running free, of the adoration of pagan beauty, which makes it possible to combat not only the repulsion toward death but also the reluctance toward life. In Belmont you do not pay with money (this is what you do in Venice), but with love. On the island—Belmont is another island in Shakespeare's archipelago—you fall out of the realm of time, out of history; there you live in the realm of a timeless Woodstock. The beautiful Portia is satisfied with pure simulacrum, and if she decides to leave the island for a while and enter history, she enters it—like in Kafka's writings—through the gate of the Law, because only the Law guarantees a relative effectiveness in the strange world, inimical to love. And she starts acting—in this world she acts like Nemesis, the goddess of revenge (for the Venetian merchant's undeserved damage), justice (consisting in the confiscation and redistribution of assets from money-lending) and destiny (all Jews are to become Christians and then—Belmontians).

For Venetians, Belmont is their regulatory idea, their dream, the aim they are striving for; it is the Arcadia of "the last people," where there is nothing else to do except share love. On the condition that one has someone to share these goods with. In this sense, "if Antonio is not to fade away into a nonentity, then the married couples must enter the lighted house and leave Antonio standing alone on the darkened stage, outside the Eden from which, not by the choice of others, but by his own nature, he is excluded."[25]

Summary

As a society, Venice is more efficient and successful than Henry IV's England. Its citizens are better off, more secure and nicer mannered.

---

25. Auden, *The Dyer's Hand*, 233–34.

Politically speaking, therefore, one may say that a mercantile society represents an advance upon a feudal society, as a feudal society represents an advance upon a tribal society. But every step forward brings with it its own dangers and evils for, the more advanced the social organization, the greater the moral demands it makes upon its members and the greater the degree of guilt which they incur if they fail to meet these demands.[26]

Shakespeare's Venice is a world without measure, where the only available measure is money. "Human flesh and money in Venice are constantly exchanged for one another. People are turned into objects of financial speculation. Mankind has become a commodity, an exchange value like any other."[27] When Bassanio expatiates on Portia's merits, he focuses on her ducats (dowry), only later mentioning her beauty and the merits of her mind.

Capitalism that is in the process of formation right in front of our eyes mocks any vital differences—cultural, national, religious. It then pours huge sums of money to obliterate the differences, then waters the differences down and forces a new concept of the human whose existence is not much different from the uninhibited growth of plants and animals. In such a world the only strategy with a chance of survival is playing a game.

In Venice everyone plays, pretends—they wear masks and live two-faced lives. This behavior is typical of the ambience of "carnival." The mask separates the wearer from himself; it is used to cover up traces, to dissolve identity. Thanks to the mask, one can hide behind "someone else." For Shylock wearing a mask is a dangerous game leading to self-annihilation. So he asks his daughter to lock the door every time she hears musicians. Why "gaze on Christian fools with varnished faces" (II.v.32–34). He feels that in a mask one can lose not only their face's features but also their face and perhaps even their soul. But what if *The Merchant of Venice* is itself a mask? If it were so, what would it be covering? In the case of Venetians—*nothing*; it simply hides their—ours—inner hollowness, their desire for cheap trinkets and trifles that Venetians hope to enjoy some day, maybe in Belmont. In the case of a Jew, the mask covers *everything*—tradition, the passion for the Law, God. Under the mask, the Jew can pretend he is like the others, that is, he can lie. Also to his God. But in reality the Jew *has* different eyes, for he sees other things, looks somewhere else; he eats differently than Christians (kosher!), also he takes care of his bodily cleanliness in a decidedly different way (mikvah!). The Jew is

---

26. Ibid., 235.
27. René Girard, *A Theatre of Envy: William Shakespeare* (New York: Oxford University Press, 1991), 542.

different and Venice tries to take his difference away, to tear it out, to condemn it. Because you wanted to cut a pound of flesh from a Christian's body,[28] we will cut a pound of your soul. This is the moment when we can hear the voice of the uncanny proselytism of early capitalism that does not accept any differences, that destroys all manifestations of cultural and religious diversity. If Shylock loses this unequal confrontation, it is exactly because he refers to "human rights," to a common denominator he hopes to fit both the Jew and the Christian. If Shakespeare's Coriolanus is an example of a Greek thrown into the Roman world, then Shylock is a Jew thrown into our world—the world of the great, incomprehensible capital.

---

28. Shylock's seemingly aberrational demand that the debtor pay back the debt with his own body derives from the Law of the Twelve Tables, which constitutes the first (451–449 BC) attempt at codifying the Roman law. It included the formulation *tertiis nundinis partis secanto* giving the creditor the right to have the debtor's body at his disposal. The regulation mainly regarded the situation where several lenders were to be paid back and they could dismember the debtor's body and divide it among themselves according to the debt owed to each one of them. Allegedly, Lucius Caecilius Iucundus, a Roman banker, took this formula very literally. Quintylian, on the other hand, believed this law to be dead letter, condemned by tradition. See Henry John Roby, *Roman Private Law in the Times of Cicero and of the Antonines*, vol. II (Cambridge: Cambridge University Press, 1902), 424. Marta Andruszkiewicz, PhD, drew my attention to the fact that Shylock's demand may refer to a form of litigation earlier than the Law of the Twelve Tables, the *legis actio* procedure, in this case expressed in the formula *legis actio per manus iniectionem* ("procedure via laying on hands"). If the court ruled in favor of the creditor, he could lay his hands on the debtor's head and pronounce the paremia stating that the debtor loses the freedom of action and may become the object of debt enforcement. In this case the creditor could sell the debtor into slavery and also had control over his body and even his life.

Chapter 4

THERE SHOULD BE TIME NO LONGER (D. H. LAWRENCE)

I wish that whatever props up the walls of light
would fall, and darkness would come hurling heavily down,
And it would be thick black dark for ever.
Not sleep, which is grey with dreams
nor death, which quivers with birth,
but heavy, sealing darkness, silence, all immovable.[1]

Sun of my soul, Thou Savior dear,
it is not night if Thou be near.[2]

A back cover of the first edition of David Herbert Lawrence's *Apocalypse* bears information in three languages—in the original, German and French—about the exact thing the reader is holding in their hands. It reads:

> In this his final attempt to make his interpretation of life understood, Lawrence uses the "Revelation of St. John" to convey what he believes to be the truth. In condemning the artificiality of all modern ways of living, he reveals by means of ancient symbols the proper relationship between man, his emotions and his environment. The last work of a dying man, "Apocalypse" deals with life not death; it is not the work of a scholar but the intuitive message of a poet.[3]

A few words about the man to begin.

---

1. D. H. Lawrence, "And Oh—That the Man I Am Might Cease to Be," in *The Complete Poems of D. H. Lawrence* (Ware: Wordsworth Editions, 2002), 154.
2. J. Keble, "Sun of My Soul," *Hymns to the Living God*, no. 329 (1820), https://hymnary.org/text/sun_of_my_soul_thou_savior.
3. Richard Aldington's introduction to D. H. Lawrence, *Apocalypse* (Hamburg: Albatross, 1932).

Life in Motion

D. H. Lawrence was born in 1885, in the small mining town of Eastwood, Nottinghamshire, where he attended local schools. He had a slight cough from his early days. His father worked down the mine; his mother was a teacher of artistic and intellectual ambition and, for the most part, the son's upbringing was her responsibility. In 1907, Lawrence became a teacher at the Davidson Road School in Croydon (now a district of London), which made his financial situation stable. He takes his first steps in literature propped up by Ford Madox Ford, who makes his poetry debut as well as publication of *The White Peacock* (1911) possible. Around this time, his mother dies of cancer, causing a nervous breakdown in the young writer and forcing him to resign from his teaching position. In March or April 1912, he makes the acquaintance of Frieda Weekley (née: von Richthofen), a mother of three children six years his senior, a Baroness and his former university lecturer's wife. Almost instantly, force of the feeling and an unconventionality of their relationship push them out of post-Victorian England toward Germany, the motherland of Lawrence's lover. "Love rather suits me. I am getting fat, and look awfully well. You don't know how surprised I am," he writes in a letter to his publisher Edward Garnett.[4] He's working intensively on his Bildungsroman, a proper classification for *Sons and Lovers*, concerned with a writer's youth and his feelings for his mother. He expounds its main idea the best he can, thus opening up a field for future arguments about meaning of the work:

> It follows this idea: a woman of character and refinement goes into the lower class, and has no satisfaction in her own life. She has a passion for her husband, so the children are born of passion, and have heaps of vitality. But as her sons grow up she selects them as lovers—first the eldest, then the second. These sons are urged into life by their reciprocal love of their mother—urged on and on. But when they come to manhood, they can't love, because their mother is the strongest power in their lives, and holds them.—It's rather like Goethe and his mother and Frau von Stein and Christiana.—As soon as the young men come into contact with women, there's a split. William gives his sex to a fribble, and his mother holds his soul. But the split kills him, because he doesn't know where he is. The next son gets a woman who fights for his soul—fights his mother. The son loves the mother—all the sons hate and are jealous of the father. The battle goes on between the mother and the girl, with

---

4. D. H. Lawrence, *The Letters of D. H. Lawrence*, ed. Aldous Huxley (New York: Viking Press, 1932), 46.

the son as object. The mother gradually proves stronger, because of the tie of blood. The son decides to leave his soul in his mother's hands, and, like his elder brother, go for passion. He gets passion. Then the split begins to tell again. But, almost unconsciously, the mother realises what is the matter, and begins to die. The son casts off his mistress, attends to his mother dying. He is left in the end naked of everything, with the drift towards death.[5]

In 1914, straight after Frieda's divorce with Ernest Weekley, Lawrence marries her. During the Great War, the couple conducts intensive friendships with Aldous Huxley, Bertrand Russell, Katherine Mansfield, John Middleton Murry and Richard Aldington. 1915 sees the creation of *Rainbow*, which many regard as Lawrence's superior work in prose. Suffused with autobiographical episodes, the work leads its author to a dubious pornographer's fame and threatens persecution by institutional moral censorship. Soon, a libel trial is spreading ever more widely. The writer and his wife are accused of spying for the enemy state of Germany—supposedly for sending signals to German submarines from a beach in Cornwall—and expelled from their county. Also, attempts at bringing out the recently completed *Women in Love* end in a fiasco. No British publisher wishes to talk to Lawrence. Eventually, the book gets self-published in 1920, in the USA. Next, he brings out *The Lost Girl*, for which he wins the prestigious James Tait Black Memorial Prize and comes into his first significant sum of money. The Lawrences leave the isles behind, embarking on a new period in their lives, which they themselves described as "savage pilgrimage," or "voluntary migration." Like their contemporary flaneurs, they can, at last, roam the world at will, staying here and there, which have always been Frieda's great dream. So, first, to Europe: Abruzzo, Capri, Sicily, Sardinia, Malta, Austria, southern Germany; next: Ceylon, Australia, Mexico, New Mexico, the States; and they end with southern France. From each of the journeys, D. H. Lawrence brings back something that makes up the so-called travel literature, or what is these days—more often and simpler—called a blog. Thus, the fruit of their Italian peregrinations are three volumes: early essays, *Twilight in Italy*; the following, collected in *Sea and Sardinia* (1921); and the posthumously published *Etruscan Places* (1932). A summary of their voyage through Australia is a novel titled (how else?!) *Kangaroo* (1923), while travels in Mexico produce *Mornings in Mexico* (1927) and *The Plumed Serpent* (1926).

---

5. D. H. Lawrence, *The Selected Letters of D. H. Lawrence*, ed. James T. Boulton (Cambridge: Cambridge University Press, 1997), 49.

"We Fucked a Flame into Being"[6]

Lawrence attains the world of popular culture 30 years after his death, on account of his final and most renowned novel *Lady Chatterley's Lover*. It already brought him a lot of trouble while he was alive. Self-published in France, the United States and the UK, in 1928, it is released a few years later in a much reduced shape. The censor's scissors prune all scenes at odds with the then Puritanical spirit of the age. A verdict allowing the book to be published without interventions of censorship is passed only at the turn of 1950s, when the 1857 Obscene Publications Act is finally liberalized, introducing a statutory provision making possible publications of works of outstanding literary value. Penguin Books does not need to wait long for a market effect: the novel becomes a bestseller overnight. On the streets of Edinburgh, stacks are built from its copies and set alight, librarians in southern Wales refuse to lend it, moralizers warn against popular depravation. In one year, three million copies are sold worldwide. Philip Larkin composes a funny little poem for the occasion, alluding to Lawrence's and the Beatles' influence on contemporary love life of the British:

> Sexual intercourse began
> In nineteen sixty-three
> (Which was rather late for me)—
> Between the end of the *Chatterley* ban
> And the Beatles' first LP.[7]

Lawrence authored several volumes of theory, including discussions of his readings,[8] Freudian psychoanalysis (*Psychoanalysis and the Unconscious* and *Fantasia of the Unconscious*, 1921–22) or essays on American literature (*Studies in Classic American Literature*, 1923). He also produced poems and plays. Considering that his frenetic creativity and interest in numerous aspects of contemporary and

---

6. D. H. Lawrence, *Lady Chatterley's Lover* (Cambridge: Cambridge University Press, 2002), 301.
7. Philip Larkin, "Annus Mirabilis," in *Collected Poems* (London: Marvell Press & Faber and Faber, 1990), 167.
8. Here I refer to Lawrence's excellent shorter texts collected in two bulky volumes: *Phoenix: The Posthumous Papers of D. H. Lawrence*, ed. E. D. McDonald (New York: Penguin Books, 1936); *Phoenix II: Uncollected, Unpublished and Other Prose Works by D. H. Lawrence*, ed. W. Roberts and H. T. Moore (New York: Viking Press, 1968). See also D. H. Lawrence, *Introductions and Reviews*, ed. N. H. Reeve and J. Worthen (Cambridge: Cambridge University Press, 2005).

historic culture lasted a little over two decades, the outcome of Lawrence's travails appears impressive indeed.

Apocalypse as his subject was taken up by Lawrence thrice. In spring 1924, he wrote, under a pseudonym, a one-page review of John Oman's *Book of Revelation*; in 1929–30, it informed his "Introduction" to Frederick Carter's *Dragon of Revelation* as well as the text proper of the *Apocalypse*. In early stages of his research, he had been interested in a psychological aspect of revelation. In a letter to Carter, Lawrence confided: "Myself I am more interested in the microcosm than in the macrocosm, and in the gates to the psyche rather than the astrological houses."[9] By the late 1929, he moves with Frieda, his unflinching companion, to the southern French town of Bandol. There he writes his final minor texts and the *Apocalypse*. Lawrence scholars date the writing of the work very exactly: December 27, 1929. Lawrence dies in March 1930 of tuberculosis and is buried in Vence, the same cemetery that, many years later, would become the final resting place of Witold Gombrowicz.

Among other sources, I collected the information about D. H. Lawrence's life from the reputable *Cambridge Guide to Literature in English*, which Margaret Atwood described in her introduction as "a testament to the amazing range and vitality of the English language itself."[10] In the olden days, such digests might have served this kind of purposes; today, however, they no longer do. The task is obstructed not so much by errors (they are, in principle, carefully edited) as by common—frequently intentional—silences and omissions. How else can the absence of a mere mention of Lawrence's final work in the *Cambridge Guide* be explained if not by a misconceived care of the poet's image as a libertarian and a nonreligious person? Should *Apocalypse* really be considered as an embarrassing piece of the author of *Lady Chatterley's Lover*'s oeuvre, spoiling the general idea of the man, or is it not—not unlike *Phaedo* with respect to the *Corpus Platonicum*—its natural complement and coronation? The editor of the critical edition of the *Apocalypse* is, therefore, right in claiming that it is

> an important document, not merely because it is Lawrence's last book, but because the ideas expressed in it—ranging over the entire system of his thought about Christianity, politics, man, God, religion, myth, art and symbol—are the summing up of issues that preoccupied him

---

9. Letter to Frederick Carter from March 8, 1923, quoted after Mara Kalnins, "Introduction," in D. H. Lawrence, *Apocalypse and the Writings on Revelation*, ed. Mara Kalnins (Cambridge: Cambridge University Press, 2002), 3.
10. Margaret Atwood, "Introduction," in *The Cambridge Guide to Literature in English*, ed. Ian Ousby (Cambridge: Cambridge University Press, 1988), i.

throughout his life and that he also explored in the writings of the final years.[11]

The editor himself did not really have a fully formed approach to the text. At first, he saw it as an extended version of the preface to Frederick Carter's book; next, an exercise in theology of little significance, fragments of which alluded to the writer's childhood; and, then, as another unfinished essay, as suggested by excerpt from correspondence Lawrence was exchanging at the time.[12]

A Book Unlike Any Other

A book is like a person—when it lies down, shut, it is silent and only pretends to be present. Unread—it simply dies. It is only enlivened by attentive reading, while a second reading transforms both sides: the book and the reader. There are books that lose in value on subsequent readings; there are also those that, reread, refresh in us the old impressions while setting alight passions muted by course of time. In other words, books serve their purpose when, every time, they are able to move us differently.

Before turning 10, Lawrence had read the Revelation of St. John 10 times. It does not matter how much he had understood; something quite different seems to matter here. The *Apocalypse* has lived in him since childhood; throughout all his eccentric life, it was pulsating in his body—through its poetry, it aroused emotions, thanks to morality, it influenced instincts. One does not outgrow such bonds easily.

The *Apocalypse* is composed of several layers. This does not mean that it should be regarded as a work of syncretism. Much rather it is a probe book, *livre-sondage*, as Gilles Deleuze terms it, probing successive areas of myth. "A pagan, a Jewish, and a Christian stratum: these are what mark the great parts of the *Apocalypse*, even if a pagan sediment slides into a fault line in the Christian stratum, filling up a Christian void."[13] The *Book of Revelation* helped Lawrence understand that Jesus's Christianity, based on a pagan affirmation of life and a wholly un-pagan commandment of unconditional mutual love, had, at a point, been replaced with a religion of self-deification of the hurt and the humiliated.

---

11. Kalnins, "Introduction," 24.
12. Ibid., 26.
13. Gilles Deleuze, "Nietzsche and St. Paul, Lawrence and John of Patmos," in *Essays Critical and Clinical*, trans. Daniel W. Smith and Michael A. Greco (London: Verso, 1998), 42.

So that religion, the Christian religion especially, became dual. The religion of the strong taught renunciation and love. And the religion of the weak taught *down with the strong and the powerful, and let the poor be glorified.* Since there are always more weak people than strong in the world, the second sort of Christianity has triumphed and will triumph. If the weak are not ruled, they will rule, and there's the end of it. And the rule of the weak is *Down with the strong!*[14]

Duality of Human Nature

A bemusing paradox of early Christianity rests on a recognition that truly democratic feelings—love, philanthropy, compassion, understanding of human frailty—had been cherished by aristocrats of the spirit. The feelings stemmed from their strength and a sense of *self*-worth. Meanwhile, Christian democrats, even if they exhibit a similar moral sensibility, tend to raise the same questions much more insistently and irrevocably, in addition, with an awareness of their limitedness. A difference between spiritual aristocracy and the common people is, therefore, decided by a quantum of power and an attitude to the power, which means that the difference is enduring, timeless and indelible. Mind you, what's at stake here is not politics but a state of the soul, a duality of human nature.

Jesus, says Lawrence, made a grand discovery, because he understood that the greatest power rests in renunciation, resignation, in breaking natural ties and stopping the use of force in relations with other people. The human was meant to be powerful by force of their character, which revealed itself in self-mastery. Ataraxy, trained in prayer, then came together with a commonplace, good, empathetic treatment of neighbors.[15] Here is the rub: such an attitude to reality simultaneously spawned people who were authentically lame, messed up, demanding revanche on the strong, independent and—good. Those were conditions that gave rise to the *Apocalypse*. It is, therefore, impossible that John the Evangelist be its author. The *Apocalypse* had to have been written by another John—John of Patmos, a choleric man full of resentment toward the world, who used his fury to influence unrefined tastes and minds of those who, like him, entertained an equally powerful wish of revenge on the visible world. His unswerving position had, initially, given rise to heterodox strains of Christianity built upon the belief that true salvation was born in

---

14. Lawrence, *Apocalypse*, 51. See also 209.
15. Wasilij Rozanow, "O radości przebaczania" [The Joy of Forgiving], in *Przez śmierć* [By Death], translated from the Polish edition: *Przez śmierć* (Warszawa: Fundacja Augusta Hrabiego Cieszkowskiego, 2017).

fire and enters the world through pain. In this sense, the Apocalypse seems to be as indispensable a part of popular, democratic Christianity as the figure of Judas Iscariot, constituting an indispensable ingredient in the economy of salvation.[16]

> For Revelation, be it said once and for all, is the revelation of the undying will-to-power in man, and its sanctification, its final triumph. If you have to suffer martyrdom, and if all the universe has to be destroyed in the process, still, still, still, oh Christian, you shall reign as a king and set your foot on the necks of the old bosses![17]

Pagan Antiquity saw in fire an element: neither evil nor good, certainly perilous. A destruction consisting in the loss of cosmic equilibrium between elements was defined as disharmony and injustice.[18] If Heraclitean worlds became renewed in fire, no one thought of it in terms of *just* regeneration. A fire was treated as a misfortune. Nonetheless, since the times of the Revelation, "*it is destruction that is called just*, it is the will to destroy that is called Justice and Holiness."[19] Hence, a role of the poor and the injured boiled down to destroying preexisting material conditions and a substitution of a univocally angry voice of the collective for aristocratic individuals.

A Sentence Ends in a Full Stop

One can become a Christian aristocrat only in solitude. Where a group is formed, instantly hierarchies turn up: Jesus is followed by apostles, while He himself becomes their "shepherd." Also Socrates has his disciples whom he kneads like dough. Only Zarathustra reaches for a stick to chase them away.[20] The difference between a solitary, self-contained, individual Jesus and a Jesus resulting from a group demand for divine vengeance creates the place from which *cometh* the sound of the trumpets of the Last Judgment.

---

16. Lawrence, *Apocalypse*, 56, 198. See also Jerzy Nowosielski, interview by Zbigniew Podgórzec, "O Judaszu i tajemnicy cierpienia" [Judas and the Mystery of Suffering], in *Rozmowy z Jerzym Nowosielskim* [Conversations with Jerzy Nowosielski] (Kraków: Znak, 2014), 385.
17. Lawrence, *Apocalypse*, 56.
18. Ibid., 147.
19. Deleuze, "Nietzsche and St. Paul, Lawrence and John of Patmos," 45.
20. Friedrich Nietzsche, "The Voluntary Beggar," in *Thus Spoke Zarathustra: A Book for Everyone and No One*, trans. R. J. Hollingdale (London: Penguin Books, 2003), 279–83.

> John of Patmos does not even assume the mask of the evangelist, nor that of Christ; he invents another mask, he fabricates another mask that unmasks Christ or, if you prefer, that is superimposed on Christ's mask. John of Patmos deals with cosmic terror and death, whereas the gospel and Christ dealt with human and spiritual love. Christ invented a religion of love (a practice, a way of living and not a belief), whereas the Apocalypse brings a religion of Power (*Pouvoir*)—a belief, a terrible manner of *judging*. Instead of the gift of Christ, an infinite debt.[21]

Contemporary concept of power has been altered. It no longer rests—as in the days of old—on self-mastery. Its popular interpretation is a resultant force of others recognizing it as power. If somebody questions the capacity of power to mold reality, they ultimately weaken themselves as well, narrowing the circle and potentiality of their own impact. No one has ever become more powerful by taking power away from others; "power minus power" by no means totals "greater power," but a "power drop." No wonder, that's a must. Christians, however, refuse to acknowledge the equation. Because the *Book of Revelation* furnishes them with a "political program," allowing them to cherish the hope for a worldly restoration of the lost order.

> He [Jesus] left it to John of Patmos, who was up against the Roman State, to formulate the Christian vision of the Christian State. John did it in the Apocalypse. It entails the destruction of the whole world, and the reign of saints in ultimate bodiless glory. Or it entails the destruction of all earthly power, and the rule of an oligarchy of martyrs (the Millennium).[22]

Here, too, lies the most significant aporia of the book: itself feeble, it wants to take power over, calling for the killing of the nobles of this world.[23] Therefore, another question matters: where does its extraordinary success within *Christianity* arise? Whence the astonishing career of the book? From an attempt at "clarification," Lawrence argues, of the work of Jesus, a need to end the sentence with a full stop "after-thought" by John of Patmos. For Christ let the weak down. He abandoned them and left in the exact same way he tended to evaporate from this world—into an utter, deafening solitude, into isolation, the circle of lunar light, into the great beyond. Thus, he stripped them of any remains of their faith that had been burning out, generation after generation,

---

21. Deleuze, "Nietzsche and St. Paul, Lawrence and John of Patmos," 36.
22. Lawrence, *Apocalypse*, 213.
23. Ibid., 60.

in the weakening hope for justice and resurrection. Soon enough, the weak moved their eschatological focus onto the *Book of Revelation*, which conserved a promise of crushing the evil of the everyday and an acceleration of the end. Authors of the bloodiest revolutions tended to be "good Christians."

The Democratic Jesus

A Jesus worthy of our contemporary, democratic dreams, Lawrence writes, is a vindictive Jesus, thirsty for revenge and blood. To this world, he brings the sword and discord, Sarajevo and Rwanda. The belied image has been woven around a media-apocalyptic representation of the Last Judgment, in which a verdict of the end of the world is being passed. This, precisely, is the meaning of the second part of the Apocalypse. Jesus becomes the lord of the planet, an impostor dressed up in sable furs, the king of all kings, the overlord of all creation, who dishes out his punishment to the world promptly and ruthlessly. John made him so.

> [The] thing that strikes us in the persistent use of the great pagan, as well as Jewish, power titles, both for God and for the Son of Man. *King of Kings and Lord of Lords* is typical throughout, and Kosmokrator, and Kosmodynamos. Always the titles of power, and never the titles of love. Always Christ the omnipotent conqueror flashing his great sword and destroying vast masses of men, till blood mounts up to the horses' bridles. Never Christ the Saviour: never. The Son of Man of the Apocalypse comes to bring a new and terrible *power* on to the earth, greater than that of any Pompey or Alexander or Cyrus. Power, terrific, smiting power. And when praise is uttered, or the hymn to the Son of Man, it is to ascribe to him power, and riches, and wisdom, and strength, and honour, and glory, and blessing—all the attributes given to the great kings and Pharaohs of the earth, but hardly suited to a crucified Jesus.[24]

And further:

There is Jesus—but there is also John the Divine. There is Christian love—and there is Christian envy. The former would "save" the

---

24. Ibid., 84–85. The perception of Christ as a Roman emperor has a long-standing tradition. See also the interesting article by Erik Peterson, "Christ as *Imperator*," in Erik Peterson, *Theological Tractates*, trans. Michael J. Hollerich (Stanford: Stanford University Press, 2011).

world—the latter will never be satisfied till it has destroyed the world. They are two sides of the same medal.[25]

We, therefore, do not really know who John of Patmos was, that man who knew the psychology of Jesus apparently pushing the world toward perdition so poorly—or so well. It does not really matter, after all. Suffice that he had been able to gather around *his own* ideas a certain species of Jewish Antinomians ("Christians") who, in time, started to create an image of a gloomy and doomed *ecclesia*.

The Jews Messed Up First

Human destiny is death. The Jews invented something significantly worse: a destiny that is postponed, not death, but *eternal* life, eternal torture.[26] Jewish prophets did not preach what the God *had told* them—they would, then, be speaking the incomprehensible and the unutterable—only *represented images* he had *revealed* to them. They knew the beginning of creation from Genesis; now, they only had to invent an ending, namely, spell out the one-of-a-kind spectacle of the end of the world in individual scenes and stages, as humanly bloody as possible. The pagans, on the contrary, did not make a habit of arranging their own final end. Since anything exists, they would repeat, it will also exist when its accidental, "day-old" life will have ceased to be. That is a normal course of things. Meanwhile, in the book of the Apocalypse, measuring out the end becomes a near-manic state, an anticipation of the grand spectacle of destruction and annihilation. The "first" death, corporeal, and that "other" one—the sounds of trumpets and gritting of teeth, of the seven seals cracking—the symbols are all too familiar. As well as a sense of perdition and abandon intertwined with a hope of rising from the dead. That is what the book of the vindictive and weak feeds us, the book of the revenge on life foretold.

On the one hand, Lawrence admits that Jews had not been able to absorb the world otherwise than through a prism of their particular ethnic consciousness, the contents of which they subsequently universalized[27]; on the other, he clearly states that they saw the world through pagan-borrowed eyes.[28] A grand

---

25. Lawrence, *Apocalypse*, 10.
26. Lawrence's thesis is risky, to which my attention was drawn by Robert Pawlik. A majority of Jews do not believe in eternal life. Immortality in Christianity is considered to be an Egyptian-Greek borrowing.
27. Lawrence, *Apocalypse*, 89.
28. Ibid., 87.

master of the vision was John of Patmos—"the terrible laborer of the last hour"[29]—who complemented his prophetic gesture with a pagan brutality. He very well knew that primordial religions had been based on a cult of power, potency, life, while the moral-principles-appealing Mosaic religion—*his* religion—suffers from a profound avitaminosis, from a lack of even a residual vitalism. He knew as well that pagans knew no other morality than good manners, rules defining conduct or decency. That is why the Jews outbid it: if one God, then only an invisible one; if a reward, then only after death, in a numerically "second," "better" life. The theme of "life after life" was subsequently taken up by Christians, of which Lawrence informs us with a truly Rozanovian gusto: "All religion, instead of being religion of *life*, here and now, became religion of postponed destiny, death, and reward *afterwards*, 'if you are good.'"[30]

John of Patmos owns his historic success to an efficient bullying of the "bad guys" by means of alluding to a mystified (as "operating" in nether-worlds) will to power. He was convinced that common people would sooner get the meaning of the endlessly laboring "penal colony" than take to their hearts the message of the Sermon on the Mountain. Hence, for the past two thousand years, we've been living within the perimeter of influence of a completely dead religious imaginary, focused on putrefying bodies and hailing post-mortem rewards. The *Apocalypse* "is a book for all those who think of themselves as survivors. It is the book of Zombies."[31]

---

29. Deleuze, "Nietzsche and St. Paul, Lawrence and John of Patmos," 44.
30. Lawrence, *Apocalypse*, 90. Convergences between Rozanov's works and Lawrence's writings are not accidental and therefore noteworthy. Both created their own *Apocalypses*; both also located themselves eschatologically in pagan cultures preceding the Classical era (ancient Egypt, Aegean culture, the Etruscans). They also shared a sacred attitude to sex and reproduction or, more broadly, to life and the body. See Anthony Burgess, *Flame into Being: The Life and Work of D. H. Lawrence* (New York: Arbor House, 1985), 157. Also Vasily Rozanov, *The Apocalypse of Our Time and Other Writings*, trans. Robert Payne and Nikita Romanoff (New York: Praeger, 1977). It is not without significance that Lawrence knew, appreciated, and wrote about Rozanov's books. See D. H. Lawrence, "Review of *Solitaria*, by V. V. Rozanov," or "Review of *Fallen Leaves*, by V. V. Rozanov," in *Introductions and Reviews* (Cambridge: Cambridge University Press, 2005). Also under the influence of Rozanov's work, Lawrence started taking Russian lessons late in life, but he lacked strength to acquire the language to a satisfactory degree. See A. Burgess, *Flame into Being*, 221. Parallels between Lawrence's thought and Nietzsche's philosophy seem too obvious to even warrant a mention. Gilles Deleuze believes that the text of Lawrence's *Apocalypse* could not have been written without his previous thorough reading of *The Antichrist*: "Lawrence takes up Nietzsche's initiative by taking John of Patmos as his target, and no longer Saint Paul." Deleuze, "Nietzsche and St. Paul, Lawrence and John of Patmos," 37.
31. Deleuze, "Nietzsche and St. Paul, Lawrence and John of Patmos," 37.

Symbols and Allegories

"The symbol is a concrete cosmic force [*puissance*]," Gilles Deleuze observes in his study of D. H. Lawrence's apocalyptics. "The symbol means nothing, and has neither to be explained nor interpreted, as opposed to the intellectual consciousness of allegory."[32] Although, in itself, it is "nothing," it nevertheless influences conditions of possibility of what is revealed to the human, what is made present before them. Images organized and self-organizing around a myth symbol become, *thanks to it*, visible and understandable. They are accompanied by "a rotative thought, in which a group of images turn ever more quickly around a mysterious point, as opposed to the linear allegorical chain," Deleuze somewhat puzzlingly explains. "This is precisely what the rotative symbol is. It has neither beginning nor end, it does not lead us anywhere, and above all it has no final point, nor even stages."[33] Lawrence makes "rotative thought" the original experience of Antiquity, whose symbols ("myths") transmute—"revolve," whirl into a vortex—concepts and categories we contemporarily use. Note that this does not concern the Greeks or their Roman imitators, but the most ancient cultures: Egypt, the Etruscans, the Aegean civilization. Lawrence writes:

> The myth of Kronos lives on beyond explanation, for it describes a profound experience of the human body and soul, an experience which is never exhausted and never will be exhausted, for it is being felt and suffered now, and it will be felt and suffered while man remains man. You may explain the myths away: but it only means you go on suffering blindly, stupidly, "in the unconscious," instead of healthily and with imaginative comprehension playing upon the suffering.[34]

Paganism is a world without the "Jewish" burden, a world "before the Apocalypse." It is difficult to think of such a world, since we had lost it, divesting ourselves of each and every connection with it, except for those, perhaps, we were able to impose ourselves. No writer has surpassed Kant in frankness on that matter:

> When Galilei experimented with balls of a definite weight on the inclined plane, when Torricelli caused the air to sustain a weight which

---

32. Ibid., 48.
33. Ibid.
34. D. H. Lawrence, "Introduction to *The Dragon of the Apocalypse* by Frederick Carter," in *Apocalypse: And the Writings on Revelation* (Cambridge: Cambridge University Press, 1980), e-book.

he had calculated beforehand to be equal to that of a definite column of water, or when Stahl, at a later period, converted metals into lime, and reconverted lime into metal, by the addition and subtraction of certain elements; a light broke upon all natural philosophers. They learned that reason only perceives that which it produces after its own design; that it must not be content to follow, as it were, in the leading-strings of nature, but must proceed in advance with principles of judgement according to unvarying laws, and compel nature to reply its questions.[35]

Our ruthless rule over nature, Lawrence claims, means that we have voluntarily renounced the wild life, as destructive as it is strength- and relief-giving; a life speaking to us in a language we used to understand, but which has been overshadowed currently by our consciousness and our speculation in lime, gasses and metals, exhaustively defined by such a causal relationship that is inseparable from a mechanical sequence of events proper to processes of production. We've forgotten that the human and the universe are one, and that the Moon, arrangements of planets, sea tides had always made the connection tremble.[36] So when the contemporary human complains about their loneliness, they do so because they've lost their cosmic ties with the universe, having turned their backs on what is written in the stars for them. "We can't get the sun in us by lying naked like pigs on a beach."[37] Is there a way back to the elemental world, or have we lost it forever? If there is, it must be leading through the body; there is no other. Because a spontaneous instinctiveness makes possible a connection with the reality of primordial forms. A human resurrection means, therefore, a regeneration of the entire cosmos, a supra-individual affirmation of solar light through the acceptance of planetary influence as one's fate. Two centuries before Christ, heavens returned to the human with the force of the rumor and the stereotype. It was the time of reading cards, horoscopes and telling fortunes from birds' entrails. Once again human fate began to be guarded by planets. To this day, however, people know nothing about their dependence on the stars; they merely experience the force of gravity and a burning when they're overexposed to sunlight. "When men become poor in life then they become anxious about their fortune and frightened about their fate."[38]

---

35. Immanuel Kant, *Critique of Pure Reason*, trans. J. M. D. Meiklejohn (London: Henry G. Bohn, 1855), xxvii.
36. Lawrence, *Apocalypse*, 127.
37. Ibid., 79.
38. Lawrence, "Introduction to *The Dragon of the Apocalypse* by Frederick Carter."

Nothing New or True

Let's not overdo it: the past is not all sweetness. Primordial people were not only afraid of the dark; they were also in panic about themselves, their unpredictable, mighty nature, over which they did not—could not at that point—exercise full power. They were threatened by (as we would say today) the unconscious, but also by sudden hunger, pain, a force of uncontrollable passions. They were scared of the dragon that lived in them. They perceived their strangeness in daemonic terms—as if they were visited by something they could not master at all. "Their" power transcended human nature and was treated as divine power, temporarily residing in a human, and sharing itself with the human to a certain extent. The human-dwelling dragon either ate them from within or combined with them and helped in overcoming some peril.[39]

Old worlds could be simultaneously religious and "non-theological."[40] True, prayers were offered in temples, but nobody asked about the existence of gods. People shared one skin with the world, hiding no secrets from it. So the gods did not have to descend; they lived in the midst of people. Like in the Cavafy's poem:

> When one of them moved through the marketplace of Selefkia
> just as it was getting dark—
> moved like a young man, tall, extremely handsome,
> with the joy of being immortal in his eyes,
> with his black and perfumed hair?
> the people going by would gaze at him,
> and one would ask the other if he knew him,
> if he was a Greek from Syria, or a stranger.
> But some who looked more carefully
> would understand and step aside;
> and as he disappeared under the arcades,
> among the shadows and the evening lights,
> going toward the quarter that lives
> only at night, with orgies and debauchery,
> with every kind of intoxication and desire,
> they would wonder which of Them it could be,
> and for what suspicious pleasure
> he had come down into the streets of Selefkia

---

39. Lawrence, *Apocalypse*, 166–69.
40. Ibid., 183.

from the August Celestial Mansions.[41]

God's presence was as obvious as sexual license or breathing. Discreteness, separation from the world, and its subsequent conquest meant the loss of gods—of their presence and care.

Pagans loved the world and did not want to lose it. They liked the fact that the sun was shining and that, shining, it created life. They could not understand the Christian feeling of vengefulness toward the visible world, their need of burying, preferably in cooled ashes, the whole empirical reality. What's more, neither could the Orthodox Jews. The former and the latter saw it as a special perversion, a near blasphemy.

> No wonder the pagans were horrified at the "impious" Christian desire to destroy the universe. How horrified even the old Jews of the Old Testament would have been! For even to them, earth and sun and stars were eternal, created in the grand creation by Almighty God. But no, these impudent martyrs must see it all go up in smoke.[42]

For the same reasons, Fathers of the Eastern Church recoiled from including the *Apocalypse* in their biblical canon.[43] They were not able to imagine how it could be incorporated without infringing upon the love of the world.

In his "savage pilgrimages," Lawrence sought sources of life unpoisoned, in the words of Anthony Burgess, "by the commercial and industrial heresy of the West."[44] And he found them. A universal symbol, on which stumble ("rotate") practically all notions used by the contemporary human, seems to be the half-mythologized culture of the Etruscans. He performed a systematic study of the culture, which allowed him to delve into the phallic religion of life. Hence, a leading theme of his late analysis of Etruscans is the destruction of a civilization that, in life, referred only to things suggested by natural instincts.

> The Etruscans, as everyone knows, were the people who occupied the middle of Italy in early Roman days, and whom the Romans, in their usual neighbourly fashion, wiped out entirely in order to make room for Rome with a very big R. They couldn't have wiped them all out, there

---

41. C. P. Cavafy, "One of Their Gods," in *Collected Poems*, trans. Edmund Keeley and Philip Sherrard (Princeton: Princeton University Press, 1992), 72.
42. Lawrence, *Apocalypse*, 208.
43. Ibid., 209.
44. Burgess, *Flame into Being*, 222.

were too many of them. But they did wipe out the Etruscan existence as a nation and a people. However, this seems to be the inevitable result of expansion with a big E, which is the sole *raison d'etre* of people like the Romans.[45]

Lawrence's "rotating" thought on post-mortem heritage of Etruscan civilization is, as a matter of fact, woven around an "Etruscan" belief (again: how Rozanovian) that earthly soil does contain not only bones of the dead but also seeds of life, ready to flower in life-encouraging moments. For this reason, the Etruscans made death the cause and condition of life. On one hill, they built a city; on another, exactly opposite the first, in plain sight, they erected a necropolis, "the near-at-hand city of their dear dead."[46] Between graves, they discovered the exact same life as in the city of the living, only lived "by other means." For this reason, into the vicinity of their graves, they brought food and wine, decorated them with jewels, dance and flute music—all this with those who were no longer there in mind.

With Animals

Lawrence liked and respected them. I might even say that he entertained a sort of cult in relation to animals, first and foremost due to their radical *otherness* to the human, intensified in its mythological layer by images of inhuman(e) dragons and monsters, familiar, for example, from the *Apocalypse*. He believed animals are always at home in themselves, whereas he spent his entire life searching for a home. Only the snake was seen as a king in exile. Burgess comments: "No other writer has this unpretentious sense of the sacredness of the world of beasts and reptiles, nor this willingness to give up his own raging ego (the curse he always carried with him) in an almost desperate desire for identification with pure being tortured by thought and being."[47] Works such as *Fantasia of the Unconscious* or *Psychoanalysis and the Unconscious* betray the writer's great longing for transformation into an element of the bestialized, animal world, aroused by his anguish brought upon his head by his own, groomed and perfumed, humanity.

In the late 1920s, he wrote to John Middleton Murry: "But I don't take myself seriously, except between 8.0 and 10.0 a.m., and at the stroke of midnight."[48] Was he thinking about the so-called minor creatures, or did he

---

45. D. H. Lawrence, *Etruscan Places*, quoted after Burgess, *Flame into Being*, 224.
46. Ibid.
47. Burgess, *Flame into Being*, 156.
48. Lawrence, *The Letters of D. H. Lawrence*, 653.

receive informal, blurred visions of them throughout the remaining hours of the day, we will never know for sure. The sentimental-pathos-laden approach to nature was, during the period, an element of the resounding, *fin de siecle* Przybyszewski's fashion creeping all over Europe.[49]

How Does He Know?

In the preface to *Fantasia of the Unconscious*, we are informed that:

> I am not a proper archeologist nor an anthropologist nor an ethnologist. I am no "scholar" of any sort. But I am very grateful to scholars for their sound work. I have found hints, suggestions for what I say here in all kinds of scholarly books, from the Yoga and Plato and St. John the Evangelist and the early Greek philosophers like Herakleitos down to Frazer and his "Golden Bough," and even Freud and Frobenius. Even then I only remember hints and I proceed by intuition.[50]

---

49. Here's a taste:

Ancient man had stood in an intimate relationship with nature. They lived directly in and with nature. They were a part of it, were one of nature's nerves that sounded at the smallest change in the environment. And if all the inventions of the human spirit were only organic projections, then the power of every polytheistic cult to bless and destroy was an organic projection as well. Just as the soul was a mechanism of the body that looked out from the inside of it and projected out into the world, nature revealed itself to the heathen cults in powerful symbols. In a confused battle the church destroyed one by one the veins through which the blood of the earth flowed in man. It destroyed the unconscious natural selection process of nature that expressed itself external beauty, strength and nobility. It defended everything that nature wanted to eliminate, that which was so powerfully repulsive, filth, ugliness, disease, the crippled and the castrated. The church would have loved it if everyone was castrated, the light extinguished, and the entire earth allowed to be consumed with acid rain. Its only desire, its burning request, was the ardent hope that the recently promised Day of Judgment would finally come at last. But the nerves, the veins of blood would not allow themselves to be torn out so easily. Especially in the country folk, those still rooted solidly in the earth. They used every smallest opportunity to return back to their beloved earth gods. The Christian death rage was directed against the heathen in blood thirsty laws, but the demon, the earth and nature, were indestructible. He went into the forests, hid himself in inaccessible grottos, collected his believers and celebrated crude bacchanals." (Stanisław Przybyszewski, *The Synagogue of Satan*, trans. Joe Bandel (Bandel Books Online, 2012), e-book.)

50. Lawrence, quoted after Kalnins, "Introduction," 8.

A true cabbage soup of ideas, where some are plastered onto others! Lawrence, indeed, honestly admits that he's not a scholar and has no academic aspirations, that he draws material from science, which he then rather freely employs. He highlights that, sometimes, he makes a conscious effort to misinterpret academic findings and to commit epistemological abuse. He can, therefore, claim (which we may or may not believe), for example, that none other than John of Patmos holds the keys to secret knowledge of the world and the human being, *the esoteric lore*, subsequently spoiled by Jewish and, then, Christian commentators.

Before the *Book of Revelation* became in Lawrence's hands an instrument of his critique of contemporary culture in the name of the unmediated order of being, the book had helped him in the process of mystical self-freeing from parochial shackles of consciousness. Such reading of the text had been influenced by occultist brochures written in French by the Russian, Helena Blavatsky, devoured by Lawrence in the years of the Great War. Besides them and authors abovementioned, he drew, in the course of creating his *Apocalypse*, on Hesiod's *Theogony*, Plutarch's texts on questions of cosmogony and cosmology, as well as Dean Inge's lecture on Plotinus[51] and the works of Gilbert Murray. He maintained that Christianity distorted the true knowledge of salvation, transferring matters related to it to the "nether-world." For this reason, the dissolution of Christianity taking place before our eyes[52] can offer an opportunity, Lawrence says, for a regaining of knowledge once already lost. All the more that salvation—especially in its spiritual aspect—cannot be awaited with arms crossed. We are faced with a painful process of tearing apart the seven seals with which the visible existence had been padded. This is also a process of becoming of the soul.

The writer had great respect for a heaven "preceding the Apocalypse," or even preceding the Orphics, as only in their world did the soul stumble and fall, searching for a way out of the circle of death and birth. For this reason, he rejected the psychophysical collation, demystifying the lie about the soul separated from its material guise. For this purpose, he turned in his works to the wisdom of *the body*, to its great "reason." He wrote to Frederick Carter:

> I do hate John's Jewish nasal sort of style—so uglily moral, condemning other people—prefer the way Osiris rises, or Adonis or Dionysus—not as Messiahs giving "heaven" to the "good"—but life-bringers for the

---

51. The dean was William Ralph Inge (1860–1954), a preacher, Classics scholar, theologian, nominated three times for the Nobel Prize in literature.
52. Lawrence, *Apocalypse*, 171.

good and the bad alike—like the falling rain—on the just and unjust—
who gives a damn?—like the sun.[53]

The Politics of Excess

A letter to Samuel Koteliansky of the 9th of January 1930 reads:

> I was just writing about the impossibility of fitting the Christian religion to the State—Send me the *Grand Inquisitor*, and I'll see if I can do an introduction. Tell me how *long* you'd like it. I did about 6,000 words for Carter's *Apocalypse* book.[54]

The words from Lawrence's letter indicate that the *Apocalypse* ends exactly where his breathtaking essay on the Grand Inquisitor begins. I would even claim that a lack of any traces of joining the two pieces suggests that they should be treated apiece. Let us have a look at this.

In practically every political regime, Lawrence argues, authorities taunt their power openly, no matter if its source is authority, money or naked force. Paradoxically, democracy does not deviate in this respect from the mean. Its "power" rests on a skillful, soft terror of minorities by intimidation. A success of the institution of political correctness in democracy is no accident, operating as a substitute for censorship in totalitarian regimes. In a democracy, as someone nicely put it, you can kill your political opponent with a newspaper. An infamy emanating from the mainstream is as efficient in destruction as a bullet, having the capacity to make someone or something invisible and useless overnight. "In democracy, bullying inevitably takes the place of power. Bullying is the negative form of power."[55] Whereas questioning the need for a hierarchical order and dogmatizing the principle of equality introduces a disorder in all spheres of life and signifies a lack of any criteria whatsoever. Lawrence observes:

> To have an ideal for the individual which regards only his individual self and ignores his collective self, is in the long-run fatal. Of the hierarchy
> To have a creed of individuality which denies the reality of the hierarchy

---

53. Letter to Carter from October 10, 1929, quoted after Kalnins, "Introduction," 16.
54. Quoted after Kalnins, "Introduction," s. 21. Samuel Solomonovich Koteliansky (Kot, 1880–1955) was a Russian emigre and a translator. He was the person who introduced Lawrence to Russian culture, including the work of Vasily Rozanov. He worked in a trio with the Woolfs (Virginia and Leonard).
55. Lawrence, *Apocalypse*, 215.

makes at last for more anarchy. Democratic man lives by cohesion and resistance, the cohesive force of "love" and the resistant force of the individual "freedom."[56]

Today, the individual experiences mediocre feelings: neither loves nor does not love. That's to say, the individual loves themselves. A chase of distinctiveness and uniqueness stifles a truth of feeling one could bestow on another—second to one both in terms of numbers and exceptionality. Love, to put it differently, clashes against the wall of solipsism and indifference separating us from someone else's *and* uninteresting world. "We *cannot bear connection*. That is our malady. We *must* break away, and be isolate. We call that being free, being individual."[57] If we want to overcome the "malady," to reach out to the other and leave the cage we've been trapped in, we first need to renounce the shells of aged and used-up human forms: Christianity, socialism, doctrinal separateness and the omnipresent, offensive power of the people.

Here another question arises: who should help the lost human monad turn in the direction of pure being unmediated by social institutions? I've already heralded the answer above: this can be achieved by the Grand Inquisitor, a Jesuit philanthropist representing Western Christianity, the new John of Patmos, who knows that the Apocalypse proper had taken place some time ago, imperceptibly, without fame. His knowledge is grounded in the long-durée experience of humanity, who stopped taking the prophecy of the Second Coming seriously at least some time ago. Well, just another eschatological rumor, a philosophical hypothesis, to which no greater importance ought to be attached. "It is reality versus illusion, and the illusion was Jesus's while time itself retorts with the reality."[58] But it was not only Jesus who had failed, putting *parousia* to bed. Also the Christianity he had prepared had to emerge with either *the already saved*—saved without deeds—or those who have strength enough to prepare their own salvation in mind. Whereas the common people are precluded from salvation by the burden of their preposterous biology. For this reason, "These are the strong, and they must be as gods, to be able to be Christians fulfilling all the Christ-demand."[59] The rest be damned.

The belief in one's exceptionality leads to a temptation (and, arguably, a requirement) of patronization with regard to common people: in order to protect them from themselves, more than plain goodness is required: contempt

---

56. Ibid., 216.
57. Ibid., 219.
58. D. H. Lawrence, introduction to *The Grand Inquisitor*, in *The Complete Works of D. H. Lawrence*, Parts Edition (Delphi Classics, 2015), e-book.
59. Ibid.

and toleration are needed. As well as science, medicine and biological experiments in particular, which fulfills the desire for miracles, making itself felt with timeless regularity. In a longer temporal perspective, humanity will definitively resolve the threat of hunger, as people will only be looking for the bread that satisfies their physical yearning in the stomach. "Heavenly bread," for which one reaches when one wants to live in truth, will be renounced as unnecessary extravagance. "Only the few, the potential heroes or the 'elect,' can see the simple distinction. The mass *cannot* see it, and will never see it."[60] Lawrence indicated here a difference in essence, not just of degree, between humans. The divide into the better and the worse, the human and the sub-human is a consequence, so to speak, of the "ontology of social being"; in any case, it certainly is not an invention of the corrupt elites or the literati.

Those wielding power over earthly bread return it to the masses in excess, as if it were their gift to them. "The mass, who do not understand the difference between money and life, should always bow down to the elect, who do."[61] Christ demonstrated a lack of political acumen in making resignation from earthly bread a universal imperative, not caring about its availability. Meanwhile, distribution of material goods is a very real power. By ceding it to the enemies, he did not only do a silly thing but also weakened Christians' political position. The human may *think* of the "nether-world," but they *live* in this one. "Money is not life, it is true. But ignoring money and leaving it to the devil means handing over the great mass of men to the devil, for the mass of men cannot distinguish between money and life."[62] The inability to distinguish between daily and heavenly bread leads to moral irrelevance. Lawrence motions: "Think how difficult it is to know the difference between good and evil! Why, sometimes it is evil to be good. And how is the ordinary man to understand that? He can't."[63] The human will not save their humanity *en masse*. He, therefore, has to depart—the point being that he has just left—unnoticed, the way birds die. Christ had lied to the common people; the Inquisitor speaks the truth and there's nothing disquieting, nothing devilish in his words. Simply, Jesus's teaching was intended for people of "another dimension," while *ordinary* people have to make do with *plain* bread.

> And here, surely, he [the Inquisitor] is right. Since man began to think and to feel vividly, seed time and harvest have been the two great sacred periods of miracle, rebirth, and rejoicing. Easter and harvest home are

---

60. Ibid.
61. Ibid.
62. Ibid.
63. Ibid.

festivals of the earthly bread, and they are festivals which go to the roots of the soul. For it is the earthly bread as a miracle, a yearly miracle. All the old religions saw it: the Catholic still sees it, by the Mediterranean. And this is not weakness. This is truth. The rapture of the Easter kiss, in old Russia, is intimately bound up with the springing of the seed and the first footstep of the new earthly bread.[64]

Preface to Dostoevsky's *The Grand Inquisitor* is not the only place in which a radicalism of the writer's beliefs comes to the fore. The protagonist of *Women in Love* argues that "one man isn't any better than another, not because they are equal, but because they are intrinsically *other*, that there is no term of comparison. The minute you begin to compare, one man is seen to be far better than another, all the inequality you can imagine is there by nature."[65] In the 11th chapter of *The Plumed Serpent*, Lawrence writes about aristocrats of the spirit who, living among people, do not regard themselves as human. Strictly speaking, they are overlords of humanity, but do not originate from it.[66] So if humans decide to bow to them, there's nothing wrong with this; it merely results from the order of things.

The Truth about Fascism, the Truth of Fascism

Bertrand Russell had really nothing good to say about his ex-friend. Although he did sense a man of considerable genius in Lawrence, he was repelled by "a positive force for evil,"[67] of which he suspected him. He even accused him of fascism long before the invention of fascism, with an utter disregard of an anachronism of such juxtapositions. The reason for the accusation was supposed to be the writer's distrust of efficiency of democratic procedures in the arrangement of the world of free people, which would rank him in the same file as Plato, Alexis de Tocqueville and Nietzsche. Russell not only failed to notice any grain of truth in premises of Lawrence's "political philosophy" but also charged him with issues others regarded as sound. In this respect, Lawrence's voluminous correspondence can be used as an address book of his declared friends and allies. Might have they also gone mad? Let us scrutinize Russell's "arguments."

---

64. Ibid.
65. Lawrence, quoted after Kalnins, "Introduction," 23.
66. Kalnins, "Introduction," 24.
67. Bertrand Russell, *Portraits from Memory and Other Essays* (New York: Simon and Schuster, 1956), 112.

But this is not to say that there was anything good in his ideas. I do not think in retrospect that they had any merit whatever. They were the ideas of a sensitive would-be despot who got angry with the world because it would not instantly obey. When he realized that other people existed, he hated them. But most of the time he lived in a solitary world of his own imaginings, peopled by phantoms as fierce as he wished them to be. [...] The world between the wars was attracted to madness. Of this attraction Nazism was the most emphatic expression. Lawrence was a suitable exponent of this cult of insanity.[68]

Anthony Burgess, the writer's biographer, echoes Russell. He sums up critical remarks with regard to democracy in a familiar fashion: "Dangerous words, perhaps. We have to remember that Lawrence died three years before Hitler came to power."[69] Deceptively put. Can the critique of democracy we come across in Plato's oeuvre, formulated two and a half thousand years ago, weaken (or reinforce) the temporal distance between Plato and the Weimar Republic? I doubt it. For the same reason—this time, due to a temporal proximity—looking for connections between Lawrence's passionate, struggling thought and the hateful message of *Mein Kampf* is not only a malpractice and thoughtlessness but also a kind of assertion of the democratic man's moral superiority.

Here, both Russell and Burgess managed to tackle a very significant problem consisting in a relatively facile attribution of the adjective "fascist" to a political opponent, especially if they come from antidemocratic milieus. Thus, the contemporary, lay "Manicheans," classifying fascism as the greatest evil, put an inalienable *moral* label on their opponents.[70] The person who, so labeled, is sent out into the world has no place amidst the civilized. If we accede to the facile stigmatization and segregation, we will understand nothing, except, perhaps, the fact that such an operation is easily conducted. Most of all, we will not be able to comprehend why intellectually responsible and deeply thoughtful individuals ("I was inclined to believe that he [Lawrence] had some insight that was denied to me"—Russell[71]) could take into consideration issues that, later, made a smooth passage onto the Fascists' flags and banners. Choosing ignorance, we will never understand reasons why 95 percent of Germans supported Hitler until the very end of the Third Reich.[72]

---

68. Ibid., 116.
69. Burgess, *Flame into Being*, 124.
70. Milan Kundera, *The Curtain: An Essay in Seven Parts*, trans. Linda Asher (New York: Harper Perennial, 2008), e-book.
71. Russell, *Portraits from Memory*, 115.
72. W. G. Sebald, *On the Natural History of Destruction*, trans. Anthea Bell (New York: Random House, 2003), e-book.

Thus, it turns out that there must be some truth in fascism. It is revealed—a truth unchallenged even by Christ—by the Grand Inquisitor: true—people fall into the worse and the better; true—for a majority of the people, the language of moral difference is as illegible and as stale as their daily bread. The truth uttered by the Grand Inquisitor is difficult to swallow, and even more difficult to debunk, because it forms a pillar of contemporary civilization. Its elements can be found as easily in fascism as in democracy. "Fascism," then, lies in everyone who accepts the world they presently inhabit without reservations. And it is of no importance that they be a monarchist, a fascist, a democrat, an anti-globalist or someone else still. In this sense, Lawrence in Deleuze's reading is right: Fyodor Dostoevsky's *The Grand Inquisitor* is a symbol "rotating" all contemporary concepts. Their "rotation" unleashes a vertigo, an anxiety in the human, disabling their dwelling in a world that has long stopped being theirs. More, still: it disables their understanding of what has happened to them ("oh, gosh, this can't be true!"), which derives from an inability to distinguish Dostoevsky from Balzac,[73] Christ from His malevolent imitator, bread from stones.

Conclusion

In a violently poetic text, Lawrence describes what produces poetry: people are constantly putting up an umbrella that shelters them and on the underside of which they draw a firmament and write their conventions and opinions. But poets, artists, make a slit in the umbrella, they tear open the firmament itself, to let in a bit of free and windy chaos and to frame in a sudden light a vision that appears through the rent-Wordsworth's spring or Cézanne's apple, the silhouettes of Macbeth or Ahab.[74]

I repeat after Dostoevsky, after Lawrence: only beauty can save the world; only the artist can become a priest of being renewed in truth and via truth, whatever the truth may be. Let us not look for a different path. And God? Better he stayed where he is. If he comes, he will fulfill John's prophecy. A thing worth remembering.

---

73. Olga Sedakova, "Nieudana epifania: dwie chrześcijańskie powieści—*Idiota* and *Doktor Żywago*" [An Unsuccessful Epiphany: Two Christian Novels—*The Idiot* and *Doctor Zhivago*], *Kronos*, no. 1 (2014): 196.
74. Gilles Deleuze and Felix Guattari, *What Is Philosophy?*, trans. Hugh Tomlison and Graham Burchell (New York: Columbia University Press, 1994), 203–4.

Chapter 5

TO LOOK UPON HIS FACE AND YET NOT DIE (JACOB TAUBES)

Rabbi Ben Levi, on the Sabbath, read
A volume of the Law, in which it said,
"No man shall look upon my face and live."
And as he read, he prayed that God would give
His faithful servant grace with mortal eye
To look upon His face and yet not die.[1]

Poseur, scribbler, provocateur, seducer, trifler, uncompromising theologian, thinker of such broad scope that the shrewdest rabbis of his time could not follow—these are all masks, costumes in which Jacob Taubes chose to dress up his uninhibited thought, his unique way of being. A little kitschy, always provocative, undoubtedly a genius, he saw everywhere "signs of the approaching End"; at the same time, as one can tell from his chaotic writing, he wanted—like Rabbi Ben Levi—to capture the first moment of the apocalypse, to spot the rising tide and even to outstrip it.

Curriculum Vitae

He was born in 1923 in Vienna into a rabbinical family. In 1936 the whole family moved to politically neutral Switzerland where Taubes's father was appointed chief rabbi. He completed his education in Basel and Zurich. In 1947 in Zurich he defended a doctoral thesis on Messianic ideas in Western culture (*Abendländische Eschatologie*), which he then published as a book—the only one published in his lifetime. He became friends with Armin Mohler, the author of the term "conservative revolution," a would-be SS man (they did not want him), later the secretary of Ernst Jünger. At the same time he maintained close intellectual ties with the Protestant theologian Karl Barth and with Hans

---

1. H. W. Longfellow, "The Spanish Jew's Tale. The Legend of Rabbi Ben Levi," in *The Poetical Works of Longfellow* (London: Henry Frowde, 1906), 358.

Urs von Balthasar, the influential Catholic priest and prominent theologian. In 1949 he was employed at the Jewish Theological Seminary in New York. He attended Leo Strauss's seminar held at the New School for Social Research. While in the United States, he also met Hannah Arendt and Paul Tillich. It's a small world.

In 1951 Taubes was awarded the Warburg scholarship and went to work at a university in Jerusalem. He was admitted by the rector of the Hebrew University, Hugo Bergman, who would later describe Taubes's intellectual abilities as "absolutely exceptional" while pointing to his characteristic "disreputable behavior [...] his chutzpah and his verve."[2] The Israeli episode is particularly interesting for it was then that Taubes began his study of the Apostle Paul's epistolography, which brought him posthumous fame when published in 1993 as four lectures on Pauline political theology.[3] His efforts focused on the creative application of some conceptual solutions to biblical issues, as developed by Carl Schmitt and Walter Benjamin. Interpreted anew, Paul, the apostle of the state of emergency, is presented as a follower of Isaac, Moses's rival in the creation of a spiritual community *ab ovo*, and finally as an uncompromising enemy of Jews who are "kept in captivity under the law" and hence as someone who is both outside and inside the law. It is possible that Taubes saw himself as such a border figure, moving between these two areas: of law and of lawlessness, of convention and of ridiculing all conventions. Suffice it to say that Gershom Scholem, who had invited Taubes to Israel, one day told him to pack up and go back where he came from. And the otherwise outstanding student and scholar was bid farewell with a rather unrefined word—*Verräter* (traitor).[4]

In Israel, Taubes became friends with Geulah Cohen, Bergman's MA student and activist of the Lechi extremist military organization that strived to actualize Jewish Messianic ideas by force. She later recalled: "When I joined the boys for one of their missions, I felt the spark of primordial fire, the same spark that would burn in me years later on giving birth."[5] And thus the end is the beginning; killing inspires the thought of the birth of a new life; a new world rises from the ruins of the old one. I think that Taubes must have had an extraordinary ear for this kind of radicalism. Taubes's letter addressed to Bergman sheds an interesting light on the relations between himself and Cohen:

---

2. Nitzan Lebovic, "The Jerusalem School: The Theopolitical Hour," *New German Critique* 105, no. 3 (2008): 107.
3. Jacob Taubes, *The Political Theology of Paul*, trans. Dana Hollander (Stanford: Stanford University Press, 2004).
4. Babette Babich, "Ad Jacob Taubes," *New Nietzsche Studies*, no. 3–4 (2008): vi.
5. Lebovic, "The Jerusalem School," 110.

> Yesterday I postponed my study of ontology and went to see Geulah (so you see I took your advice finally), eventually finding her. We sat together till after midnight, and I came to see that her nationalist thinking is full of truly messianic yearning. I said, "The goal should not be to reach the kingdom [*Malchut*], but first to produce a man worthy of it." [...] Geulah answered, "The empty vessel is ready to accept the wealth of sacredness [*Shefa Kodesh*]."[6]

Partly a soldier and partly a radio journalist, in her journalistic activity Cohen made use of something that might be called "antinormative messianic discourse," which Taubes greatly admired. Using Schmitt's language, she voiced the rights and interests of the majority of Jewish settlers: "There is no hatred between me and the Palestinians," she would emphasize. "They are the enemy in a legitimate struggle over land."[7] Cohen's opinion was that the legitimacy of the Arab–Jewish confrontation was due to its political-theological character. "Cohen is a nonpracticing Jew," to cite Nitzan Lebovic, "and she does not see her messianic perspective as in any way religious. Her politics ascribes sacredness to the Zionist enterprise without appealing to divine law."[8] The very right to free life and the freedom to determine one's own fate seemed "holy" enough.

At the time of its formation, Israel was a country in a state of emergency. It struggled for existence and its own substance using all means available and all possible forces. Jews would find some surprisingly good solutions to crisis situations in the writings of Carl Schmitt, which Taubes noted—with considerable amusement—in his famous essay on this German political theologian:

> Not only was Jerusalem a divided city in the 1940s and 1950s, but the Hebrew University had been exiled from Mount Scopus and was located in a monastery in the city center. The great library was locked up on Mount Scopus, where an Israeli guard changed every fortnight under the supervision of the United Nations.
>
> Contrary to the terms of the official truce, which said that nothing could be taken from Mount Scopus into the city, and nothing from the city to Mount Scopus, the decree was circumvented with the help of members of the guard who, when they came back to the city, filled their trousers and bags with books that the university library had labeled "urgent."

---

6. Ibid., 111.
7. Ibid.
8. Ibid.

So it came about that, as a novice, I was to give lectures on the philosophy of the seventeenth century. I went to the library director and told him of my problem. For a lecture on Descartes I needed a historical and philosophical sketch of the term *law* in both its natural scientific and juridico-theological senses.

The differing conceptions that came together in the term *Gesetz* had to be identified more exactly. The only source that could help me deal with this problem was Carl Schmitt's *Verfassungslehre*, which dealt with the problem of *nomos / lex / Gesetz*.

The chief librarian listened carefully, but explained that he was powerless to speed the book ordering process. It could take two or three months before I got hold of the book. This was little help, since in three months the semester would be over.

You can imagine how surprised I was when, three weeks later, just before the beginning of the semester, I was called to the library and was able to pick up a copy of Schmitt's *Verfassungslehre*. The chief librarian quickly explained that I should not get any big ideas; the day after I had put in a request for the *Verfassungslehre* they had received an urgent call from the Ministry of Justice: the minister of justice, Pinchas Rosen (formerly Rosenblüth), needed Schmitt's *Verfassungslehre* so that he could deal with some difficult problems in the drafting of a constitution for the state of Israel. The book was therefore immediately brought from Mount Scopus and had now arrived in the library on its return journey, where my urgent request had been kept against an "opportune moment."

There is a subsequent European and American history to this. I must admit to being more bemused than taken with the idea that the constitution of the State of Israel (a constitution which fortunately still does not exist) would be drafted using Schmitt's *Verfassungslehre* as a guide.

I wrote about this to my "Swiss" school friend Armin Mohler and added to it a reflection on the problem of the Fascist intelligentsia. I wrote something like: for me, Martin Heidegger and Carl Schmitt are the most significant exponents of German intellect from the later 1920s and early 1930s. That both involved themselves with the Hitler regime presents me with a problem that I cannot resolve by appealing to the inner bastard of Nazism. I mentioned also that both came from a Catholic background, just like Hitler and Goebbels actually.[9]

---

9. Jacob Taubes, "Carl Schmitt: Apocalyptic Prophet of the Counterrevolution," in *To Carl Schmitt: Letters and Reflections*, trans. Keith Tribe (New York: Columbia University Press, 2013), 9–11.

Martin Buber, Hugo Bergman, Geulah Cohen, Jacob Taubes—these are the four names of the most prominent representatives of Jewish political theology of that time. In that minefield, that reality which was unfavorable to Jews, the contestants' political colors ceased to be of much importance. They shared hostility toward "the world as it is," the world that pushed against them from all sides. But one more thing brought them close together. It was a liking for the books of Carl Schmitt whose theory provided them with a basis for their actions, resulting in very specific political and theological outcomes. They agreed with the German constitutionalist as to the fact that the basic theological concepts and terms became secularized, that is, misrepresented, thus losing their divine power and sanction and gaining an impure power, a "devilish," "infernal" one. As Taubes puts it, "Secularization is thus not a positive concept for Schmitt. On the contrary, to him it is the devil."[10] Under the new conditions, God is no longer the source of the supernatural, nor is it Him who suspends the laws of nature for "a certain time." Sovereign is he who decides on the state of exception, who has the authority to determine exceptions. A sovereign decision constitutes all possible relations, including the most important one that defines the difference between an enemy and a friend, between the unfriendly time of the past and the future time that is filled with hope.

> The present becomes an unreal boundary between the "no-longer" of the past and the "not-yet" of the future. Time is not the place of life, but contains the pestilential smell of death, and plunges life into the Sheol of the past. Not until the End Time, at the end of time, when transience itself passes away, will eternity triumph over the deadly principle of time. It is the work of magic.[11]

Neither of magic nor of art, but politics, as Taubes would modify his view while in Jerusalem. If, whether one wants it or not, one abides in a place where the substance of time and the substance of eternity, death and life, intersect, one must—for some pious reason, in the name of the "not-yet-existing" God—turn to the means of destruction, the means that are used to carry out a massacre. "God," Taubes writes, "will annihilate the world and then appear in his might. [...] If the demonic, destructive element is missing, the

---

10. Taubes, *The Political Theology of Paul*, 66.
11. Jacob Taubes, *Occidental Eschatology*, trans. David Ratmoko (Stanford: Stanford University Press, 2009), 8.

petrified order, the prevailing positivity of the world cannot be overcome."[12] (I will return to this issue later on.)

The above quoted words seemed to Geulah Cohen to theologically support the fight against the Arabs, while both Hugo Bergman and Martin Buber, in their political calculations, regarded Zionism as "a mistake": "I have a bad feeling," Buber wrote to Bergman in 1927, "because we came here without asking permission from those populating the land."[13] Taubes's attitude to Zionism was also critical but out of different, not quite sentimental reasons. He believed that the attempt to transform the movement into political messianism ended in complete failure. Israel was created in the shape and likeness of a nineteenth-century nation-state. Thus, the cardinal and most significant sin of Zionism was its "negation of Jewish avant-garde"—Jewish spirituality was reduced by the Zionists to "normal existence."[14]

Having returned to the United States from Israel, Taubes found a job at Beacon Press, where he was asked to supervise a series on "radical philosophy." And thus he commissioned books from Schmitt and Buber. The former refused politely; the latter published his famous *Paths in Utopia*.[15]

Starting in 1949, Taubes lectured in philosophy of religion in New York, then in Jerusalem between 1951 and 1953, and then, by a symptomatic stroke of luck, at Harvard, Princeton and Columbia Universities. In 1996 he became professor at the Freie Universität in Berlin. Almost everybody in Germany agreed with Gadamer when he said that Taubes was "a wastrel of his talents."[16]

Taubes's first wife, Susan (*primo voto* Feldman, 1928–69), the writer and cultural anthropologist, described the nightmare of their relationship in her novel titled *Divorcing*. Their toxic entanglements are best illustrated in a passage at the beginning of the novel in which Sophie (Susan) vivisects the confrontational personality of her husband Ezra (Taubes):

> Ezra began with a very small point. So small that Sophie didn't realize at all that he was starting a quarrel. A little thing that can be settled in a minute, she thought, or a little thing there's nothing to be done about that can be dismissed in a minute. Then as Ezra went on developing his point for an immoderately long time, it dawned on Sophie that the issue wasn't

---

12. Ibid., 10.
13. Lebovic, "The Jerusalem School," 114.
14. An undated letter from Jacob Taubes to Hugo Bergman (early 1952), in Lebovic, "The Jerusalem School," 117.
15. From Taubes's letter to Schmitt, dated August 2, 1955, it can be inferred that the book in question is *The Conservative Tradition*, an anthology of texts by authors such as Schmitt, Bonald, Donoso Cortés, and even Pope Pius IX.
16. Babich, "Ad Jacob Taubes," viii.

simply a particular tie he couldn't locate and blamed her for failing to pack, or her having failed to pack other items on other occasions, or her disregard for his appearance, or for her own appearance—her disregard for appearances in general. The issue was really all the consequences this had on their lives and would continue to accumulate. The issue was enormous.[17]

She committed suicide when she discovered that Taubes had left her and their two children for Margherita von Brentano, the Kant specialist at Freie Universität. The presumption is, though, that the reason behind Taubes's second marriage was other than love. "Von Brentano," as Taubes would always address his new wife, was to him the embodiment of the highest virtues and values of the German spirit, which is possibly why he decided to marry her, thus breaking the law that had been in force in Germany 30 years earlier.[18]

Jacob Taubes was a great womanizer, a fact that in itself would not be worth dwelling on were it not that he himself, like a Don Juan, was keen on communicating his sexual conquests to a broad audience. "If you sleep with the same woman twice, you've joined the establishment," he liked to repeat the famous 1960s slogan. Whenever he went to Rome with Ingeborg Bachmann, he would always assume a false identity, in case someone was following in his footsteps.

He was famous for his lack of tact and his untidiness. He always wore black, did not change his clothes for weeks. He was a messy eater. He was always in a hurry. He made free use of other people's belongings (his writings are mostly made up of cryptoquotations, verging on plagiarism) and attributed to others that which was his (he considered his thoughts to be some foreign secretion that he must get rid of as soon as possible). I will now try to relate one more scene (after Babette Babich whose memoir I am relying on here), a very revealing one in which they both took part.

When in Paris, Taubes took her to a synagogue. It was shrouded in darkness. Being a woman, Babich could only take her seat in the balcony, nowhere else. Taubes sat below, in the immediate vicinity of the sanctuary. She looked at him as if he contained within himself the entire history of the Jewish nation. She saw in him at once a man and a prophet. Next to her was an old Jewish woman, focused on her prayer, the mother of a little girl who was carelessly running around the balcony. The exalted mood was suddenly interrupted by Taubes's monotonous snore. But it was not only the synagogue's dead silence that would put him in the mood for an afternoon nap; he was in the habit of

---

17. Susan Taubes, *Divorcing* (New York: Random House, 1969), 12.
18. Babich, "Ad Jacob Taubes," viii.

falling asleep almost everywhere—at countless conferences he attended in his lifetime, or even during his own seminars.

> The contrast between the dark balcony above and the dull daylight of the sanctuary below wrenched in my throat and I found my face wet with tears. Surprised because I was not sure whether I was crying for my own lack, for the beauty of her faith or else for the contrast between the worlds of prayer, above and below.[19]

It was February 1986. Despite his advanced disease, Taubes continued teaching, in a lying position, his last seminar on the political theology of the Apostle Paul. He died seven weeks later.

The Theology of Paul of Tarsus

The main intention of Taubes's lectures on Paul, and their central meaning, was "gathering the heretic back into the fold," that is, returning Paul to the Jewish community. The Christianity of the Apostle Paul corresponded with the Jewish apocalyptic experience. The universalism of this religious movement, which today is so eagerly pointed to,[20] was conceived not only as a means of incorporating the Gentiles into the circle of the Jewish perception of the world but rather as a means of converting the Jews to the right path to salvation—a path that they either abandoned themselves or were coerced to abandon. The dramatic circumstances on his way to Damascus made Paul break with the Old Faith, with the Law, with the Mosaic religion, and establish a new people and a new faith based on a new kind of covenant, focused around a new center—similarly to Moses who had formed an entirely new nation of the faithful. The critical point, namely, that which makes it possible to distinguish the new chosen ones from the usurpers, is neither a hastily enacted law nor any rule that is of this world and that aims to organize it anew, but the death and resurrection of the Crucified One. "It isn't *nomos* but rather the one who was nailed to the cross by *nomos* who is the imperator!"[21] From now on, it is spiritual kinship ("by way of faith"), and not corporeal kinship, that constitutes the foundation of the community of believers. "For they *are* not all Israel, which are of Israel"—this means that salvation is to be in salvation "according to the promise" and not "according

---

19. Ibid., ix–x.
20. Alain Badiou, *Saint Paul: The Foundation of Universalism*, trans. Ray Brassier (Stanford: Stanford University Press, 2003).
21. Taubes, *The Political Theology of Paul*, 24.

to the blood."²² Salvation will depend upon whether one is a member of the new community. The old people of God are to immerse, to "dissolve" in a newly engendered people of God.²³ Taubes suggests that the relationship of Jews and early Christians (even though they did not call themselves so²⁴) before 70 AD (the destruction of the Second Temple) should be contrasted with what happened later. In other words, the strictly apostolic period should be contrasted with the folly of Christian proselytism, every manifestation of which resulted in anti-Semitism.²⁵ It would be a mistake to see Paul as an irreconcilable enemy of the Synagogue, or to see the Synagogue as a generalized enemy of Judeo-Christians or the Judeo-Christian spirit. Everything was intertwined and quite muddled in the fluid reality of the Roman Empire. Christians were spiritually restless Jews, Jewish antinomians who from time to time radicalized the vapid message of the Torah. Therefore, as Paul intuited, the most interesting questions were born not in the Synagogue but in the course of contact with the external environment—with the Gentiles converted to Christianity (proto-Judaism!). What determined their inclusion in the economy of salvation was not law—any law—but their belief in Christ's resurrection. Questions would arise as to what it really meant to be a Jew in those conditions. Does it make any sense to destabilize the fragile political balance based on respect for positive law? And finally—what is positive law when confronted with messianic hope? Taubes argues that in order to grasp the meaning of these questions more fully, one has to bear in mind the fact that early Christians ("new Jews") were possessed by the eschatological longing for the Second Coming that was "at hand", that their faith was fueled by visions of an imminent apocalypse. Thus, Paul's theology seems to express the collective longings; his politico-theological calculations are oriented toward legitimizing a political community and do not focus on the inner life of its members. For Jews always consider faith—*emuna*—to reach far beyond the

---

22. Ibid.
23. Ibid.
24. Ibid., 19.
25. There is nothing surprising in it, argues Carl Schmitt. Anti-Semitism, or rather anti-Judaism, is intrinsic to the new situation from the outset. It is either we, Christians, or you, Jews, who are right as to final matters. There is no room for deliberating, one needs to take a stand, make a decision of fundamental importance (to salvation). This world is thus organized, Taubes echoes Schmitt—it is filled with either Jews or Christians, and no conciliatory gestures will ever change it. "You" *versus* "we" is the true face of political theology. In other words, there is no room for neutrality in the theological-political argument. In the reality contemporary to Paul, it was a matter of decision whether one was a Jew or not. And though it was not possible to become a Jew, one could stop being a Jew or remain so.

horizon of individual experience; it constitutes the basis of the whole nation's existence and creates its history.

Apocalypse is a miracle of humanity's deliverance from the slavery of death—through death—as well as from the oppression of necessity, from the cycle of natural transformation. "Consequently, Taubes argues that apocalypse must guard against its own destructive impulses without relinquishing its antagonism towards profane authority."[26] Its impetus is directed against the law that glues together the loosened structures of temporal reality (the structures of meaning and power). On the one hand, there is the apocalyptic understanding of time as delay—as a respite or reprieve ("everything has its end"); on the other, in case the former vision is negated, there is simple metabolism, an endless and senseless natural repetition.[27] Therefore, if man wants to break away from the inhuman rhythm of experiencing the world, to grow independent of the pulse of biological transformation ("the pulse of life"), he must be prepared, at any time, to confront the dark, unknown, uncontrollable and untamable forces. This precisely is history. It is a field of action for some undefined powers, but also an arena where man's character is being forged, a place of humanization and—at the end of time—of deification ("to look upon His face and yet not die"). Nature poses a natural threat to this type of vocation due to its dehumanizing force and its gradual naturalization of all symptoms of human life. Faced with this breach—between the order created by man and the chaos that he yields to, between history and nature—man must decide what is closer to him: he himself or the murmur of a stream and the flight of birds. "Endless infinity," Taubes writes, "characterizes indifferent happening [*das gleich-gültige Geschehen*] that does not call for decision. History separates itself from this indifferent happening by placing one into the decision for truth."[28] Apocalypse, that unhistorical element of history, abolishes chronology, undermines the concept of progress and even of evolution: everything advances toward its end that gives meaning to history. By posing the question of the Eschaton, history surpasses its limitations; it becomes visible and sensible to itself. However, for the naturalized *hyletics* there is always "time" to decide; they are not in any hurry. For cyclicality changes decision into an empty gesture. Immersed in the natural sequence of events (Thursday–weekend–Monday), they are completely indifferent as to the act of decision and as to history. They do not—in a sense it is not even possible—take responsibility for anything. Ethics is replaced with law that tells them what one must not do and

---

26. J. R. Gold, "Jacob Taubes: 'Apocalypse from Below,'" *Telos* 134 (2006): 142.
27. This is Alexandre Kojève's post-historical vision of the world, criticized by Taubes in his essay "Asthetisierung der Wahrheit im Posthistoire."
28. Taubes, *Occidental Eschatology*, 5.

what goes unpunished. In this seemingly living, restless world, everybody is at once dead and rejected by death. "Creation," to cite Taubes again, is "decay [...] without hope."[29] Those, in turn, who feel the course of human history are urged for decision by every historical occurrence, including the *final* and most important one. So haste is very advisable. Historical time is running out and coming to an end, as opposed to the barren μεταβολή; the need to decide is growing more and more urgent day by day: be as little children no longer! As Taubes once noted of apocalypse: "Whether one knows it or not is entirely irrelevant, whether one takes it for fancy or sees it as dangerous is completely uninteresting in view of the intellectual breakthrough and experience of time as respite. [...] There is no eternal return, time does not enable nonchalance; rather, it is distress."[30] And further on in the interview:

> But from a Christian perspective one has no time, because God's Kingdom is at hand. It is not important for me what God's Kingdom expresses in the assumption "God's Kingdom is at hand." What matters is the plausibility of its being close [Nah-Sein]. Whoever presumes to think in a Christian way, but refuses to think of respite, is mentally deficient.[31]

Law of whatever kind: positive, given (to Jews) by God, or natural—law as κατέχον—turns out to be faulty in the context of a "reprieve"; something groundless, arbitrary and inoperative. "This is the secret knowledge promised by apocalyptic thought that worldly authority would prefer to pass over in silence."[32] Taubes sees apocalypse as the abolition of all law, including the natural one: the world ends; death ceases to exist (or only it "exists"). "Paul defines the time between the death of Jesus and the Parousia of Christ as the kairos, which is characterized by the crossing over of the still natural and the already supernatural states of the world. With the death and resurrection of Jesus, the turning point [*Wende*] is reached: the fashion [*das Wesen*] of this world will pass away."[33] Since it always arrives from the future, apocalypse is an empty, unwritten "story"—an event devoid of any traces or memories whatsoever. Its unstoppable, destructive movement, its progression toward the catastrophe of the world—pregnant with memories and full of traces of past events—is

---

29. Gold, "Jacob Taubes: 'Apocalypse from Below,'" 155.
30. Interview with Jacob Taubes, in *Denken, das an der Zeit ist*, ed. Florian Roetzer (Frankfurt am Main: Suhrkamp, 1987), quoted in Taubes, *Occidental Eschatology*, xiii.
31. Interview with Jacob Taubes, in *Denken, das an der Zeit ist*, 318.
32. Gold, "Jacob Taubes: 'Apocalypse from Below,'" 156.
33. Taubes, *Occidental Eschatology*, 68. If there is no hope for love, then the last sentence of this passage has very little to do with common sense and becomes somewhat nihilistic

due to the emptiness that draws everything in. At the moment of catastrophe, impatience interweaves with the hope that the apocalyptic fire, though it engulfs everything, does not incinerate everything, that it contains within itself "the time that remains." As in César Vallejo's poem about a house that is brimming with absence:

> —No one lives in the house anymore—you tell me—; all have gone. The living room, the bedroom, the patio, are deserted. No one remains any longer, since everyone has departed.
>
> And I say to you: When someone leaves, someone remains. The point through which a man passed, is no longer empty. The only place that is empty, with human solitude, is that through which no man has passed. New houses are deader than old ones, for their walls are of stone or steel, but not of men. A house comes into the world, not when people finish building it, but when they begin to inhabit it. A house lives only off men, like a tomb. That is why there is an irresistible resemblance between a house and a tomb. Except that the house is nourished by the life of man, while the tomb is nourished by the death of man. That is why the first is standing, while the second is laid out.
>
> Everyone has departed from the house, in reality, but all have remained in truth. And it is not their memory that remains, but they themselves. Nor is it that they remain in the house, but that they continue about the house. Functions and acts leave the house by train or by plane or on horseback, walking or crawling. What continues in the house is the organ, the agent in gerund and in circle. The steps have left, the kisses, the pardons, the crimes. What continues in the house are the foot, the lips, the eyes, the heart. Negations and affirmations, good and evil, have dispersed. What continues in the house, is the subject of the act.[34]

Marcion, Our Contemporary

Over two thousand years have passed since the Lord promised man the Second Coming, and he has not kept his promise. Jews, who have already had many messiahs, such as Jesus or Sabbatai Zevi, have been awaiting salvation even longer. One might ask, what is it that has made them wait—in vain, or so it seems. Perhaps

---

in its tone. (See also Gold, "Jacob Taubes: 'Apocalypse from Below,'" 156; and Taubes, *The Political Theology of Paul*, 72.)

34. César Vallejo, "No One Lives in the House Anymore…," in *The Complete Posthumous Poetry*, trans. Clayton Eshleman and J. R. Barcia (Berkeley: University of California Press, 1980), 26–27.

the messianic idea itself has been misread from the start? Perhaps the message containing the idea of the parousia has been intentionally misinterpreted—by conservative rabbinic Judaism on the one side, and by Christian orthodoxy on the other? All the sources have been distorted and thus, when reading them, one should reverse the perspective—as Overbeck suggests.[35]

The first to venture to do this was Marcion. He came to Rome from Asia Minor when the last members of the Bar Kokhba revolt were being executed. Marcion—the self-appointed successor of the Apostle Paul—followed the spirit of the time and began purging the Christian canon of Jewish traces and influences. First, he threw out the Old Testament, a useless thing, then purged the New Testament of the Gospels, except for Luke (from which he still cut out the first chapters devoted to the childhood of Jesus), and finally he got rid of the letters (three out of thirteen) he considered to be Jewish "interpolations."[36]

At the root of his religious doctrine was the crisis of the Messianic idea. It influenced the early Christians' will to escape from the mainstream of history, which was connected with their interiorization of the hope for the coming of the Messiah, who, this time, was to come—if he comes at all—from the inside, from within, and not, as it was expected, from the outside world. They assumed that the temporal world is ruled by a Demiurge who is just but who knows no pity. This God is just as imperfect as the world he had created. He knows neither love nor compassion—the Messiah cannot reveal himself in such conditions, and if he does, he will perish as Christ did. At the antipodes of the Creator-God is the *Deus alienus*, "the alien God." He has no direct contact with his creation, with life. He is the "black sun" whose light makes all living things wither. He is characterized by infinite, unworldly love and compassion for man. Marcion only presumes him to possess these traits. But he must possess them, just like his Son who was sent to the people as Jesus Christ to tell them about the paradoxical existence of his "nonexistent" father.

Marcion's doctrine should not be identified with Gnosticism, as Harnack stresses.[37] Gnosticism teaches the doctrine of two gods in terms of a struggle between good and evil, a battle to the death between two antagonistic principles. According to Marcion, the just Lord of creation does not enter into any relation with the *Deus alienus*—as if they did not know each other. However, both are interested in man who seems to be a curious commodity to "haggle over."

---

35. Taubes, *The Political Theology of Paul*, 20.
36. *Apokryfy Nowego Testamentu: Ewangelie apokryficzne* [The Apocrypha of the New Testament: Apocryphal Gospels], vol. 1, ed. Marek Starowieyski (Kraków: Wydawnictwo WAM, 2003), 125.
37. Kurt Rudolph, *Gnosis. The Nature & History of Gnosticism*, trans. R. McL. Wilson (Edinburgh: T&T Clark, 1998), 313.

In fact, every part of him needs mending—not only the body is bad but also the soul that is tied to the body. One solution is to destroy both these areas, as postulated by the Encratites (ἐγκρατίται means "abstinent," "renouncing all worldly goods"), or to radically withdraw from the world (ἀναχώρησις is "an ebb," "a shelter," but also "a return"). "Marcion places the redeemed soul on one side and the existing society on the other, and on the improvement of the latter, no thought is to be wasted. The Church did not follow Marcion. It knew that by "tearing apart creation and salvation its authority to influence the order of this world would be lost."[38] However, although it rejected Marcion's theology, the Church "recompensed him" with the celibacy of the priests and the elitism of the Jansenists. By doing so it colluded with him against life.

How is it that twentieth-century culture, so stirred up by life, had so much reverence for Marcion's anti-vitalistic speculation? This can be partly explained by its anti-Judaism that is always in demand.[39] According to Taubes, the main cause of the revival of Marcion's doctrine is to be sought in the belief that something important, some precious knowledge, has been concealed from man, for example, that "the sense of the world must be outside the world" (Wittgenstein). What has proved to be of particular value in this respect is the message about the radically transcendent God who sent his Son to the world so that people could be saved through Him. God's voluntary self-degradation, the fact that He humiliated and humbled himself by incarnation, would bring to mind the idea of God who is "weak" and just as powerless as we are in the face of the demonic powers of history. Despite the vagueness of such images, one can find some consolation in them, some hope for the return to a changed world that will be our common home rather than a cage in which people are imprisoned.

"In the apocalypses no one 'acts' but rather everything 'happens,'"[40] writes Taubes. One is overwhelmed by passivity. "The drawbridge comes from the other side," so there is no point striving for salvation.[41] But the Marcionic

---

38. Jacob Taubes, "Das stählerne Gehäuse und der Exodus daraus oder Ein Streit um Marcion, einst und jetzt," in *Vom Kult zur Kultur: Bausteine zu einer Kritik der historischen Vernunft: Gesammelte Aufsätze zur Religions- und Geistesgeschichte* (München: Wilhelm Fink Verlag, 1996), 177.
39. Hence Buber's remark: "Harnack died in 1930, three years later his thought, the thought of Marcion, was put into action, not by means of thought but through violence and terror. Marcion's gift to Hadrian had passed over to other hands." Taubes, "Das stählerne Gehäuse und der Exodus daraus oder Ein Streit um Marcion, einst und jetzt," 182.
40. Taubes, *Occidental Eschatology*, 34. See also Gold, "Jacob Taubes: 'Apocalypse from Below,'" 148.
41. Taubes, *The Political Theology of Paul*, 76.

separation of "the alien God" and creation forecloses the possibility of apocalypse: the sacred will not—it is not able to—cope with the profane; justice will triumph over love; the inertia of legalistic structures will withstand the pressure of inertness and the loss of meaning. The Marcionic version of Gnosticism is thus a misguided response to the apocalyptic crisis, to a situation when apocalypse refuses to come, especially if its arrival is not a question of "some indeterminate future but [is] entirely proximate."

Conclusion

For the Jews, revelation has a public dimension—its arena is human history: God is coming from the direction of their history. Revelation is always connected with that which already came to pass. For Christians, however, it is a spiritual event that wholly belongs to their private, apolitical world. But the Messiah does not come simply in order to change the hearts of individual sinful beings. Revelation does not relate only to the sphere of pure spirit. Its power must encompass the whole sublunary world and cause the miracle of its successful re-creation. The salvation of the visible world is at the same time the end of its previous form—the Parousia occurs in the form of apocalypse. Thus, "every moment must be ready to receive the plenitude of eternity, the furthest distance is that which is expected at the nearest moment."[42] Theology, being an attempt to rationally speak of final matters, interweaves with politics that administers the impermanent form of this world.

The venerable kings, David and Solomon, the biblical prophets and also one Greek astronomer placed God at the very top of the hierarchy of being, pictured as a vertical axis of the universe. God, who previously had a sacrificial table and his tent among the people, was deprived of his body and then banished to heaven. He became a subject of faith, a "symbol," that is, someone who is believed in (πείθω, πίστις) but who is not trusted. For hierarchies weaken religious instinct and openness. Aristarchus of Samos, the first "heliocentrist," tried to change this, but it was only Copernicus who managed to refute the bipolar reality of the Ptolemaic cave. In his view, the temporal order is no longer an emanation of heaven's perfection, because there is no heaven. There is—which in fact is good news—no hell either (in its place we have the nightmare of history). Strictly speaking, one is confused as to what is above, what is below, what revolves around what (allegedly the Sun is in the center, but how much longer?). Modern cosmology has destroyed not only the prevailing hierarchical system but also any possibility of any hierarchy,

---

42. Franz Rosenzweig, *The Star of Redemption*, trans. B. E. Galli (Madison: University of Wisconsin Press, 2005), 245.

including the difference between what is natural and what is supernatural. Ethics and her younger (and uglier) sister, political correctness, are perched on the peg of the historical moment; they constitute a desacralized form of religion; they are temporary and to a great extent revocable. In his letter to Armin Mohler, Taubes asks: "How does a system of law [*Recht*] look, given that atheism is our fate?"[43] Thus, ethics and law, along with the whole sphere of contemporary politics, might have, and indeed do have, only so much to do with religion that they are its degenerate, late forms. While relying solely on their own efforts, they do not believe in "ghosts" or "miracles" and thus capitulate before any state of emergency any thought they find "unthinkable" and can neither interpret nor make lucid. A planetary ban on political power is being introduced; the legitimacy of its acts is being revoked. The world is ruled by foppish lookalikes. Yet no one seems to mind, for it makes no difference.

The Copernican revolution caused yet another "salutary" effect. Cast down from heaven, "the Lord" found himself among people again, though no one noticed it. "His" presence today can be felt by the effects of "a transcendental dynamic discharge," as Oskar Goldberg claimed at the beginning of the past century. We know neither who nor where "He" is; we cannot tell the course that he is set for. Surely he is not Marcion's *Deus alienus* as there is no such God, or at least he is beyond any possible, human experience. Even the Son, whom he sent to save mankind, did not die because he had never lived. His "body" was fashioned out of foam, out of something "phantasmal," hallucinatory (δόξα derives from δοκεῖν—"to appear," "to seem"), some pseudo-matter in which he had to clothe himself so that he could seem to suffer. Man is thus to take comfort from God who does not exist, from meaning that does not exist either, and from novelty that does not have to justify itself: its advantage over traditional values consists in the fact that it is fresh, brand new. Success proves the usefulness of novelty; it is its legitimacy. What is venerable is not taken into account, but simply destroyed. In other words, tradition is not even hostile; it is not to be combated; it simply is not taken into account in discussing the future shape of the human world.[44]

In the twentieth century, we experienced the presence of "the other god." Everywhere around the world, "He" manifested himself in spasmodic convulsions, in "His" successive, though gradually less and less successful incarnations. The Shoah, world wars, global dehumanization, Tutsi-Hutu—all

---

43. Taubes, *The Political Theology of Paul*, 109.
44. M. Terpstra, "'God's Love for His Enemies': Jacob Taubes' Conversation with Carl Schmitt on Paul," *International Journal in Philosophy and Theology* 70 (2009): 202.

this is "Yahweh's" delirious dance. In "His" song he promises: "This is the final struggle"—it is in fact a promise of an apocalypse that will not be followed by any other struggle, because there will be no world worth fighting for, not even a cracked shell of it. Ultimately, sociology and political science provide no explanations, so one needs to dig deeper, into theology—political theology.

If called by the right name, "He" will supposedly come, although it is not certain as whom: an enemy or a friend. Perhaps it would be better not to summon "God" at all. Yet this is impossible, argues Taubes, for, today, every gesture, even the least spectacular one, turns out to be theology, "invoking" God, summoning Him.[45]

> On such a day the Messiah advances to the edge of the horizon and looks down on the earth. And when He sees it, white, silent, surrounded by azure and contemplation, He may lose sight of the boundary of clouds that arrange themselves into a passage, and, not knowing what He is doing, He may descend upon earth. And in its reverie the earth won't even notice Him, who has descended onto its roads, and people will wake up from their afternoon nap remembering nothing. The whole event will be rubbed out, and everything will be as it has been for centuries, as it was before history began.[46]

---

45. "Taubes is right: today everything is theology, with the exception of what the theologians talk about...": Carl Schmitt, "Four Passages from Letters of Carl Schmitt to Armin Mohler," in Taubes, *To Carl Schmitt: Letters and Reflections*, 26.
46. Bruno Schulz, *Sanatorium under the Sign of the Hourglass*, trans. Celina Wieniewska (New York: Walker, 1978), 21.

Chapter 6

EX ORIENTE LUX? (JOSEPH ROTH, PRIMO LEVI)

When a Jew—asked by a friend how distant is the country to which they are heading—offers their notorious answer, "How far from what?," they do not, thereby, underscore a quality of all places and, therefore, all paths (which would entail a meaninglessness of any journey whatsoever), but express their desperate pain that it is impossible to arrive at that unique place the reaching of which appears necessary.[1]

Why don't the Jews from the East see the advantages of their position and prefer the others' to their own? Why do they choose to wander and abandon places that are also their places? After all, Jewish bones had for centuries been buried in the Borderlands of the former Polish Commonwealth. What force propels them to where no one awaits the Jews? And, lastly, why doesn't the Jew "see the goodness of the Slav people, whose coarseness remains more decent than the housetrained animality of the Western European, his secretive perversions, his cringing before the law, with his well-bred hat in his apprehensive hand"?[2] Some Jews abandoned, as they would have it, a land of eternal oppression where, alternately, they were under threat of war or pogromos. Hence, far, far away from here, everywhere, but not here! Still others kept believing that the Jews' only motherland is Palestine, because that is what the Bible says and the Zionists teach, but also because, outside of that land, the Jews would not be at home in any other place on Earth. A great number of Jewish émigrés were also drawn to an attractiveness of industrial civilization developing at an ever higher pace, felt particularly west of the Lusatian Neisse and in the Soviet Union. The mere reason Eastern Jews arrived in a new place as new blood, with fresh vitality, entrusted them with the task "to break up the

---

1. Sergio Quinzio, *Radici ebraiche del Moderno*, translated from the Polish edition: *Hebrajskie korzenie nowożytności* (Kraków: Homini, 2005), 69.
2. Joseph Roth, *The Wandering Jews*, trans. Michael Hofmann (New York: W.W. Norton, 2000), 6.

deadly, antiseptic boredom of its civilisation,"[3] to shake it up from within, to revolutionize.

Considerations of that order fill the opening pages of Joseph Roth's book about the world-wandering Jews, as he ponders the question whence all their buzz, what is the source of their energy and faith in the fact that life must doubtlessly be better somewhere else. *The Wandering Jews* was brought out in 1927 by the German publishing house Die Schmiede. The book is a moving account of a world sliding into inexistence right before its author's eyes. In spite of the writer's remarkable perspicacity, Roth does not know that, this time, he is creating no metaphors, that, in the course of less than a generation, Occidental Jews would really cease to exist. Fortunately, he will not live to see it. Half a century later, Eastern Jews would be spoken about just as the Etruscans and Mayans had been: with an admixture of fascination with an alien culture and a disbelief they had once really existed.

The Shtetl

Words such as "nation" or "nationality" are no music to soothe Jewish ears. They pass for a nineteenth-century invention and, as history had demonstrated, a very dangerous one to boot, enlivening national antagonisms and group ressentiments. In places where multiethnicity was once a cultural pattern, where simple people spoke several languages since childhood, a sense of the state border as well as understanding a necessity of its existence were greatly weakened. In this sense, also, the shtetl—a small Jewish town or a village situated at some distance from central agglomerations and located somewhere in the hinterlands of the former Polish Commonwealth or within the borders of the Russian state—seemed to pass for an "extraterritoriality," a space "out of this world."

Several reasons for the state of things can be listed, and each will be somewhat bound up with religiousness of the Jews. The first reason is its "manic" intensification (according to the original meaning of the word mania, namely, "God's visitation"). The Jews pray three times a day, wherever they can. Besides a synagogue and a church, there are a few tens of small shuls in a shtetl. A learned man in Western Europe is satisfied with an antiquarian bookseller and a library, while a small-town Jew studies the Torah in his shul. Which man is the wiser? Answering the question posed no challenge to Eastern Jews. Here, one needs to realize what knowledge, religion and nationality are for Eastern Jews, namely, that "learning is religion, and religion—nationality. Their clergy

---

3. Ibid., 11.

are their men of learning, and their prayer is an expression of nationhood," Roth observes.[4]

Prayer, therefore, rather than being a festive ritual (a "Sunday"), is tightly interwoven with everyday life of a Jewish town, wherein no time can be spared on follies or evil thoughts. Its necessary complement in Eastern lands was the Hasidic Movement associated with the name of Baal Shem Tov of Medzhybizh, its creator.

Even in its most embryonic shape, Hasidism was a religious formation founded primarily on faith in miracles, on a belief in a miraculousness of being. As a movement exploiting irrational resources of the human soul, it was unacceptable to enlightened and cultured Jews, who did away with miraculousness and mystical flights in their prayer. But also, conversely: the Hasidim rejected their contemporary civilization with its overblown ambitions, rationalism, the pursuit of happiness and comfort. They could not imagine a life without a yearning for a messiah. No temptation affected them strongly enough, so they be pushed toward apostasy. As late as 1927, Julian Tuwim would still claim: "There is only one type [of the Jew] I know and value. That old Jew in a caftan, not yet infected with European culture [...] I do not believe in assimilation, it is impossible."[5]

Miracles in the tzadik's court awed Eastern Jews no less than their Western brothers were awed by the cinema, microscope or airplane flight. The tzadik had more life in himself because of God, rather than thanks to his contemporaries. Even to his wife, he was connected by a complicated relationship of enjoyment and duty. He helped everyone who turned to him for help. And he read a lot, read voraciously, obsessively, read nonstop, since God had revealed himself to man in letters: through and in the Word.

Eastern Jews were disbelieving of those who had or pursued power. A title for lordship arose their intuitive and deep distrust. In turn, they believed anyone who did *believe*, who was marked by a fervent, unfeigned religiousness, hence one who sensed more than they were allowed to know.

Generally, the village population exhibited, euphemistically speaking, a far-reaching reticence toward the Jews. The state of things comprised several elements. One of them was a closed character of Jewish culture; another, the Jews' sobriety, who sold vodka but did not drink it, which could not have been to the simple-minded peasants' taste. Roth subverts both stereotypes.

---

4. Ibid., 113.
5. "Wywiady z pisarzami pochodzenia żydowskiego. Rozmowa z Julianem Tuwimem" [Interviews with Writers of Jewish Origin. A Conversation with Julian Tuwim], *Dziennik Warszawski* (February 6–7, 1927). Quoted after *Rozmowy z Tuwimem* [Conversations with Tuwim], ed. Tadeusz Januszewski (Warszawa: Wydawnictwo Naukowe Semper, 1994), 25–26.

Dance, vodka and a healthy, "enthusiastic" madness, originating from the Greek ἔνθεος ("possession by a god"), precisely, occupied a prominent place in Hassidic rituality, leading at the same time to relieving a spiritual tension. True, not infrequently did the Jews lose consciousness, but there was always a religious reason behind the loss, not a regular drunkenness. The Hasidic religiousness created a highly sensual, quasi-erotic bond;[6] faith was supposed to trigger a spontaneous joy in the believers, rather than a concern for what may come after death; it was meant to release and appreciate the sensual side of the human, rather than negating it, coaxing them, to take the first example, into a necessity of months-long fasting. Stripped of sensuality, religion promptly turns into fear (Catholicism) or a barren, intellectual speculation (Protestantism).

Jews in the West celebrate Yom Kippur, which many of them see as the most important holiday, being the day of reconciliation. For the *Ostjuden*, it is the day of atonement and therefore a farewell to the material world, rather than making matters up with it. The Jews had learnt not to take conflicts that consumed them outside; they did not want the world to resolve those for them. They expected that tensions life brought with it could be soothed by God the Lord, that the man could not do this. The Eastern Jew was entirely convinced of God's protection, thanks to which, he trusted, he could come to no evil or harm. (At that time, 70 years before the events, he hadn't surmised that his God could be a weak God.[7]) Therefore, a "genuine Jew"—Roth's own term—is a godly Jew. His belonging to the community does not arise from any "national character," because it is completely unrelated to anything as modern as the nation. In this sense, if the Zionists' dream of their own state one day comes true, the whole affair could be arranged in such a manner that, in such a state—Roth's prophetic words—there will be no Jews—"who are forced to become a 'nation' by the nationalism of the others"[8]—and it will be inhabited, for example, by Israelis. Because being, or not being, a Jew is not decided by a passport, an administration or a place of birth, but by God.

The culture of Eastern European shtetl—an incessant rumpus—created by Jews around them brought to mind oriental bazaars. Only during the Yom Kippur did all the commotion stop. One proof of a nether-worldliness of the festival and its extraction from the framework of everyday life may be the fact

---

6. Wasilij Rozanow, "Magiczna stronica u Gogola" [Gogol's Magic Page], translated from the Polish edition: *Kronos*, no. 3 (2013).
7. Sergio Quinzio, *La sconfitta di Dio*, translated from the Polish edition: *Przegrana Boga* (Kraków: Homini, 2008), 41. See also Hans Jonas, "The Concept of God after Auschwitz: A Jewish Voice," *Journal of Religion* 67, no. 1 (January 1987).
8. Roth, *The Wandering Jews*, 52.

that in the sudden silence, the intense focus, "every enemy begs all the others for forgiveness."

> In all the prayerhouses, the people stand, crowded together. Some prostrate themselves on the ground, lie there for a long time, then get up, sit on footstools or flagstones, hunker there, and suddenly leap to their feet, sway back and forth from the waist, and run around incessantly in the tiny space like ecstatic sentries of prayer. Entire buildings are filled with white funeral shirts, with the living who are absent, with the dead who are alive. Not a single drop is permitted to moisten the parched lips and refresh the dry throats that cry out in so much pain—not to the world but to the heavens. They will not break their fast today or tomorrow. It is a shocking thing to know that not one Jew in this town is going to eat or drink. All have suddenly turned into spirits, with the attributes of spirits. [...] superhuman, because this is the day on which he wants to reach God. All stretch out their hands to touch the hem of his garment. All without distinction: The rich are no better off than the poor, as none of them will have anything to eat. All are sinners, and all pray. A giddiness comes over them, they reel, they rant, they whisper, they hurt themselves; they sing, shout, wail. Heavy tears trickle down their old beards, and their hunger is taken away by so much pain in their souls and by the immemorial melodies that fill their ecstatic ears.[9]

Another stereotype dismantled by Roth, in his peculiar manner, is an exclusivism of Jewish culture: a self-enclosed culture, maintaining a careful and unbending distance toward all external phenomena. Such an image of the culture, the writer claims, does not live up to facts that speak of *"relatively frequently"* encountered landowners' conversions to Judaism.[10] I have got to admit I do not understand this passage of *The Wandering Jews*. Since God branded the Jews with the mark of selection, merely this is the reason why one cannot subscribe to them as one would volunteer to join a select social group. The fragment is unclear, unconvincing, especially against the background of remarks about a specificity of the Mosaic religion that demands an activeness manifested, for example, in the reading of the Torah. It would be difficult to imagine an illiterate, fair-haired peasant from the whereabouts of Kałuszyn or Brody in (the Austro-Hungarian) Galicia with his back bent over the Jews' sacred text written in Hebrew.

---

9. Ibid., 42–43.
10. Ibid., 53.

A puzzle within Jewish culture, Roth writes, is its haste in burying the dead. Why so great? What is the reason behind the rule that "a body is not allowed to remain unburied for more than twenty-four hours"? Is the pain assisting a burial of the beloved dead so great that it has to be curtailed at any cost? "The most shattering scenes take place at the cemetery. Women refuse to leave the graves; they have to be dragged away; they require taming as much as comforting. The melody for the prayer for the dead is of a monumental plainness, the burial ceremony is almost curt in its brevity."[11] Pain in such places seems oblong, having no beginning or end. The *Gehenna* of the beloved's burial always keeps being relived by the living, anew.

The Wander

In the second part of Roth's book, Jews from the East head out for the horizon. Propelled by dreams of a better world—since real life is always "elsewhere"—they are everywhere. Literally everywhere. In Vienna, no Jew would leave another Jew in need. Such is their tacit existential agreement, consisting in providing mutual assistance in a foreign world, usually unwelcoming to the Jews.

> The worst of it is: He can't just be left to perish. He's not a stranger. He is a Jew and a compatriot. Someone will be found to take him in. Someone else will advance him a small loan or get him a credit. Someone else will organize a territory for him, or turn over his own. The new arrival will go into installment selling.[12]

In this respect, life in Vienna resembled their life in a Russian village beyond the Polar Circle, where no mischief or thievery was to be found, and doors to

---

11. Ibid., 43–44. A question I have always asked myself, since I can remember, relates to a certain aspect of the German death industry. Why did the Nazis, carrying out their extermination of the Jewish population combined with the holocaust of their whole culture, leave Jewish cemeteries intact? Such was the case of the Bródno (district) cemetery for Warsaw Jews, established in 1780 by Szmul Jakubowicz Zbytkower, the court banker to the Polish king Stanislaus II Augustus. Untouched by the Nazis, it was destroyed in 1951 by the Communists by order of Paweł Hoffman, a "Soviet Jew" (*iudaeus sovieticus*). The term does not signify "a Jew from the Soviet Union," but an uprooted Jew, hence one in whom the old blood is still running, but the historical Jewish community is no longer their point of reference; a "Soviet Jew" refers to Communism and the USSR. *Iudaei sovietici* are discussed in a latter part of this essay.
12. Ibid., 57.

every thatched house were always open, since nature itself proved humanely hostile.

Berlin seems completely different, and nobody in their right mind goes there, says Roth. Itinerant trade may be forbidden in Berlin, but it is kind of tolerated. And the eternal heckling with the forces of order… Indeed, the Jews' Berlin stalls resembled the so-called metal jaws marring the landscape of Polish cities in the nineties of the previous century. They were removed, because they transformed the city into the bazaar, into "the East." The 1920s Berlin resembled Baghdad. Here, a question may be asked whether such really are the looks and behaviors of "movers and shakers over the whole world," of those who "are plotting" against it.

Against Berlin walls, the Jews stand out with their flavor, uniqueness, religiousness: their "Asia." In the East, amidst Polish and Little Russian peasants, they were "at home." Here, however, they repelled even the Jews themselves, that is, the assimilated ones, those reconciled to the European culture of Jewish upstarts, who had come to see God only as some element of a distant tradition.

Nonetheless, German is nearly Yiddish and, even amidst the Germans, one can find a piece of their kitschy—*gemütlich*—warmth. According to Heine, "the tongue of Eastern Jews is the German language spoken in a Polish vein, intertwined with Hebrew words."[13] Hence, even if things between the three nations—Jews, Poles and Germans—went quite "neighborly," so to speak, the French language is, plainly, unlike any human tongue whatsoever. This might be the reason prompting the Jews to avoid the Romance countries: after all, they had been expelled from no other place than Spain, on which rabbis, until fairly recently, put their curses. In Romance countries, the world is translated from the foreign to the familiar and the other way round, regardless of what the "familiarity" might mean. To the Jew, "foreign" equals "French." That is the language from which one does not translate; French, as any other Romance language, is usually figured out. The difficult art of translation from the foreign into the familiar, or into even more foreign, receives a colorful discussion from Roth:

> A few, a very few, stay in Marseilles. They become interpreters. Interpreting is a Jewish calling. It is nothing to do with translating, say, from English into French, from Russian into French, from German into French. It has to do with translating the stranger, even if he hasn't said [anything]. He doesn't have to open his mouth. Christian interpreters

---

13. Heinrich Heine, *O Polsce* [On Poland], translated from the Polish edition: *Dzieła wybrane: Utwory prozą* [Collected Prose Works] (Warszawa: Państwowy Instytut Wydawniczy, 1956), 635.

might translate. Jewish ones intuit. They earn money. [...] They go down to the harbor, they get on a ship, and they go to South America.[14]

Yiddish is the most popular language in the world, but not statistically, only geographically. Also in the United States, it is, therefore, recognizable and completely understandable. But to get there, the Jews have to cross the ocean, of which they are more scared than of fire. As the seas are roadless and, at any moment, they can lead the Jew into disorientation. If, then, the sea roads are tangled, also the most important one, leading to God, is tangled. Besides, onboard a ship—and here is another "cabal"—the way back is cut off, which spells out extremely untoward news to those who have constantly, throughout their lives, run away from something. What if a pogrom breaks out aboard? Where, then, should one go? How to behave? Where to look for help? And what if one happens to die at sea? Is it at all possible to pick oneself up from the seabed and head onto a post-mortem pilgrimage to Jerusalem? Since, for Jews, those were difficult questions, many of them clang tightly onto land. In an uncertain world, we read in Tolstoy, "One must have an idea of the promised land, in order to have the strength to move."[15]

But, then, where to go if "genuine Jews" ought to shun Berlin and the Romance countries, while the road to the United States seems such a very risky enterprise (one can drown one's soul in murky oceanic depths) and not straightforward (due to the maritime no-man's land)? Those among them who have chosen to head south often returned to the house of Europe—to their own detriment, a while before the Shoah. They could not cope with challenges of labor in Palestine kibbutzim.[16] One reason, among others, why many chose the ghetto, a place of respite for a person in continual motion, or to agitate for a direction that was *opposite*—in every meaning of the word—championing the Union of Soviet Socialist Republics.

The Soviet Men

"A narrative gift is something frequently found in the East," Roth observes. "In every family there is an uncle who is good at storytelling."[17] Unfortunately, too

---

14. Roth, *The Wandering Jews*, 88.
15. Leo Tolstoy, *The Complete Works of Count Tolstoy: War and Peace*, trans. Leo Wiener (New York: AMS Press, 1968), 165.
16. "Many return," Roth affirms (*The Wandering Jews*, 11), without supplying any numbers. A statistics regarding the Jews' return to the East a few years before the Shoah could be very interesting. Unfortunately, I have not come across any such to date.
17. Roth, *The Wandering Jews*, 47.

many uncles, bewitched with the idea of lay salvation, were well spoken enough so as to have managed to persuade their closer and more distant relatives into participating in the creation of a reality, "a land, where tomorrow is already yesterday."[18]

The slogan about the supranational community of the proletariat ("the excluded," "blacks,"[19] etc.) had a particularly powerful impact on the Jewish imagination, since it had initially created an obscure illusion and, then, an actual opportunity of setting out conditions, by way of which the Jews could be differentiated from other people.

The old Russia had not strived for the Jews' assimilation. More often, they were fenced off and barred from settling in larger towns or cities. Their presence was demonized, and persecutions were organized, imitating the tzar, who pretended to be afraid of the Jews—aliens—and therefore—due to their incomprehensible otherness—harassed them with pogroms.

> Characteristics were therefore ascribed to them that made them appear dangerous to every class: To the simple "man of the people" they were ritual murderers; to the small landowner they were destroyers of property; to the senior official they were common swindlers; to the nobility, clever—and therefore dangerous—serfs; and finally, to the bureaucrat, the quintessential petty official, they were ritual murderers, hucksters, revolutionaries, and plebeians—everything rolled into one.[20]

Meanwhile functionaries of the Communist regime condemned anti-Semitism *en bloc*. While at it, they could murder a fifth of their own without batting an eyelid. A brutal, accelerated modernization of the whole country brought about a series of various oppressions on regular people. One had to watch every word one spoke. Errors in print could cost a typesetter their life or freedom, one false note made for pretext enough to send a musician to Siberia. Usually, however, one ended up in the GULAG for no reason, by accident. Owing to the ruthless industrialization of the backward country, of such violent effects, Jews could, at last, stop being identified by their religion, because, from 1917 at least, they were defined by the Soviet citizenship. Like many others, Jews also became *homines sovietici* in Soviet Russia, the same species of "Soviet men" as engineers, NKVD agents, farmer workers or Marxist–Leninist politruks.

---

18. Julius Fučík, *V zemi, kde zítra již znamená včera* (Praha: Karel Borecký, 1932).
19. In America, "they have people who are more Jewish than the Jews, which is to say the Negroes." Roth, *The Wandering Jews*, 102.
20. Roth, *The Wandering Jews*, 106.

"The old questions, the crucial questions aren't even addressed by the Revolution: Are the Jews a nation like any other, or are they more or less; are they a religious community, a tribal community,"[21] or merely a spiritual unity; can a people who have survived millennia solely, thanks to their religion and exceptional position in Europe, be considered "a people" irrespective of religion; does their special case allow for a separation of the "church" and nationality; can people of inherited spiritual interests be turned into peasants, firmly formed individuals—into entities churned out by a psychology of the masses?

Instead of the Jew—"the Soviet man," in place of ancient tradition—a false "proof of identity" and a neo-primitivism: such was the price to be paid for a removal of anti-Semitism. In this sense, the "Soviet Jews" (or "the circle squared") did not take after their ancestors; they merely consented to coming after them. Lightly, yeshiva got transformed into Party academies, synagogues and *shuls*—into Communist Party houses, their existential angst—into a surety of a Socialist tomorrow, thinking about salvation—into the idea of permanent, world-embracing revolution.

Still, this was not quite as easy to implement. It has not been for nothing, we read in *The Wandering Jews*, that, for four thousand years, the Jews had been a wholly literate people.[22] It is not easy to deceive them. Not only "the new man" is formed under the new conditions, but also a reaction to the "man"; hence, a justified, new "anti-Semitism." "In some sense, I am an anti-Semite myself," Roth writes in a letter to Stefan Zweig. "I hate vulgarity, vileness, stupidity and, above all, so much I could slaughter, baseness."[23] The writer found all those unpleasant things in the order newly created by the Communists. And, ultimately, being an Eastern Jew, he adroitly plied the seas of Socialism and Catholicism, of Jewish orthodoxy and upper-class aspirations (he maintained he is one Habsburg's illegitimate son); he exhibited a remarkable sobriety (despite his love of drink) and a skepticism in relation to novel, miracle-promising social ideologies, spreading like vermin in the early decades of the twentieth century.

Ponary—The Base

In the early days of the war, so also shortly after Roth's death, Germany developed two programs of systemic genocide. The first one alluded to Soviet

---

21. Ibid., 110.
22. Ibid.
23. Letter of February 27, 1927, as quoted in the afterword to the Polish edition of *The Wandering Jews*. Joseph Roth, *Żydzi na tułaczce* (Kraków-Budapeszt: Austeria, 2017), 149–50.

terror, consisting in stoking up a plague of hunger on a grand scale. In a short period of time, thirty million human lives were supposed to be put to death by hunger. When the program misfired, they moved onto the second one, the aim of which was the murder of all European Jews. To achieve a greater efficiency in the annihilation, special SS squads, trained in killing Communist elites, were set apart. A mere change of orders was sufficient for the priority to become the holocaust of the whole Jewry. The SS squads were soon joined by units of the Wehrmacht, the Nazi Order Police, as well as battalions formed from thrill- and beef-craving "local" thugs and their "ideological" guides, for whom murdering Jews became a continuation of their bloody crackdown on global Bolshevism.

In June 1941, the territory of the former Lithuanian state was inhabited by two hundred thousand Jews, more or less their number in the whole of Germany. When the Nazi army was invading Lithuania, the resident population had a fresh memory of Soviet deportations, tortures and death sentences, which had recently come to be executed in the local NKVD offices. Hence, the Lithuanian military man and diplomat Kazys Škirpa—for some the leader of Lithuanian collaborationists, or of patriots for others—could very successfully invoke ethnic ressentiments, pointing at "Soviet Jews" as perpetrators of the recent sufferings of a greater part of the population. Pogroms that followed consumed two-and-a-half thousand victims and were an overture proper to the more organized massacre. From July to December 1941, a million people were murdered in the borderlands of the former Polish Commonwealth, thereby bringing the "Jewish question" in the East to its "ultimate conclusion."[24]

Victims were shot in the village of Ponary near Vilnius. They were transported on trains to the terminus where, first, their dignity, then, possessions and, finally, their lives were taken. In his shocking short story, "Ponary—'Baza'" (Ponary—"The Base"), Józef Mackiewicz draws attention to this precise aspect of the Shoah: a preceding dehumanization of the murdered. "Neither in their moves, nor in their escape, manner of hiding, their hunger and fright-mumbled language, in their fantastical rags and pangs was anything human left," he writes. Indeed, not only those who died partook in the loss of humanity. Those who managed to escape lost it in equal measure. Mackiewicz continues:

---

24. Timothy Snyder, *Bloodlands: Europe between Hitler and Stalin* (New York: Basic Books, 2010), 194. As always, numbers are a subject of controversy also in this case. Even as thorough a historian of Eastern Europe as Timothy Snyder—from whom I draw those dreadful counts (192), in an extended endnote—quotes yet another, no less dreadful (but much humbler, as halved) number of "457,436 Jews" (485). So, a million or half a million it was?

Jews, led no longer by a human impulse, but an animal instinct of premortal flight, exactly like animals, eschewed human dwellings, dogs, stupid kids who ran to the village with their watchful cries and news revelation, pointing their fingers at a site where they had, accidentally, spotted the human monster. A ruthlessly applied rule of law put any man to death who gave shelter, a mere piece of bread, or even a clue to a Jew, or one who, having the knowledge, did not inform the police.[25]

In time, the local populace got accustomed to the incessant, daily and monthly, surging cannonade of constantly renewed executions. If one could get used to killing animals in a slaughterhouse, a habituation to a planned extermination of the civil population was only a matter of time. Except...

I can't bear to watch. The air is torn by such a racket of murdered people and, yet, children's voices, several notes higher, can be discerned amidst the cries, exactly like a cat wailing in the night. It cannot be reiterated by any human-contrived letter. [...]

A Jewish woman falls, first to her face, then jerks herself onto her back and, waving her hand in the air, looks for her child's tiny hand. I cannot hear, but can see from the movements of the little girl's mouth that she's calling: "*Mame!*" [...] On her head, a rag-made ribbon quivers and, bending forward, she grabs her mother by the hair. "Do you think that those oppressors, tormentors, the Gestapo and the SS men, and all the police hordes, conscripted for killing, were never born like us, did not have their own mothers? Women?" "You're wrong. They are made of that very same human clay, humanly—bestialised, as pale as the snow that might fall here one day, they are like madmen, like savages dancing, in their moves, their insane gestures, their murdering, their shooting" [...] How else could one explain that the entirely crazed policeman grabs the Jewish woman by her right leg and tries to drag her between railway tracks, all bent over, with his muck so contorted as if slashed with a sabre, where to?! wherefore?! The woman's legs are spread, the left one is caught by a rail, her skirt slides below her waist, revealing her dirt-grayed underpants, while the child picks on her mother's hair tagging on stones and pulls it to herself, and one cannot hear, only see how she screams: "*Mammme!*" [...]

---

25. Józef Mackiewicz, *Fakty i ludzie* [Facts and People] (Warszawa: Officyna Liberałów, 1988), 7–8. This is an abbreviated, "underground" edition of Józef Mackiewicz's *Fakty, przyroda i ludzie* [Facts, Nature and People] (Londyn: Kontra, 1984). The short story was first published in the *Orzeł Biały* magazine, in 1945.

Now, the dragged woman's mouth erupts with blood [...] For a moment, a thick wall of uniforms blocks the view [...] And, then, some Latvian raised a butt over the tiny ruffled hair, tied at the crown with a small piece of the tiny rag into the ribbon and [...] I closed my eyes and seemed to hear somebody ring. They rang, indeed, a railwayman, clenching my bike handlebars convulsively, sunk his fingers into the bell, jerked it in clutching, bent forward and is puking; he's puking on the platform gravel, on the front wheel tyre, on his own hand, on my shoes, puking in shivers, similar to convulsions of those who are dying there, on the rails.[26]

Mackiewicz's account of what he accidentally witnessed in Ponary is complemented with a later account, recollected half a century after the events, in Timothy Snyder's *Bloodlands*:

Ita Straż was one of the very few survivors among the Jews of Vilnius. She was pulled by Lithuanian policemen to a pit that was already full of corpses. Nineteen years old at the time, she thought: "This is the end. And what have I seen of life?" The shots missed her, but she fell from fear into the pit. She was then covered by the corpses of the people who came after. Someone marched over the pile and fired downward, to make sure that everyone was dead. A bullet hit her hand, but she made no sound. She crept away later: "I was barefoot. I walked and walked over corpses. There seemed to be no end to it."[27]

From Auschwitz to Turin

Not even in part is Primo Levi's *The Truce* as good a literature as Roth's work or Józef Mackiewicz's novels and nonfiction. Nonetheless, it furnishes a significant testimony that ought to be taken into account whenever a place occupied by the Jews from the Commonwealth borderlands in Polish culture is being considered.

Levi's odyssey begins on January 7, 1945, the day the Red Army frees Auschwitz, where he spent nearly a year. In spite of the liberators' swift decision to equip him with a spade and force him to work, he sees them as providential men of the hour, whose tanks arrived, literally, at the final hour. The book contains a whole plethora of approving remarks and reverences to the frank, albeit somewhat chaotic, but certainly magnanimous Russians, who "lived together with friendly simplicity."[28] The remarks demonstrate Levi's

---

26. Mackiewicz, *Fakty i ludzie*, 11–12.
27. Timothy Snyder, *Bloodlands*, 193.
28. Primo Levi, *If This Is a Man: The Truce*, trans. S. Woolf (London: Abacus, 2013), e-book.

unenforced, trusting attitude to "the Soviet men." At once, they are expression and example of the leftist intellectual's blindness; for him, a drab NKVD officer in the rank of lieutenant, fluent in Italian, is barely different from drunk Red Army soldiers riding a tram through Vienna, who "hung out of the windows and cheered, while others incited and threatened the driver into increasing his speed."[29] In this respect, Roth could boast of a better eye and a much greater discretion.

Levi knows that he escaped death at the last minute and ascribes the change in his situation to the do-good Russians. At once, he grapples with shame he felt throughout his stay behind the wires, mostly at the sight of suffering, humiliation and martyrdom of thousands of human existences. "We did not know; but we knew that on the thresholds of our homes, for good or ill, a trial awaited us, and we anticipated it with fear. We felt in our veins the poison of Auschwitz, flowing together with our thin blood."[30] The trial was to be rehearsed in his books, poems, conversations to come.[31] *The Truce*, however, seems slightly different in this respect. As much as the time Levi experiences still is a hiatus between one massacre and the other (the title "truce"[32]), I discovered in the picaresque tale an enclosed corner of the world, as if an inexplicable hope shone through the accumulation of evil and bad fortune—a hope of meeting a kind of better people, be them "Soviet." No less interesting aspect of the book seems to be all those things the author of *The Truce* refused to notice, the things he truly overlooked and, ultimately, things made unobservable because of civilizational clichés.

The stereotype of "new human happiness," mass-produced in the Soviet Union, has already been discussed. In Levi's book, the stereotype successively becomes deeper and sharper in comparison with images of the sad (curiously, why so?), old Poland.[33] Let us have a look at the images.

The first time the author partook of the "Polish sadness" was in Katowice (rather than on the occasion when he watched Polish peasant girls' "open desire"[34] for close encounters with chance men in the absence of husbands and lovers long gone to the front line). In the city, Levi was—or so was his impression, may I add: how deeply mistaken!—the first man in the striped uniform. A local crowd greeted him with a mixture of curiosity, horror and

---

29. Ibid. The writer's almost idolatrous attitude toward the Soviet Union is definitely one of those threads in the book that seem worth tracing.
30. Ibid.
31. *If This Is a Man. The Truce* (memoir); *The Drowned and the Saved* (essays); *The Voice of Memory: Interviews, 1961–1987*; *The Survivor* (poems).
32. Levi, *If This Is a Man. The Truce*.
33. Ibid.
34. Ibid.

pity. Stories he shared with his listeners were related to his stay at the camp. They were translated by a chance encounter, a polyglot Polish lawyer, whom Levi regarded as enlightened and empathetic. Except that his translations weren't faithful. When Levi, who only spoke a few random words in Polish, realized that the interpreter changes the phrase "Italian Jew" into an "Italian political prisoner," he asked why the distortion of his stories. He heard, then, that he should be wary of the Poles. *C'est mieux pour vous. La guerre n'est pas finie.* ("That'd be better for you. The war hasn't yet finished."[35]) In other words, never again will any Jew feel safe in those lands. The lasting truce is a fragile and passing state.

If This Is a Man was written right after leaving the camp; *The Truce* came out two years after Eichmann's trial, in a very different reality. Both books mark two eras and, at once, two manners of narrating the Shoah. In the former, the survivors were treated like rams who accidentally escaped the shepherds of nothingness' hand. Indeed, their right to life, once toppled, has never been fully recovered. The camp compromised everyone: the perpetrators, the survivors and the whole world as its by-stander; all those things were shameful, such that no one really knew what to do with them. So silence was decided upon. This changed with the coming of the latter era, based on a cult of the victim. Beginning in the 1960s, namely, after Eichmann's hanging, survivors of the Shoah were gradually equaled in being with others. They no longer had to blame themselves for their survival. On moral grounds, a difference between them and the creators of the state of Israel was annulled. Hence, it is difficult to determine whether the conversation with the lawyer recalled by Levi, but written after many years, under completely new conditions, had actually taken place, or if it is an extrapolation of the phenomenon of the cult of the victim, slowly emerging at the time, connected to what is, today, ever more eagerly and vocally described as "religion of the Shoah."

Another thing that kept me awake when reading *The Truce* was an utter absence of even the slightest traces of Jewish culture in the book, a culture so colorfully, so vividly captured by Roth only two decades before events here described. In the first part of Roth's book, we encounter a strong and rich tradition, based entirely on the Mosaic religion, which Levi, coming from a family of Italian Jews that had for centuries been assimilated, could not notice, even though he crossed the same lands as Roth before him. What, then, did he see? Mainly nature and its resident "noble savages."

> We became aware, to our own amazement, that this endless land, these fields and woods which had witnessed the battle to which we owed our

---

35. Ibid.

salvation, these virgin primordial horizons, this vigorous people full of the love of life, had entered our hearts, had penetrated into us and would remain there for a long time, glorious and living images of a unique season of our existence.[36]

There are not any rare Jews, who have managed to survive, returning to their homes. No matzevot, no *shuls*, no synagogues. Nothing. A void. A hydrogen bomb crater. The inability of noticing or, at least, guessing any traces of Jewish life on the territories of the former Polish Commonwealth and the Soviet Union comes to prominence with a particular emphasis in Levi's conversation with two accidentally encountered "local" Jewish women. Initially, he tries to strike up a conversation in German, claiming that he and his three companions are Jews.

> I asked them in German if they were Jewish, and declared that we four were also Jewish. The girls (they were perhaps sixteen or eighteen years old) burst out laughing. "Ihr sprecht keyn Jiddisch; ihr seyd ja keyne Jiden!" "You do not speak Yiddish; so you cannot be Jews!" In their language, the phrase amounted to rigorous logic.
>
> Yet we really were Jews, I explained. Italian Jews: Jews in Italy, and in all Western Europe, do not speak Yiddish.[37]

A Jew from the West could not meet or see Eastern Jews through a lack of a common (in the broadest possible meaning) language, which would have established a middle ground between. Not even a dumb "Russian" sailor (the inverted commas seem necessary here, as every Slavic language east of the Bug Levi took to be Russian), who, listing numerals, at one point had to resort to Yiddish, as he forgot his native tongue, could set Levi on the Eastern Jews. Not even then did the young "traveler" ask himself the question wherefrom the fair-haired simpleton got his residual knowledge of the language.

Summary

The Holocaust of European Jews was not a product of chance or an effect of anti-Semitism that, in its invoking of meagre passions of weak and vicious people, is capable of inciting a pogrom, but not of organizing an industrial-scale massacre. The Shoah was a necessary result of processes of modernization annihilating, one by one, every element of the old world, which came to

---

36. Ibid.
37. Ibid.

be regarded as "swamped in gross superstitions,"[38] unfit for assimilation, and anachronistic. Eastern Jews, due to their incorruptible attitude to religion and tradition, played no accidental role of the victim in the work of destruction. It turned out that negotiating conditions of renouncing their forefathers' faith with the chosen people was impossible. They valued their religion over the miracles of the latest technology or the newest social solutions prompted by ideologies and lay prophets. This could not be to the taste of the protagonists of the world "without God," a world in which practically every choice has become infantilized and every symptom of freedom turns out to be a meaningless gesture, where any superstition whatsoever is afforded seriousness, on the condition that it fits within a framework of the so-called popular culture.

The requiem over the world of Eastern Jews is a mourning after the loss of truly human values: God, tradition, remembrance of the dead, after a fierce religiousness unharmed by an aggressive atheism and thoughtless boredom. Without them, without Jews, whose very own tradition transformed them into guardians of human values, we have been diminished in our very essence.

> There are no more Jewish towns in Poland, no more,
> In Hrubieszów, Karczew, Brody, Falenica,
> You'd loon in vain for lit candles, or try to catch
> The sounds of singing from a wooden temple.
> The last remains disappeared, Jewish rags,
> Blood scattered like sand, traces cleared away
> And walls whitewashed clean with strong lime
> As after some plague or for a high holy day.
> [...]
> Those towns are no longer, they've passed like shadows,
> And these shadows will fall between our words,
> Before two nations, nourished by the suffering of centuries,
> Will approach each other fraternally and again unite.[39]

All those things could not have been known to Roth, although he wrote about a twilight of the world he did know. The tragedy was never fully understood by Primo Levi. The Jews' demise, the holocaust of the human collided with the optimism of left-wing ideologies, Levi's compass. Because of them, he noticed nothing during his passage through the "bloodlands," and what he managed to see, he promptly belied, dressing up his *personal* tragedy as a picaresque novel.

---

38. Heine, *O Polsce*, 635.
39. Antoni Słonimski, "Elegy of Jewish Towns," in *Stranger in Our Midst: Images of the Jew in Polish Literature*, ed. Harold B. Segel (Ithaca, NY: Cornell University Press, 1996), 363.

Chapter 7

PILLORIED BY NECESSITY (JEAN AMÉRY)

> At forty the bladder beginning to leak—
> was it for such louts, do you think, that the earth
> grew from sun to moon—?[1]

There are books that should be required reading but—let us not kid ourselves—not at all times and not for everyone. I mean books that grow out of a radical experience, from facing an event too rich in meanings or, conversely, devoid of any meaning at all, not making any sense. Jean Améry's writing belongs in the second category. A response to the absurdity of the twentieth-century history, it constitutes its ultimate result. Améry is not a historian, or, if he is one, he is the historian of his own suffering. He infects us with a knowledge that then becomes addictive; we can no longer do without it. It is the kind of knowledge one does not inherit, but painstakingly acquires.

The Loss of Language

In *At the Mind's Limits*, his only book where he explicitly refers to his incarceration, first at Fort Breendonk, then in Auschwitz, Améry tries, in my opinion, to relate the helplessness of his mind, its uselessness and powerlessness in face of extreme oppression. Because only in the fiery pit of genuine hell one learns whether the mind—thinking, rationality—is everything or serves no purpose at all.

Intellectuals, that is, a certain species of creatures for whom the "natural" environment is the system of intellectual references—be it a poem, some sheet music or Bach's *Brandenburg Concertos*—usually trust the power of their

---

1. Gottfried Benn, "The Doctor," in *Selected Poems and Prose*, trans. David Paisey (Manchester: Carcanet Press, 2013), 48.

intellect as it constitutes an important support, hell; in fact it is their lives' very essence.

In the first chapter, "At the Mind's Limits," Améry revises this view. There are conditions, he says, in which the mind is of no use; it can even do harm. In a death camp, for someone suffering from cachexia, the mind is not just useless; it actually lowers one's chances of survival. An intellectual who in his previous life worked with his brains not his hands cannot cope with the new kind of work that mainly consists in digging holes and backfilling them. In the camp the intellectual first becomes isolated from the others as *the weaker one*, the worse one, the one who is all thumbs, and then he becomes separated from himself.

Améry mentions a philosophy professor from the Sorbonne, in the free world an expert on Hölderlin, who inside the camp communicated with others using not more than ten words. "Is the explanation that his senses had become blunted? Definitely not. The man had not become insensitive, no more than I had. He simply no longer believed in the reality of the world of the mind, and he rejected an intellectual word game that here no longer had any social relevance."[2] We are talking about a total indifference to everything that used to seem close and unique—to Rilke's poems, the music of the Romantics and other creations of the human spirit. To the oppressed person it all begins to seem "idle talk" and "lightness of concepts" that lost their validity. It means a radical loneliness of an intellectual who "does not understand" and "does not believe," a loneliness qualitatively different from the loneliness of ordinary people who worry about their families out there in the free world.

Thus, the experience of the concentration camp annihilates the intellectual experience, in particular, language, discourse. Permanently? It would seem so: "We emerged from the camp stripped, robbed, emptied out, disoriented—and it was a long time before we were able even to learn the ordinary language of freedom. Still today, incidentally, we speak it with discomfort and without real trust in its validity."[3] The plural in this sentence is not accidental as—this is Améry's thesis—the concentration camp experience extends to all of us: the children and heirs of Shoah. *Our* helplessness in face of the fact that some thugs brutally tore out our tongue—the tongue that spoke the language of values that showed us where to go—we now call relativism, we cover it with a story about "overcoming metaphysics," hiding behind the authority of mainly German, but also French, philosophers. This desolation has one more very current dimension: it carries the conviction that playing at understanding

---

2. Jean Améry, *At the Mind's Limits: Contemplations by a Survivor of Auschwitz and Its Realities*, trans. Sidney and Stella P. Rosenfeld (Bloomington: Indiana University Press, 1980), 7–8.
3. Ibid., 20.

is a pagan pastime, a noncommittal juggling of a few notions, a game of quotations, that the human being is first of all *homo ludens*, and then *homo patiens*, and nothing suggests this state of affairs is about to suddenly change. Améry, then, loses the language in which he could describe freedom, and even if he speaks it sometimes, he no longer has faith in the importance of the uttered statements.

> Améry […] knew that if he wished to say anything about himself he must begin by reconstructing the medium in which his unspoken thoughts moved. […] Language is indeed the means whereby he counters the disturbance to his existential equilibrium, but it too ultimately proves inadequate as a cure for the precarious condition of a man losing faith in the world again daily when, on getting up, he sees his Auschwitz number tattooed on his forearm.[4]

Pain, Dying, Nakedness

There is no more horrible feast for the body than prolonged torture when the naked, crass violence reaches the most intimate of thresholds—the threshold of pain endurance. The first blow is like rape—it imposes someone's unwanted physical presence. "For, by an inscrutable decree of Nature," Gombrowicz wrote, "even the strongest person has one single thing foreordained in this world that is stronger than him, that is above him and that he cannot tolerate!"[5] It is the finding of this "one single thing" that torturers are intent on, at all latitudes (even democracies are not free from the enormity of torture[6]). Evil is not banal then—Améry argues with the famous thesis of Hannah Arendt—there is in evil a certain dark imperative of self-actualization. The tortured person in the horrible ordeal experiences an extreme form of mastery, of the power to spare life or take it away. The torturer seems like "an evil god" who confirms his or her might and inaccessibility. "The plain, ordinary faces finally become Gestapo faces after all, and […] evil overlays and exceeds banality. For there is no 'banality of evil,' and Hannah Arendt, who wrote about it in her Eichmann book, knew the enemy of mankind only from hearsay, saw him only through the glass cage."[7] Améry, as opposed to Arendt, has experienced a

---

4. W. G. Sebald, "Against the Irreversible. On Jean Améry," in *On the Natural History of Destruction*, trans. Anthea Bell (New York: Random House, 2003), e-book.
5. Witold Gombrowicz, *Bacacay*, trans. Bill Johnston (New York: Archipelago Books, 2004), e-book.
6. Améry, *At the Mind's Limits*, 27.
7. Ibid., 396.

different kind of evil, an evil that has forever questioned his trust in reality. In other words, if one becomes a victim once, one is a victim forever.

> The hook gripped into the shackle that held my hands together behind my back. Then I was raised with the chain until I hung about a metre above the floor. [...] And now there was a cracking and splintering in my shoulders that my body has not forgotten to this hour. The balls sprang from their sockets. My own body weight caused luxation; I fell into a void and now hung by my dislocated arms which had been torn high from behind and were now twisted over my head. Torture, from Latin *torquere*, to twist. What visual instruction in etymology![8]

"No help from anywhere"—this is the extreme experience of the tortured person; extreme, as it is an inalienable human right—it is even a valid law in the world of wild animals—to be allowed to defend oneself and to have hope that someone will come to the rescue. A tortured victim has no such hope. The experience of helplessness in face of the evil one is subjected to causes something inside the person to die, something that cannot be by any means brought back to life or reconstructed.

The tortured person is conquered by pain. They experience the body in an exceptional way, at any rate differently than in everyday life—their existence is suddenly reduced to naked life, to the sphere of sensual presence. The greater the suffering—Améry writes—the more horrifying our connection to the body, this swollen "punchbag" one becomes, a "bag" that only stands upright thanks to gravity. Torture then—this would be its ultimate purpose—leads to a gradual putting out of the mind: the tortured person stops longing for anything, imagining, thinking. He or she forgets symphonies, the poems recited in their youth, and finally they forget their close ones. They become a piece of meat. They do not fear death. They do fear, however, a prolonged dying. Is it going to hurt, or is it going to go fast and smoothly? —this is the only question the tortured person's drifting attention turns to. "Améry describes extremes of torture and the pain they cause as an approach to the death to which otherwise 'no road that can be travelled by logic' leads."[9] Therefore, it is impossible to forget, "to suppress," the experience of the reduction of one's humanity to its bodily, vulnerable aspect, to mere physical presence. If one hang by one's dislocated, limp arms once, one hangs like this forever, endlessly.

---

8. Sebald, "Against the Irreversible."
9. Ibid.

Old Age

On Aging is in a sense a continuation of the story Améry tells in *At the Mind's Limits*. The protagonist of the narrative is still the body, only the torturer changes—in *On Aging* it is time.

From a certain age, this shell, our body, starts "leaking," stops protecting us. Every time our health fails and we recover, we never do so fully, we land one step lower than before. If we used to have the tendency to slouch over a book, we can be sure that the hump of knowledge on our back will only grow with age. In other words, from a certain point in time our body starts betraying us. It no longer opens up the world for us; instead, it separates us from it more and more effectively—with arthritis, dyspepsia, myopia. The saying, probably of Orphic origins, that our body is the prison of the soul becomes valid in our old age or, more exactly, when we start to physically feel the passing of time. I do not know how general this sentiment is—I fearfully avoid discussing it with my peers; I have nothing to discuss with younger people; and I hardly ever ask the older ones about anything. Yet, sometimes when I am asleep, there is something inside me fluttering as if trying to "take off," something that is not fully in sync with my body and my life as I live it in my waking hours. In old-fashioned books one can read that this is soul thrashing and tossing because it does not want to die with the body. In theory the soul "knows" it is immortal, but even so it "panics," it is afraid of these moments when something lifts it up and "liberates" it from the body.

> Each morning I wake up from sleep like from fire
> A fiery darkness pushes me out
> without name without existence
> with a dwindling memory
> Surprised charred
> where how who
> One must mould oneself again from ashes.[10]

In Améry's writings we won't find even such a (fleeing, tentative, dreamy) "split." He knows, just like the readers of *At the Mind's Limits* know, that *nothing but* the body exists, that the soul, if it ever existed, went up the chimney more than half a century ago. In Améry nothing "lifts off"; he simply knows very well what to do with a used-up body. He wants to dispose of it, just like you dispose of a leaky, increasingly useless liquid container—preferably by putting a gun in his mouth. That's all. "It is still day, they say as they talk to themselves

---

10. Wiktor Woroszylski, "Lustro" [Mirror], in *Lustro; Dziennik internowania; Tutaj* (Londyn: Aneks, 1984). Trans. Adam Zdrodowski.

and want to be active like men and women. But the night has already set in, even before its actual entrance, and now they are only able to have an effect as society requires, allows, or forbids."[11]

Old age—both the one socially defined and the one felt subjectively—forces us, through the body, to act in a conformist fashion—we want, at all cost, to "strike a deal" with the world, concerning the passing time. We never say about unambitious, conformist people—this is a revelatory observation of Améry's—that they are old, that they're aging.

> A subordinate official, for example, is socially an old man at forty-five when, and only when, he has tried to attain a higher position. As long as he never tries to rise in the hierarchy, has never spoken of his hopes for advancement either with his family, with his friends, or with his superiors, his social age is not defined and not definable. In his subordinate position, there is no social relevance in being thirty or fifty. He lives on in his position without history, a man without biography—and only the weight of memory or his burdensome body lets him become aware one day that he is aged.[12]

Old age is the existential terror of the individual, bodily dissolution, but it is also a certain social reality, a social stigma, all kinds of stereotypes and "superstitions." Améry confronts both forms of oppression. After all, if we have had enough of our own biological decay—he writes in *On Suicide: A Discourse on Voluntary Death*—of being pilloried by physical necessity, we can always choose voluntary death. It is our freedom, at any rate it is its extreme manifestation; and it is our freedom that makes us choose the road that leads to no place that could be conceived.

Necessity and Impossibility of Being a Jew

But aging also means becoming "dependent to an increasing degree on the memory of the past,"[13] when our thoughts focus on our schooldays and not on what we are to do now. Old age is also characterized by the lack of vigor, the lack of self-confidence and moral flites—this never-ending senile whining, the constant dissatisfaction. Eventually an old man ends up ceasing to act at all. From now on he no longer decides; he becomes a plaything of others. "The

---

11. Jean Améry, *On Aging: Revolt and Resignation*, trans. John D. Barlow (Bloomington: Indiana University Press, 1994), 64.
12. Ibid., 59–60.
13. Améry, *At the Mind's Limits*, 57.

future is no longer around him and therefore also not within him. He cannot plead change. He shows the world a naked present."[14] An old person is pushed out of the social *space* to the margins of biological, personally experienced *time*. His behavior is determined by severe dementia and the accompanying, never-ending, pathetic tales, usually about what a great figure he used to be. In other words, he is defined by what he has lost. Contrary to an old person, a young one is not only what he or she is—a young person is also what he or she is going to become. Young people's actions are characterized by the pathos of novelty. Young people never feel that they are doing (if they are doing anything, they're usually sleeping) something wrong. They are only interested in power plays, fireworks, the pyrotechnician's handbook.[15] The old ones, however, if they still have some vigor energy left, jump into action—the longer, the farther, the better—hoping that this mobility will weaken their exhaustion and save them from death. Vitality precedes essence—they keep saying. "Action is a manifestation of our levity toward death," observes Vladimir Jankélévitch in a conversation with Daniel Diné, "even though it cannot help us accept it, it can diminish its importance. Acting is like building a footbridge over death, creating projects for the future, for the coming generations, for the world in which we are not going to be alive."[16]

The struggle between youth and old age, "the war of generations," is, according to Améry, one more incarnation of totalitarianism—a movement that ruins everything to start anew, from scratch. In this sense, in this strange world designed for the young, old age is a stigma similar to the yellow patch that had to be worn by every Jew in Europe. It is a state of danger that one should—at least in the social dimension—prevent. This is enough to make "being a Jew" a necessity. For the author of *At the Mind's Limits*, "Being a Jew" means solidarity with those suffering from harm; it means taking the side of the weak, defenseless person. In this sense it is all the same whether "the Jew" is a Black person, a worker in communist Poland, and old person or a Jew—it is about feeling an elementary solidarity in the situation of danger. Yet the necessity of "being a Jew" entails the impossibility of being a Jew; a Jew, that is, someone aware of their Jewish tradition and their Jewish deracination.

---

14. Ibid., 58.
15. The lack of any inhibitions in doing away with the remnants of the old world, motivated not by anger but by the feeling of power, is discussed—brilliantly and honestly, it seems—by Leszek Kołakowski in his conversation with Zbigniew Mentzel. *Czas ciekawy, czas niespokojny. Z Leszkiem Kołakowskim rozmawia Zbigniew Mentzel. Część I* (Kraków: Znak, 2007). Chapters 6 and 7 are particularly interesting. See also Alfred Mombert's letter to his friend, in Améry, "Against the Irreversible," 59–60.
16. Vladimir Jankélévitch, *Penser la mort?*, translated from the Polish edition: *To, co nieuchronne* (Warszawa: Państwowy Instytut Wydawniczy, 2005), 31.

Améry recalls how he once went with a Jewish friend to see Schönberg's *A Survivor from Warsaw*. When they heard the opening words of "Sch'ma Israel," the most important Jewish prayer, his friend turned "as white as chalk," while Améry was trying to understand why he couldn't care less. He thought then that he could be a Jew "only in fear and anger."[17] "Seen in this light, Améry's suicide in Salzburg resolved the insoluble conflict between being both at home and in exile, 'entre le foyer et le lointain.'"[18]

Resentments

Améry does not know how to, and, most importantly, doesn't want to, get rid of them. An Austrian Jew devoid of both traditions—Austrian, because it was taken away from him, and Jewish, because it was never strong enough anyway—just does not want to join the universal choir of mutual forgiving and patting each other's shoulders. He is not one of those ashamed of their misery. He knows that the society needs agreement between people, because it wants to organize itself well, that is, peacefully, and that to do so, it needs oblivion. Améry refuses to acknowledge it. His "resentments are there in order that the crime become a moral reality for the criminal, in order that he be swept into the truth of his atrocity."[19] Reconciliation? A moral forgiveness for those who trespass against us? But of course. Only when, however, they have stood in front of the shooting squad.

"One of the most impressive aspects of Améry's stance as a writer is," in Sebald's opinion,

> that although he knew the real limits of the power to resist as few others did, he maintains the validity of resistance even to the point of absurdity. Resistance without any confidence that it will be effective, resistance quand même, out of a principle of solidarity with victims and as a deliberate affront to those who simply let the stream of history sweep them along, is the essence of Améry's philosophy.[20]

In their old age the executioner loses memory, retaining little from what they have done to people. Yet the pain the victims experienced forever inscribes in their bodies what they suffered.

---

17. Améry, *At the Mind's Limits*, 100.
18. Sebald, "Against the Irreversible."
19. Améry, *At the Mind's Limits*, 70.
20. Sebald, "Against the Irreversible."

[The victims] try, usually in vain and at great expense of energy, to banish what has happened to them from their minds. Unlike the agents of terror, they obviously no longer have reliable mechanisms of repression at their command. [...] Existence prolonged beyond the experience of death has its affective center in a sense of guilt, the guilt of the survivor, which Niederland [contemporary German psychoanalyst, the author of, among others, *Folgen der Verfolgung*] describes as the worst psychological burden weighing on those of his patients who had escaped being murdered. It is a particularly macabre irony, as Niederland says, that the survivors and not those who committed Nazi crimes should bear the burden of such guilt. Trapped in a feeling of "being overpowered and reduced," plagued by constant "personal discomfort, states of depression and apathetic withdrawal," these surviving victims carry in them a permanent "deep scar left by the encounter with death in its most terrible forms."[21]

The language of the contemporary human, functional to extremes, "Machiavellian," or reduced to pure expression, goes against the strife for moral autonomy. In this language you can experience the world or receive orders, but you cannot think, ponder on the meaning of your actions. This is the language in which you hear all these completely used-up clichés that time will heal all wounds, that the nature of things will overgrow everything.

I see the sanatorium on its lofty rise, see everything simultaneously, the building as a whole and also the minutest detail; and I know that the woodwork, the roof beams, door posts and paneling, the floorboards and staircases, the rails and banisters, the lintels and ledges, have already been hollowed out under the surface, and that at any moment, as soon as the chosen one amongst the blind armies of beetles dispatches the very last, scarcely material resistance with its jaws, the entire lot will come down. And that is precisely what does happen in my dream, before my very eyes, infinitely slowly, and a great yellowish cloud billows out and disperses, and where the sanatorium once stood there is merely a heap of powder-fine wood dust, like pollen.[22]

Juxtaposed with the crumbling sanatorium, annihilated by elementary forces of nature—beetles, grass, moisture, heat—Améry's resentments are just good

---

21. Ibid., 162, 176–77.
22. W. G. Sebald, *The Emigrants*, trans. Michael Hulse (New York: New Directions, 1996), 186.

memory and a lack of acceptance for "natural" "solutions" that result from the nature of passing time.

Resentments result from a hurt sense of justice. We should—and this is Améry's only positive message—angrily nurse these sentiments. And those who, like Gabriel Marcel, mentioned in *At the Mind's Limits*, call for brotherhood between people, a general forgiveness for scumbags and bandits in the end become spokespersons for amnesia—a social disease typical of the entire free world.

Chapter 8

GERMAN RUBBLE (W. G. SEBALD)

Seven cities stood there.
So we think.
They were meant to stand forever.
We suppose. […]
A meteor fell.
Not a meteor.
A volcano exploded.
Not a volcano.
Someone summoned something.
Nothing was called.
On this more-or-less Atlantis.[1]

The Allied Forces' air raids of Germany happening toward the end of the Second World War were broadcast live by the BBC Radio. During one of the first air raids on Berlin, the live commentator was the (then) famous British journalist Wynford Vaughan-Thomas. The circumstances seemed banal: the steady roar of the Lancaster bombers, the impenetrable night—and only the journalist's genuine emotions imbued the situation with a sense of unusual dread: "Now, right before us lies darkness and Germany,"[2] he commented in a tense voice. Moments before they reach the air defense Kammhuber Line, the aircraft's crew is presented to the listeners: Scottie, the flight engineer, in private—a cinema projectionist from Glasgow; Sparky—the bombardier; Connolly—the navigator; there is also the rear gunner, a Sussex farmer, and the skipper—who, however, choses to remain anonymous. The plot gathers speed once they are above the city. Shafts of light making the bombers easy targets for the German air defense, then the flashes of exploding anti-aircraft missiles,

---

1. Wisława Szymborska, "Atlantis," in *Poems New and Collected*, trans. Stanisław Barańczak and Clare Cavanagh (San Diego: Harcourt, 1998), 17.
2. W. G. Sebald, *On the Natural History of Destruction*, trans. Anthea Bell (New York: Random House, 2003), e-book.

eventually some hits and the Allied Forces' bombers plummeting down—this is what the citizens of the British Isles learn from the correspondent's report. Finally the order is given to drop the bombs on the city. Everything is happening very fast. The task has been accomplished. They are going back home. They unwind by becoming suddenly very talkative. "By God, that looks like a bloody good show. Best I've ever seen. Look at that fire! Oh boy!" And here's a literary rendition of a similar kind of awe:

> A tiny hamlet that you wouldn't even notice in the daytime, with ugly, uninteresting country around it, you can't imagine how impressive it can be when it's on fire at night! You'd think it was Notre-Dame! A village, even a small one, takes at least all night to burn, in the end it looks like an enormous flower, then there's only a bud, and after that nothing. Smoke rises, and then it's morning.[3]

Statistics

Presently—some numbers. According to German statistics during the final phase of the war, the Royal Air Force dropped on Germany over a million tons of bombs. One hundred thirty-one towns and cities were attacked—some only once, others repeatedly —most of which were razed to the ground. Six hundred thousand German civilians were killed in the raids. Three and a half million homes were destroyed, and as a result in the last months of the war, seven and a half million Germans were left homeless. In Cologne there was 31.1 cubic meters of rubble per person; in Dresden, a little more—42.8. In Pforzheim, a town where during one night (February 22, 1945) one-third of all its citizens were killed, one could still see makeshift wooden crosses stuck into the rubble, as late as 1950. This is what Janet Flanner wrote in March 1947—"the appalling smells which were released from the yawning cellars of Warsaw by the first warm spring weather pervaded the German cities, too, in the immediate postwar period."[4]

Those who criticized the raids—both Germans (which is understandable) and the Allies—pointed out their remarkable counter-efficiency: as late as spring 1944 the majority of German citizens showed a considerable fortitude, no defeatism, and even a degree of boldness, as if the raids only strengthened and consolidated the entire society. What is more, the bombings failed to destroy the arms industry that worked at full capacity until the last days of Hitler's

---

3. Louis-Ferdinand Céline, *Journey to the End of the Night*, trans. Ralph Manheim (New York: New Directions, 2006), 60–61.
4. Sebald, *On the Natural History of Destruction*.

Reich. Looking at the numbers that Sebald quotes, one can conclude that, at the end of the war, the front line, where soldiers fighting face to face with bullets and bayonets at least stood a chance of becoming prisoners of war, was a safer place than a cellar turned into a bomb shelter where a mother would want to hide her small children.

What was it then that made the army headquarters move the war inside the Reich? What were the factual reasons for opening a new, inner front line and taking up a fight—a fight?—with civilians? There were none, Sebald answers. No political or military considerations stood behind the decision to start the raids. At its source lay the desire for retaliation, anger, a human need for total destruction. For there always are—both during wars and in times of peace— people like the Russian generals or Sir Arthur Harris, the commander-in-chief of bomber command, whose fascination with naked force is expressed in "the growing number of its accumulated victims."[5] For them the annihilation itself is the purpose, while human suffering is merely numbers. This aspect of recent history was perfectly grasped by Jarosław Marek Rymkiewicz in his book on the Warsaw Uprising. In the chapter "Masakra w stylu Greima" (Bloodbath in the Style of Greim), he analyses the mentality of the German general who came up with the idea of finishing Warsaw off from the air, of razing it to the ground along with the city's entire civilian population. "The use of technology," we read in *Kinderszenen*,

> applying perfect tools makes the perpetrators and the organisers of the carnage disappear (remain in hiding); their faces, emotions, feelings, thoughts, everything they could hide in their minds disappears—so does their fury, anger, hate, their satisfaction along with something dark that must remain nameless (which we can't name, which I am not able to name). In other words, the bloodbath in the style of Greim takes away from the murderers the pleasure they could get from murdering.[6]

An integral part of *On the Natural History of Destruction* are black-and-white pictures of the attacked and systematically destroyed Germany. Yet it is not the photos that make the strongest impression. The readers begin to partake in Sebald's reflections once they begin to realize that there are places devoid of light in a human being, places that question our moral development (whatever this strange notion means). No matter how technically advanced, well trained, educated humans are, the arguments in favor of destruction—or, more precisely, self-destruction—will remain a mystery. Because it turns out that the

---

5. Ibid.
6. Jarosław Marek Rymkiewicz, *Kinderszenen* (Warszawa: Sic!, 2008), 212.

human mind, the enormous work of generations and resources accumulated for years in the end only serve the purpose of a carefully planned destruction of the human world. Therefore, it is not the sight of burned cities that fills Sebald with terror, but the people who decide to wipe them out. "If they are right," Charles Simic writes in a beautiful essay on Sebald's book, "and I'm not convinced they are, that may be the most terrifying thing of all. No matter what history books have told us, bombing is a form of collective punishment premised on collective guilt."[7]

During the war, W. H. Auden, one of the most outstanding poets of the twentieth century, served as bombing research analyst at Morale Division of the US Strategic Bombing Survey. His tasks included investigating the level of terror among the German civilians in bombed cities. "I know they had *asked* for it," he would say during the breaks between interrogations, "but still, this kind of total destruction is beyond reasoning […] It seems like madness! […] [I]s it justified to reply to *their* mass murder by *our* mass murder? It seems terrifying to me […]? And I cannot help but ask myself, 'Was there no other way?'"[8] After the war, Auden for a short time considered the idea of describing the raid victims' feelings. In a letter to his friend, James Stern's wife, he wrote: "The work is very interesting but I'm near crying sometimes […] The people, though, are sad beyond belief."[9]

The poet's task is to sing human harm no matter who suffers from it. Propaganda gimmicks and slogans do not have enough power to weaken his moral instinct. The officially preached Manichaeism—the bad "Krauts," the angelic Yankees—is just another of many impersonations of the tyranny of values that lets us tread down our enemy ("disvalues"). Even more so, since the enemy was asking for it. "Disvalue has no rights over value," Carl Schmitt writes,

> and there is no price too high to pay in order to force the highest value through. Thus, one deals here only with the annihilator and the

---

7. Charles Simic, "Conspiracy of Silence," *New York Review of Books* (February 27, 2003), 10. I have written more extensively about the antinomies of the idea of progress in the foreword to the Polish edition of Hannah Arendt's *Lectures on Kant's Political Philosophy*: Arendt, *Wykłady o filozofii politycznej Kanta* (Warszawa: Fundacja Augusta hr. Cieszkowskiego, 2012).
8. W. H. Auden, quoted after Vladimir Nabokov, "Excerpts from Memories," in *W. H. Auden: A Tribute*, ed. Stephen Spender (New York: Macmillan, 1975), 145.
9. W. H. Auden, quoted after James Stern, "The Indispensable Presence," in *W. H. Auden: A Tribute*, 126. Both James and Tania Sterns were important figures in Auden's life. He dedicated to them *The Sea and the Mirror*, his poetic commentary on Shakespeare's *The Tempest*.

annihilated. All the concepts of the classical law of warfare of the *Jus Publicum Europaeum* (the European Civil Law)—such as the just enemy, the just motive of war, the proportionality of the means, the prescribed course of action, the *debitus modus*—fall hopelessly victim to this valuelessness. The urge to make values prevail becomes a coercion to enact values directly.[10]

In the world of "disvalues," the enemy stops being an enemy; he or she becomes a dispensable obstacle on the way to a world without our enemy, a stumbling block that needs to be crushed, ground to dust and forgotten.

> We drifted downstream under a scattering of stars
> and slept until the sun rose. When we got to the capital,
> which lay in ruins, we built a large fire out of what chairs
> and table we could find. The heat was so fierce that birds
> overhead caught fire and fell flaming to earth.
> These we ate, then continued on foot into regions
> where the sea is frozen and the ground is strewn
> with moonlike boulders.[11]

Taboo

W. G. Sebald grew up convinced that something was being hidden from him, not discussed either in school or at home, that—as Simic put it—there was, among adults in their postwar world, a peculiar "conspiracy of silence." The first taboo subject—which is in some way understandable—was the Holocaust; the second—the carpet bombings of civilian objects in the last phase of the war; the third—the nation's support of the NSDAP. Shoah first started being talked about in Germany as late as the early 1960s, after Adolf Eichmann's execution in Jerusalem. This is also when other, minor Nazi torturers were starting to go on trial and were usually treated indulgently. The shame linked to the support for the National Socialist Party had nothing to do with the NSDAP's murderous character, but with its *inefficiency*. The dynamically growing democratic Germany had no understanding for "losers." Why is it, however, that the question of air raids was only first touched upon by an American comic

---

10. Carl Schmitt, *The Tyranny of Values*, trans. Simona Draghici (1959), https://www.counter-currents.com/2014/07/the-tyranny-of-values-1959/.
11. Mark Strand, "Error," in *Man and Camel* (New York: Alfred A. Knopf, 2006), 10.

writer?[12] Why had the great German literature not even raised the question until the 1990s? There are several reasons. The first was a universal stupefaction. "The death by fire," writes Sebald, "within a few hours of an entire city, with all its buildings and its trees, its inhabitants, its domestic pets, its fixtures and fittings of every kind, must inevitably have led to overload, to paralysis of the capacity to think and feel in those who succeeded in escaping."[13] What truly terrifies the reader in Sebald's book is his description of the effects of Operation Gomorrah whose aim was to turn Hamburg into a city of ashes. In the summer of 1943, the Royal Air Force together with the Eighth Army of American Air Force performed air raids destroying the city completely. The flames that, according to the pilots' testimony, rose 2 kilometers over the city sucked in oxygen so fiercely that the air currents reached hurricane speed "resonating like mighty organs."[14]

> The water in some of the canals was ablaze. The glass in the tram car windows melted; stocks of sugar boiled in the bakery cellars. Those who had fled from their air-raid shelters sank, with grotesque contortions, in the thick bubbles thrown up by the melting asphalt. No one knows for certain how many lost their lives that night, or how many went mad before they died. When day broke, the summer dawn could not penetrate the leaden gloom above the city. The smoke had risen to a height of eight thousand meters, where it spread like a vast, anvil-shaped cumulonimbus cloud. A wavering heat, which the bomber pilots said they had felt through the sides of their planes, continued to rise from the smoking, glowing mounds of stone. Residential districts so large that their total street length amounted to two hundred kilometers were utterly destroyed. Horribly disfigured corpses lay everywhere. Bluish little phosphorous flames still flickered around many of them; others had been roasted brown or purple and reduced to a third of their normal size. They lay doubled up in pools of their own melted fat, which had sometimes already congealed. The central death zone was declared off-limits in the next few days. When punishment labor gangs and camp inmates could begin clearing it in August, after the rubble had cooled down, they found people still sitting at tables or up against walls where they had been overcome by monoxide gas. Elsewhere, clumps of flesh and bone or whole heaps of bodies had cooked in the water gushing from bursting

---

12. Kurt Vonnegut, *Slaughterhouse-Five or the Children's Crusade: A Duty-Dance with Death* (New York: Delacorte Press, 1969).
13. Sebald, *On the Natural History of Destruction*.
14. Ibid.

boilers. Other victims had been so badly charred and reduced to ashes by the heat, which had risen to a thousand degrees or more, that the remains of families consisting of several people could be carried away in a single laundry basket.[15]

No wonder that Germans felt a hysterical will to survive alternating with clinical apathy and a resignation in face of an inescapable fate. Something else, however, strikes me most in Sebald's description—it is the fact that so many people did not acknowledge at all what happened to their lives. We see a woman cleaning windows in the only building that remained standing in the street, even though the sky is overdrawn with clouds of smoke. Or the crowded trains where you can easily recognize foreigners—mostly war correspondents—because they, as opposed to the local people, look out the windows, dumbfounded by the scale of destruction. The Germans' lack of response to what had happened to them harmonized with the deadly silence of the destroyed cities. The people's apparent indifference resembled the parable of Lot's wife who, having broken God's prohibition and looked behind her, turned into a pillar of salt. "It was the fear of turning to stone of one who looks behind their shoulder at what is already gone."[16]

The universal aphasia was not limited to millions of common Germans. What is perhaps even more significant is that German writers suffered from it as well. It seems as if the rubble from burned cities buried memory, communal sensitivity and the ability to experience reality together—nobody wanted to know anything, remember about anything—because of fear, shame, stupefaction. Writers dealt with trifles. Literally: a tin drum, a midget, another metaphor. No major war epic was written. And those who had been writing in the years 1930–50—and they were not so few—painstakingly labored at redefining their life stories. Others, younger ones, having returned from the front, focused solely on their wounds, healing them partially with their more or less successful writerly attempts. Authors had their fingers broken, their souls bombed—the two rather important elements in the creative process. Books by Alexander Kluge, Gert Ledig, Hans Erich Nossack (some of them very good) had one serious shortcoming: they did not smell of cinders; they lacked *realism*, characteristic of the prose by Borowski or Primo Levi. A testimony to the muteness, the fear of "letting the cat out of the bag"—feelings so well intuited and described by Gombrowicz in his *Dziennik berliński* (Berlin Diary)—is the fact that the only book that could testify to the Germans' defeat

---

15. Ibid.
16. W. G. Sebald, interview by Volker Hage, *Zeugen der Zerstörung: Die Literaten und der Luftkrieg. Essays und Gespräche* (Frankfurt am Main: S. Fischer, 2003), 268.

and the scope of their suffering, Heinrich Böll's *Der Engel schwieg*, came out in 1992, 40 years after it was written.

"There is a new element present in politics that goes deep, and which former victors knew nothing of, or at least they made no conscious use of it," Jacob Burckhardt wrote many years before the twentieth-century cataclysms. "They try to humiliate the vanquished profoundly in his own eyes, so that he should never again really trust himself to achieve anything. It is possible that this aim will be achieved; but whether things will be any better and happier is another matter."[17] German writers had their inner world crushed, their sensitivity taken away, their credibility—and thus the value of their testimonies—questioned. They were sent back to school of manners, then reeducated with the entire nation. In the conditions where the newly passed law of "self-revenge" told one to feel contemptuous toward oneself, no convincing book could have been written, no masterpiece. The culture and philosophy of the second part of the twentieth century belongs to those who won the war.

The Right to Suffering

I was brought up in the hatred of Germans, their Nazi jabber, the swastika, the teutonic arrogance. From early childhood, my life has been inseparable from the war and the German occupation—beginning with my grandma's tales, my friend's grandmother's stories, the character of Stirlitz, *Four Tank-Men and the Dog* TV series, up onto a child's fascination with the Nuremberg trials ("serves them right"). We, the Poles, suffered for real (much later I learned that Jews suffered as well, which seemed rather abstract because where were they, the Jews?), whereas in my eyes the Germans were dealt a well-deserved punishment for the homicide on my nation. When they died—here's a 15-year-old's dilemma—did they suffer just like we did? Perhaps, I would tell myself, after all, ants feel pain too. Yet their—ants' and Germans'—right to *suffering* was another matter. Obviously this is what I denied them, demanding that they compensate for their crimes, the kind of compensation Jean Améry demanded in his book *At the Mind's Limits. Contemplations by a Survivor on Auschwitz and its Realities*:

> For as long as the German nation, including its young and youngest age groups, does not decide to live entirely without history—and there is no sign that *the world's most history-conscious* national community suddenly

---

17. Jacob Burckhardt in a letter to Friedrich von Preen from September 27, 1870. Burckhardt, *The Letters of Jacob Burckhardt*, trans. Alexander Dru (London: Routledge & Kegan Paul, 1955), 143–44.

would assume such a position—then it must continue to bear the responsibility for those twelve years that it certainly did not terminate itself.[18]

Sebald's book met with a variety of responses, but more often than not, it was being misread. Critics claimed that it aestheticizes disaster and gives fabrication the status of testimony by applying the technique of "creative montage,"[19] or that it makes the Germans' guilt relative, that it blurs the line between the torturer and the victim showing Germans as suffering—and what is worse, showing them as having the right to suffer to the same extent (or more, because nobody sympathizes with them) as other nations. In Germany too the book caused a lot of controversy. Its author was flooded with more or less credible testimonials of suffering to which he invariably responded:

> I repeat, I do not doubt that there were and are memories of those nights of destruction; I simply do not trust the form—including the literary form—in which they are expressed, and I do not believe they were a significant factor in the public consciousness of the new Federal Republic in any sense except as encouraging the will to reconstruction.[20]

Thus, Améry's claim that the German nation is a community characterized by a special historical consciousness seems faulty—there is no evidence to support it. On the contrary, for many years the German nation had been doing justice to Jewish tribulations in the same way the loser pays reparations to the winner, splashing Deutschmarks with the same mindless zeal with which it rebuilt the country. "It had a short memory so it bore no grudge." The postwar German Republic suffered from amnesia. From the moment the new state took shape, the young and the old have never ceased their efforts to evade national history and culture; they treat their past greatness with a strange sense of indifference and disapproval. Choosing the technological civilization and "common Europe," they turn in the direction of *future* tasks. The amnesia has been complemented by fabrication that Sebald called an artificial perspective on history, "the synoptic regard." But when he himself traveled through Germany, he had the impression that everything was "ablaze." "Why when I take the S-Bahn toward Stuttgart's city center do I think, every time we reach Feuersee Station," he asked rhetorically, "that the fires are still blazing above

---

18. Jean Améry, *At the Mind's Limits: Contemplations by a Survivor of Auschwitz and Its Realities*, trans. Sidney and Stella P. Rosenfeld (Bloomington: Indiana University Press, 1980), 77.
19. Ruth Franklin, *A Thousand Darknesses: Lies and Truth in Holocaust Fiction* (Oxford: Oxford University Press, 2010), 184–98.
20. Sebald, *On the Natural History of Destruction*.

us, and that since the terrors of the last war years, even though we have rebuilt our surroundings so wonderfully well, we have been living in a kind of underground zone?"[21] In Sebald's description, the Germans make the impression of a nation that is afraid of itself. For is it not the case that their economic and political success is based on principles that have remained unchanged since Hitler's times: on invention and improvisation forced by war, on their experience in using foreign labor, on a wartime work ethics, on the loss of memory? Sebald is perhaps the only German writer who did not let himself be fooled into believing that the ruins of the old world can be replaced with something new, or that one can restore their past appearance and luster. He claimed that there is something profoundly wrong with the communal memory of a nation that does not want anything to remind it about their recent past.

In Germany the rubble is loquacious. Stones speak instead of people—a never rebuilt church next to the Berlin Zoo; a completely new Hamburg—a city of glass and aluminum; finally, Königsberg, wiped out from the world map, with the grotesque tomb of Kant without his body inside. The dates of war catastrophes are estimated based on the height of grass growing on the ruins. The deepest human suffering—one can see it in the spring in all green cities in bloom—is covered by inhuman nature. This is how the pain of individual people, their families and, eventually, the traumas of entire nations become, as Sebald observes, "a botanical question." Human history becomes part of inhuman nature because human actions are classified as natural disasters. (The English title of Sebald's *Luftkrieg und Literatur* is *On the Natural History of Destruction*.) Should, however, the disasters of history be considered solely as natural discharges or disasters? Is not such an approach too facile, underpinned by resignation in the face of all-encompassing disintegration? In his *A Treatise on Poetry*, Miłosz expresses his conviction that ironic poetry can—is able to—stop the forces of natural inertia. The temptation to keep returning to nature that is governed by its own laws is overcome by poetic effort—"Grass, defeated by the irony of a song."[22]

Sebald's prose overcomes the words' resistance, breaks an important taboo. To a no lesser degree than the bringing down of the Berlin Wall, Sebald's writing contributed to an awakening of Germans' self-knowledge. To us, it gave a chance to see Germans' suffering in a new light—in a humane way, with no unnecessary affectation, no *Schadenfreude*.

---

21. W. G. Sebald, "An Attempt at Restitution. A Memory of a German City," trans. Anthea Bell, *New Yorker* (December 20 & 27, 2004), 112.
22. Czesław Miłosz, *A Treatise on Poetry*, trans. author and Robert Hass (New York: Ecco Press, 2001), 40.

Gloria victis, vae victoribus

A surprising—Kojèveian—conclusion to Sebald's analyses was provided by Wolfgang Schivelbusch, a German history professor, the writer's age-mate and, just like Sebald, an emigrant, a New Yorker by choice.

Germany's defeat in 1945 was the entire nation's existential failure. The defeat was indisputable and nonnegotiable. The Germans were stripped of their memory, the pride of their past cultural accomplishments and their desire for revenge on the winners. The loss of self-confidence, the erasure of the moral reason that pushed the country toward war caused "a great fear" that paralyzed all activity. Soon the guilty parties were found—these were the apparatchiks of the past political system, a system that, until recently, had been almost unanimously supported by the entire German nation. Now these culprits were being burdened with all the anger, responsibility and "metaphysical guilt." The painstaking process of cleansing the national body of the concretions of the *ancien régime*, readying the "new Germans" to a life in the European democratic family, was a good way of scoring a new victory—this time over oneself. The victory consisted in a perseverant overcoming of "the past that won't go away," in liberating oneself from the German "national character." The courtroom, the workplace, the university or the sports stadium became a sort of psychoanalyst's couch where Germany underwent therapy. Simultaneously, their past enemy—the Allies—literally overnight became a dear friend and supporter of the entire nation's "wellness therapy" while also being a perfect example to follow (the so-called imitative transformation). Gradually the gratitude for the freedom given to them was replaced by the questions: "how could it happen?" How could the culture of merchants defeat the Germans' chivalrous spirit? Why is it that material power outweighed spiritual organization and moral advantage of the defeated? Thus, one day the "slaves," freed of the burden of the not-so-distant past, awoke to new tasks.

A victory must be honorable, achieved according to rules agreed upon by equals—otherwise it is not a victory at all. A butcher or some shopkeeper—people devoid of the capacity for honor—are denied victory even when they win.

> The more victory becomes a matter of winning in the sense of profiting, the more it becomes, from the perspective of the militarily oriented culture of the loser, the realm of tradesmen and merchants. Once material gain supplants the laurels of victory, the heroic loser is left with little more than the materially disinterested beau geste—the satisfaction of having fought bravely and honorably, if hopelessly, to the bitter end.[23]

---

23. Wolfgang Schivelbusch, *The Culture of Defeat: On National Trauma, Mourning, and Recovery*, trans. Jefferson Chase (London: Picador, 2004), 17.

Therefore, *gloria victis, vae victoribus*—glory be to the weak and defeated, and woe to the victors—for the victorious force is for the human world a natural disaster, an inhuman calamity. "The fear of being overrun and destroyed by barbarian hordes is as old as the history of civilized culture itself."[24] Meanwhile, highly developed cultures—and this has been pointed out by visionaries such as Edward Gibbon, Oswald Spengler, Gottfried Benn—although defeated, do not perish. On the contrary, their barbarian enemies adopt their ways. Thus, Macedonians soaked up Greek culture; German tribes adopted the habits and institutions of the defeated Romans; Mongolians took everything that was valuable from China; and the Arabs—from the Persians. Upon victory the winners absorb that which does not belong to them—the "poison" that takes away their singularity. Yet, from the perspective of the losers, the situation does not look well, at least initially. Barbarians take away their estates, their opera seats; they marry their daughters. The lack of hope for a quick retaliation, an instantaneous revenge on the cavemen breeds the culture of defeat. "The one great consolation for the defeated is their faith in their cultural and moral superiority over the newly empowered who have ousted them."[25] Yet the defeated party knows what the victor has not even begun to suspect, namely, that fortune is fickle and that its change is as natural as it is inevitable. "To see victory as a curse and defeat as moral purification and salvation is to combine the ancient idea of hubris with the Christian virtue of humility, catharsis with apocalypse."[26] Schivelbusch suggests that Germany's defeat in the Second World War gave the country an opportunity to cleanse the system, redefine its power and translate the fathers' defeat into the sons' triumph. What would their success consist in? In a successful undermining of the arrogant power of American materialism, in subverting the good intentions of the winners who, depending on circumstances, treated Germany as a dependable partner in beer-brewing or as the manufacturer of reliable cars or as a metaphysical enemy of the entire world. "Anchoring one's defeat within the tradition of history's great losers offers both meaning and consolation."[27] The situation where the borrower leaves the bank broke, a dialectical movement of history where masters and servants change places, that is, a broadly understood "logic of change," enabled Germans to gradually take back the victory from the victorious by mimicking the victorious in everything that led them to their triumph. Whether one should be afraid of it or not is another matter.

---

24. Ibid., 19.
25. Ibid.
26. Ibid., 20.
27. Ibid., 30.

Summary

History—the stage for the triumphant and the defeated—is the only tribunal available to man where his involvement and efficiency are assessed. "History to the defeated / May say Alas but cannot help nor pardon."[28] It seems, however, that it can—and to do so, it needs time as measured by the turning of "the wheel of fortune," because the bigger the prize, the greater the risk of later defeat. It is particularly apparent in the difference between the historiography of the defeated and that of the victorious. "While history may be temporarily made by victors, who hold on to it for a while, it never allows itself to be ruled for long [...] The historian who stands on the side of the victorious is easily tempted to interpret triumphs of the moment as the lasting outcomes of an ex post facto teleology."[29] Victorious chroniclers rarely have anything interesting to say about past events. They consider history a sort of teleological chain where the most recent victories of the side they are on are proclaimed the ultimate ones, the final rings in the chain that make history complete—the proper telos. The "losers" see things from a different perspective and in another arrangement. Nothing goes according to their plan, which they realize quite quickly while trying to figure out why this is the case. History—the realm of defeat—is for them a burden or a lesson, never a good opportunity. It is true that history is written by the victorious, yet this truth never becomes part of their self-knowledge. A full historic self-knowledge belongs to the defeated. "Victories are often deceptive, but defeats are always instructive."[30]

The dialectic method used by the defeated to describe (and understand) reality consists in ascribing great value to the power of denial, negation, negativity. Psychoanalysis—the self-narrative of neurotics, disappointed and defeated by the world—reduces the gist of this method to "repression." "The whole theory of psycho-analysis," Freud wrote, "is, as you know, in fact built up on the perception of the resistance offered to us by the patient when we attempt to make his unconscious conscious to him."[31] While repression is the condition for interpreting the old world in new categories, negation remains its—repression's—outer and active expression. Therefore, one can say that, only thanks to negation, "thinking frees itself from the restrictions of

---

28. W. H. Auden, "Spain," in *Selected Poems* (New York: Vintage, 2007), 57.
29. Reinhart Koselleck, "Erfahrungswandel und Methodenwechsel: Eine historisch-antropologische Skizze," quoted after Schivelbusch, *The Culture of Defeat*, 4–5.
30. Jean-Marie Domenach, quoted after Schivelbusch, *The Culture of Defeat*, 245.
31. Sigmund Freud, "Negation," in *The Standard Edition of the Complete Psychological Works of Sigmund Freud, Volume XIX (1923–1925): The Ego and the Id and Other Works* (London: Hogarth Press, 1964), 67.

repression and enriches itself with material that is indispensable for its proper functioning."[32]

Eventually all those who have tasted defeat have come out as winners; it is they who—through the dialectics of history that in the last century adopted the name of the psychoanalytic method—gave the world an unappealing yet stable and comprehensible shape. Having repressed what is old and used up, they try to define and order the world anew, in their own way. In the end, only the weak and defeated have hope for a tomorrow; those who have attained everything cannot stop being who they are.

---

32. Sigmund Freud, "New Introductory Lectures on Psycho-Analysis," in *The Standard Edition of the Complete Psychological Works of Sigmund Freud, Volume XXII (1932–1936): New Introductory Lectures on Psycho-Analysis and Other Works* (London: Hogarth Press, 1964), 235.

Chapter 9

LONG LIVE! (K. K. BACZYŃSKI)

Rainer Maria Rilke's inscription to Marina Tsvetaeva in a copy of his *Duino Elegies*, which the Austrian gifted the Russian poet in the 1920s, is a concluding remark of his entire poetic message:

> We touch each other. How? With wings that beat,
> With very distance touch each other's ken.
> *One* poet only lives, and now and then
> Who bore him, and who bears him now, will meet.[1]

For this reason, a round anniversary of the birth of a great poet—and in 2021 we celebrated the centenary of Krzysztof Kamil Baczyński's birth—is, at the same time, the birthday of entire Polish poetry. Long live!

In Poland, "ground" that receives everything of importance is culture. A series of historical events points to this. Above all, over 120 years of geographical and political nonexistence the Poles had survived thanks to culture of the highest merit, thanks to works by the world's greatest poets. Since Polish poets are the best of the best and—as a result—untranslatable, hence, specific, national. They are of absolute importance and urgently needed, indispensable.

We take part in national culture unawares—and willy-nilly. It is as indispensable as oxygen, because, like oxygen, it allows us to breathe freely. What, then, is the nation? Well, the nation has always presented itself to me as the thing that precedes me before I learn to speak. It is, therefore, a language, customs, ethical norms, shared history, as well as shared geography, a space of communal living. In the nation is my origin. The nation has always preceded me and forms me even when it is not quite to my liking. And it will be there when I am gone. The nation is a force that enlightened reformers, every now and then, want to bridle, reform and modernize. Tadeusz Różewicz once wrote that "the poet is certainly

---

1. Rainer Maria Rilke, in *Letters: Summer 1926: Pasternak, Tsvetayeva, Rilke*, trans. Margaret Wettlin and Walter Arndt (San Diego, CA: Harcourt Brace Jovanovich, 1985), 81.

someone."[2] I am not sure that Krzysztof Kamil Baczyński was a great poet. But I do know he is a Polish poet and "certainly someone."

But Rilke meant much more. He suspected that there is no plural of the word "poet," that they all strive to sing one and the same song out to the world. There is something to it. In Juliusz Słowacki's *Król Duch* (The Spirit King), spirits of the dead become incorporated into various people. And even if it is just a metaphor, such as the Polish expression *"kamień spadł mi z serca"* ("weight was lifted off my chest," literally "a stone fell from my heart"), there exist ancient ideas that are taken up anew in the modern era. New poets give old and eternal ideas a new life. It has always been so, but only Rilke drew attention to this fact with his beautiful inscription in the *Duino Elegies*.

The same concept governs Jerzy Zagórski's brilliant essay, where he draws parallels between Słowacki and Baczyński. He wrote it straight after the Warsaw Uprising. Zagórski underscores the fact that both poets favored military action. A well-known fact about Słowacki is his participation in the November Uprising (1830–31); their motherland—"the cruel beast"—demanded of both poets a nearly "Aztec worship."[3] Bitter words. Surely Baczyński emerged from the Romantic tradition, and Zagórski tended to believe that he was, in some profounder, unobvious sense, Słowacki's incarnation. Baczyński's death filled Zagórski with gall, with resentment. He could not reconcile to the loss of his close friend, one of such immense inner beauty. He also blamed himself that he had not been able to stop Baczyński in time, holding him back from involvement in military action. Nonetheless, could Zagórski's efforts have ever been successful, when an element of self-destruction had long been ingrained into the young poet's life and writing?

Krzysztof Kamil Baczyński's figure, throughout all those years, has undergone a manner, so to speak, of mythologization.[4] A soldier, an excellent poet, a scout who dies for his country at such an early age! The news of the poet's death was said to provoke Stanisław Pigoń to conclude: "Oh, well, we belong to that sort of nation that has to shoot the enemy with diamonds."[5] But,

---

2. Tadeusz Różewicz, "Włosek poety" [The Hair of the Poet], in *Uśmiechy* (Wrocław: Wydawnictwo Dolnośląskie, 2000). Trans. Renata Senktas.
3. Jerzy Zagórski, "Śmierć Słowackiego" [Słowacki's Death], in *Żołnierz, poeta, czasu kurz … Wspomnienia o K.K. Baczyńskim* [Soldier, Poet, the Dust of Time… Memories of K. K. Baczyński], ed. Zenon Wasilewski (Kraków: Wydawnictwo Literackie, 1979), 397.
4. Stefan Zabierowski, "Legendotwórczy charakter biografii Krzysztofa Kamila Baczyńskiego" [The Legendary Nature of Krzysztof Kamil Baczyński's Biography], *Prace Polonistyczne* XLIII (1987), 41.
5. Quoted after Aniela Kmita-Piorunowa, "Zaczęło się od *Listu do Jana Bugaja*," in *Kazimierz Wyka*, ed. Henryk Markiewicz and Andrzej Fiut (Kraków: Wydawnictwo Literackie, 1978), 333–34.

perhaps, it's always the case that a biography of every outstanding artist, not only Baczyński's, is liable to mythologization. Suffice to think of Brzozowski, Przybyszewski, Witkacy. The lives of Borowski, Stachura, Wojaczek got surrounded in myths. They all died tragically. The reason why Jarosław Iwaszkiewicz went underground dressed as a miner can only be surmised. In Iwaszkiewicz's case, the myth of *poètes maudits* was compounded with an element of self-created mythologization, partly self-aggrandizing and grotesque (suffice to mention the status enjoyed by miners under the first secretary of the Polish United Workers' Party in the Polish People's Republic, Edward Gierek), partly real (demonstrating a chthonic element present in Iwaszkiewicz's work). But as often happens with myths: some have a powerful influence over one generation only to disappear later, while others live longer and fade away slower. Baczyński's legend has survived relatively long, because his myth is rooted in the myth of the last world war, the most hideous of those that have sedimented in the Poles. Both myths are further superimposed with the myth of the Warsaw Uprising and that of the "Generation of Columbuses," which flowered very briefly and sunk into the ground promptly. There are painful spots in recent history of Poland, and they keep bleeding, they do not heal.

But what do we know about a demythologized Krzysztof Kamil Baczyński? Which facts of his private life make up the material of his poems? First of all, he did a dreadful thing, a thing nobody should ever do. As a single child, he let his mother go through his death. His mother was an author of children's books and handbooks. She had an excellent knowledge of poetry and was very religious. His father, too, had a professional connection to literature. We learn from Jerzy Zagórski's commemorative essay that

> the Baczyńskis originate from Volhynia, the very same Volhynia that bore the remarkable fruit of Słowacki onto the soil of Polish poetry. Like Juliusz Słowacki, Kszysztof Baczyński's father was a humanities scholar, a literary man, a remarkable critic: Stanisław Baczyński, whose son surpassed him with the force of his talent, just like Juliusz had done to Euzebiusz. [...] From his father, Krzysztof took also his military inheritance, with which Juliusz had not been burdened. Just like Juliusz Słowacki, Krzysztof Baczyński had a mother who loved poetry more than anything. For such mothers to outlive their sons is a harm hardly comparable to any other anyone can suffer. [...] However, to uncover some differences between Słowacki and Baczyński, let us mention not only the fact that Baczyński received cadet training and fought in the war [...] Juliusz died in solitude, not having the good fortune of

experiencing what is commonly referred to as "personal happiness." Krzysztof married at a very early age.[6]

The poet, we learn, was from a good family and a fairly decent student, who passed his school-leaving exam in—!—May 1939, at the Batory High School in Warsaw. His classmates were Tadeusz Zawadzki ("Zośka"), Jan Bytnar ("Rudy"), Maciej Aleksy Dawidowski ("Alek"), so the myth of the poet became intertwined with the myth of "Grey Ranks."[7] He went underground, was a member of the Home Army. He dressed in such a manner that one could smell the underground from a kilometer away. He was blessed with a love requited. A number of his poems are marked by a home-grown religiosity. My personal favorite is the poem addressed to both parents:

And so this is all you have, then.
I was like the linden's rustle;
Krzysztof was the name I was given,
and my body—so very little.

And up to my knees in the dazzle,
like the saint, I was to bear the Lord across
a river of animals, sand, people,
wading in earth to my knees.

Why such a name for a child?
Why wings shaped in this way, mother?
Why a struggle, father, for such a fault?
The earth wet and bloody from my tears.

"He'll bear it all," you thought, mother:
"he'll name the pain, bring understanding,
raise within me what's fallen; o flower—
you said—bloom with the fire of meanings."

Father, it's hard at the war.
You said in your longing, your pain
for earth: "You'll not know human scorn,
but you'll carry a cumbersome fame."

---

6. Zagórski, "Śmierć Słowackiego," 399–400.
7. J. Gorecki [real name Aleksander Kamiński], *Stones for the Rampart: The Story of Two Lads in the Polish Underground Movement* (London: Polish Boy Scouts' and Girl Guides' Association, 1945).

Why should a child need such faith, and why
a legacy like a house of flames?
Before twenty years have gone by,
life will die in his glittering hands. [...]

Mother, I cannot name, the pain is too great,
death strikes too powerfully from every side.
Love—mother, I no longer know if it is;
From far away my flared nostrils smell God.
Love—what will it give birth to—hatred, streams of tears.[8]

And the obsession of premature death permeating almost every poem of his! Including *The Gaze*, a poem of extraordinary beauty containing metamorphosis, love, hate, pain and, in the end, the end:

Nothing will return. They are forgotten
already, these times; in mirrors alone
the darkness curdles into a reflection
evil and empty, yet my own.

I know them by heart, and yet I refuse
to name them; ahead I cannot in truth
know my forms. And so I die
with God half-manifested in my mouth.
And now we sit in the circle once more,

and the walls resound from the rain of the planets
and over the table a rope-heavy stare
and hanging in the air are billows of silence.

And one of us—he is the me
who fell in love. My world blossomed out
like a mighty cloud, like fire in a dream
and like a tree I am upright.

Another of us—he is the me
who gave birth to a tremulous hatred. The glitter
you see is my knife. No tear will there be
to fall from my eyes as torpid as water.

---

8. Krzysztof Kamil Baczyński, "To My Parents," in *White Magic and Other Poems*, trans. Bill Johnston (Los Angeles, CA: Green Integer, 2006), 150–55.

A third of us—he is the me
reflected in tears that were mine to weep
and like massive darkness is my pain.

The fourth is one I have known; he
once again takes my purposeless hours
and teaches them humility
and my ailing heart, so it prepares
for the death that is hatching inside of me.[9]

His work is accompanied by a sense of his life having been taken as opportunity, a sense of a possibility of realizing his talent, his truth being taken away. I'm not familiar with any photo of his in which he smiles. He was reticent and very serious at that. When, in 1942, his wedding to Barbara took place at a church in the Warsaw district of Powiśle, the couple looked as if they were attending their first communion; they were so slight and childlike. Two years later, neither was alive.

Were his Jewish roots—under conditions of extreme German Nazi terror—a known fact at the time? As Iwaszkiewicz often said, "Everyone knew everything about everyone, and pretended to know nothing."[10]

We can learn about his Jewish heritage from *Miłosz's ABC's*, which was probably the first instance I became familiar with the fact. Baczyński's mother came from a Polonized Jewish family; this might have also been the father's case. Stefania Baczyńska's brother, Adam Zieleńczyk—who translated German philosophers, including Fichte's *The Vocation of Man*, into Polish before the war—ended up in the ghetto, managed to escape and was hiding in Warsaw with an "Aryan" ID. Shmaltsovniks reported him and his family. In the summer of 1943, they were arrested and killed by the German Nazis.

Baczyński, Miłosz argues, must have, therefore, been aware that he was destined for the ghetto. Miłosz also indicates "an irresolvable problem of solidarity" with the Jewish people, "to whom he was connected not only by blood, but by the history of several millennia."[11] Baczyński's double loyalty—to the Poles and the Jews—was, apparently, evident in some of his poems.

I should add here that the poet's Jewish origins are yet another ingredient of his myth. After all, a greater number of shaky associations could be made,

---

9. Baczyński, "The Gaze," in *White Magic and Other* Poems, 170–73.
10. Jarosław Iwaszkiewicz, "A śpieszył się z pisaniem…" [And He Hurried Writing…], in *Żołnierz, poeta, czasu kurz…*, 151.
11. Czesław Miłosz, *Miłosz's ABC's*, trans. Madeline G. Levine (New York: Farrar, Straus & Giroux, 2001), 52.

for instance, between the two Messianisms, the Polish and the Jewish, growing not so much from the same root but certainly from the same soil.[12] A follow-up to the latter origin story is usually the highlighting of an aspect of lost identity on the part of the Jews who miss Poland, as much as on the part of the Poles who miss the Jews. All told, those are awfully uncertain conclusions. How do we know, for example, that Miłosz did not hold some grudge towards Baczyński and did not force-feed the Jewishness into his work a little?

Kazimierz Wyka, author of the first monograph study of Baczyński, lists names of four poets whom he considers main inspirations on his work. They were Słowacki, Norwid, Miłosz and Czechowicz. Miłosz was the only one of the listed four Baczyński could have met in person, and he, in fact, did. Presumably, their relationship was far from ideal. During one of the underground literary readings, Miłosz was supposed to approach Baczyński and say to him: "You're likely to be greater than me." Baczyński was to respond: "I already am." The patronizing attitude to a younger colleague is symptomatic of Miłosz. Did he really perceive him as a competitor in the realm of the spirit? Does such a thing as competition really operate in the realm of the spirit? Could he have been jealous of the toughness he himself could not muster? It was probably Iwaszkiewicz who noted that Baczyński was a terribly tough man. That is to say: soft and delicate, but capable of self-imposing the toughness.

Baczyński's poetry saw recognition alongside the occupation. Even other poets, his polemicists such as Tadeusz Gajcy, could not deny the force of his poetic persuasion. "In general, the poems are very uneven," Gajcy wrote.

> Differences are striking. There are four, five good ones, the rest is readable or poor. There is, however, a feature of the poorer pieces relating them to the more fortunate achievements. The feature is that of a certain inner dignity, a certain spiritual elevation, which is, at times, manifested unpleasantly, pretentiously. Bugaj's poetry [Bugaj was Baczyński's pen name] is not so much reflective as meditative, philosophizing.[13]

Baczyński himself was convinced of the high value of his literary productions. So, when Wyka gave his poetry enthusiastic grades, he was not so much proud

---

12. At the same time, we should bear in mind that Jewish Messianism was rooted in time, rather than in space. Herder writes that "the ruins of Jerusalem are rooted, so to speak, in the heart of time." Johann Gottfried Herder, *Denkmale der Vorwelt*, quoted after Hannah Arendt, *The Jewish Writings* (New York: Schocken Books, 2007), 12.
13. Karol Topornicki (real name Tadeusz Gajcy), "Poezja o nucie dostojnej" [A Dignified Poetry], *Sztuka i Naród*, no. 5 (1942).

as relieved.[14] The poet assured his friend: "I will survive the war, since I have so much more to express."[15] Clearly, poetry cannot always protect one from the world. But even if it could, how long could it last? Wouldn't he have faced—as a Home Army soldier—the postwar Communist oppression? And if he had given into his left-wing leanings, what would his poems have looked like? Would he have praised the new order, or Stalin? In his old age, would he have been one of Trznadel's interviewees?[16] Better not to imagine. Wyka concludes: "Albeit the twenty-three-year-old poet's death remains premature and, therefore, tragic, even as the death was chosen, in battle, Krzysztof Baczyński did not interrupt his output midway, in some quarter misshapen phrase. [...] He achieved poetic maturity astonishingly quickly, and the achievement was complete, his poetry is a full and finished sentence."[17] Wyka's hypothesis of the completeness of Baczyński's poetry was interestingly—going my way—developed and detailed by Anna Kamieńska. "His youthful death fulfils the destiny of a generation," she writes in her "Ostatnie wcielenie *Króla Ducha*" ("The Spirit King's Last Incarnation"). "The bullet that killed him chose well. However cruel this may sound, Baczyński's death was an artistic and a moral, to use Norwid's language, completion of his oeuvre. Besides, heroes who survive usually stop being heroes, they carry their briefcases to work in the morning, and sometimes write bad poems. They are tired."[18] But already the second page of her interesting study contradicts what the poet wrote on the first: "Even granting Baczyński an ingenious gift, it would be really difficult to agree with the conclusion that the twenty-three-year-old boy realized his full potential as a poet. This would have been a narrowing down of the potential. Better to believe that his tragic death interrupted a development of the beautifully promising talent."[19] Also Stanisław Piętak—a poet consummately forgotten these days—conjectured about a direction Baczyński's postwar literary work could have taken. He did not foresee a poetic career. He saw Baczyński as author of more prosaic, fictional forms. Piętak speculated:

---

14. Kazimierz Wyka's letter to Jan Bugaj from 1943, quoted after Zabierowski, "Legendotwórczy charakter biografii Krzysztofa Kamila Baczyńskiego," 246.
15. Marcin Czerwiński, "Krzysztof," in *Żołnierz, poeta, czasu kurz...*," 252.
16. Jacek Trznadel, *Hańba domowa: Rozmowy z pisarzami* [Home Shame. Conversations with Writers] (Paryż: Instytut Literacki, 1986).
17. Kazimierz Wyka's preface to Baczyński's collected poems. Wyka, "Wstęp," in *Krzysztof Kamil Baczyński: Utwory zebrane*, quoted after Zabierowski, "Legendotwórczy charakter biografii Krzysztofa Kamila Baczyńskiego," 256.
18. Anna Kamieńska, "Ostatnie wcielenie 'Króla Ducha,'" in *Od Leśmiana: Najpiękniejsze wiersze polskie* [From Leśmian: The Most Beautiful Polish Poems] (Warszawa: Iskry, 1974), 223.
19. Ibid., 224.

One can speculate what would have happened had Baczyński survived the occupation? Which course would his work have followed? I think that, as for poetry, no blast could have been expected: Baczyński was a poet of national gloom, and he expressed his time and himself therein; he might have not managed a fresh, inspired poetic flight he did exhibit in 1940–44, and he would have developed other literary genres, in which he had begun to excel, seeking his grand achievements in those, for instance, in fiction.[20]

He might have or might have not. No use in guessing. The premature death of the author of the most beautiful war poetry ("Heavens of Gold Opened Be") clearly demonstrates the futility and gratuity of such ruminations. Would he have become a best-selling novelist, a respected screenwriter or "merely" a poet of intense experience of wartime—we will never know. What do we know about him for sure? Perhaps no more than the fact that Krzysztof Kamil Baczyński was certainly someone.

---

20. Stanisław Piętak, "Jeden z bohaterów" [One of the Heros], in *Żołnierz, poeta, czasu kurz…*, 211.

Chapter 10

THE LIVING AGAINST THE DEAD (CZESŁAW MIŁOSZ)

Miłosz is like the world and, just like the world, he has a lot of secrets. One of them is his attitude to those he lost in the war—his colleagues, friends, peers. I want to tear it from him; I want to interview his shadow about the rules that determined his relationships. What was he ashamed of? What was he trying to escape? Who did he protect? Why writing about the living he failed to mention the dead? Why did he shift attention away from his own person? What hurt him? And why so much?

The Religious Apprehension of the World

Haunted by fears and vague metaphysical intuitions, imagination today is subject to irreversible erosion. God is not thought of otherwise than in quotation marks, and so is used mainly as a rhetorical figure expressing what is not completely apprehensible or possible to encompass. In such a world, poetry, too, struggles with the loss of meaning. It cannot provide convincing answers to the questions that life poses to it, thus becoming heavy, incomprehensible, unable to exceed itself, with the result that it eats its own tail. This is why it must be simplified at all costs, first by giving up any unnecessary formal complexities—one should learn about a pine tree from the tree itself. In this respect, certain patterns can be found in the poetry of the East, except that it generally remains deaf to the questions that have puzzled the Old Continent for thousands of years: the difference between good and evil, God and creation, freedom and necessity, mind and body. "I do not hide the fact," as Miłosz writes in one of his essays,

> that I seek in poems a revelation of reality, of what is known in Greek as *epifaneia*. This word used to mean, in the first instance, manifestation, the appearance of the Divinity among mortals, and also our recognition of the divine in an ordinary, familiar form, as for example, in the form of a man. Epiphany thus interrupts the everyday flow of time and enters as

one privileged moment when we intuitively grasp deeper, more essential reality hidden in things or persons.[1]

Clearly, the anthology of religious poetry intended by Miłosz in the 1990s had a specific aim, just as did all the other anthologies that he managed to edit and publish. The aging poet yearns for metaphysical comfort, declares his wish to sit at one table with gods and point to "It," using less and less sophisticated poetic means, like a man struck dumb.[2]

Californian Russianists

Quite different reasons, I suppose, served as the basis for the *Postwar Polish Poetry* anthology, published by Doubleday & Company half a century ago. At first the anthology seems to be a matter of coincidence, as do Miłosz's essays on Dostoevsky, which he started to work on rather unexpectedly and purely for his own sake. "It so happens that these things take place as if by chance," Miłosz recalls in an interview with Aleksander Fiut. "I was asked if I would like to run a course on Dostoevsky, as the professor who had previously taught Dostoevsky died, and it appeared there was no one to substitute him. 'Fine,' I said. If I had been offered to run a course on Tolstoy, I would have said 'no.' But it was Dostoevsky, so I said 'fine.'"[3]

In 1960, Miłosz had been offered a job at Berkeley's Department of Slavic Languages and Literatures, where from 1961 he conducted a seminar on the art of translation. It was at that time that he first tried his hand in the translation of Polish poems into English, the language he had learned from Shakespeare, in German-occupied Warsaw.[4] Miłosz's students formed a small seminar group. His classes were usually held in English, yet the language would naturally switch to Russian whenever Aleksander Wat joined the seminar (Wat was on a scholarship in the United States). The students did not know Polish or knew it insufficiently, as Miłosz wrote to Jerzy Giedroyc in his letter of November 1964:

---

1. Czesław Miłosz, "Against Incomprehensible Poetry," in *To Begin Where I Am: Selected Essays*, trans. Bogdana Carpenter and Madeline G. Levine (New York: Farrar, Straus & Giroux, 2002), 383.
2. Ibid. "It" is also the title of Miłosz's (2001) penultimate poetic collection.
3. Czesław Miłosz, in *Czesława Miłosza autoportret przekorny* [Czesław Miłosz's Willful Self-Portrait], interviews by Aleksander Fiut (Kraków: Wydawnictwo Literackie, 1988), 125.
4. Czesław Miłosz, "Gorliwość tłumacza" [The Translator's Zeal], in *Ogród nauk* [The Garden of Science] (Lublin: Norbertinum, 1991), 175.

A number of our recent seminar meetings have been devoted to Tadeusz Borowski's work. Aleksander Wat was also present at the last two meetings, and he told us many interesting things about Borowski, in Russian, because most of the students don't speak Polish well enough. About Borowski, in California, in Russian; I hope you appreciate the strangeness of this situation.

In another letter, written in March 1965, he pointed to the distinctive character of those meetings: "What is more, I record the seminars which he participates in. Discussions about the poetry of Różewicz, in Russian, in California, between Wat and Miłosz—a most piquant case. (Russian became our lingua franca)."[5] Miłosz wrestled with the medium of three languages at the same time, but it was the process of translating from Polish into English that presented him with the greatest difficulties. "I've translated two poems by Czaykowski into English and they sound nicely," he wrote in May 1964. "The Skamandrites are hardly translatable, the reason being the thinness of their images and the fact that they rely upon melody. I didn't want to omit them, though, so somehow I managed to translate a couple of poems by Słonimski, as well as one by Iwaszkiewicz and Wierzyński."[6] The idea of publishing a volume of poems by Polish poets in English translation seems to have emerged directly from the American publisher's enthusiasm for Urszula Kozioł's poem "Alarum."

I've only recently translated a poem by a poetess who is 20 years old or so, called Urszula Kozioł; I came across the poem "Alarum" in the Warsaw-based *Kultura. Mais qelle dignité!* When you show post-1956 Polish poetry to Americans, they just go crazy about it; never before in my life have I got a letter from a publisher like the one in response to the sample of translations I sent to New York. And it's not the *Westernness* of this poetry that they value, but its otherness and uniqueness.[7]

One cannot underestimate the role Thomas Merton played in promoting Polish poetry in the American market. Merton, a Trappist monk, thinker and writer, was himself an ardent devotee of Miłosz's work after he had read *The Captive Mind*. As Miłosz would recall years later: "I didn't need to

---

5. Jerzy Giedroyc and Czesław Miłosz, *Listy 1964–1972* [Letters], ed. Marek Kornat (Warszawa: Czytelnik, 2011).
6. Ibid., 48.
7. Ibid., 34.

look for a publisher of my *Postwar Polish Poetry*; having read the manuscript, Merton immediately sent an enthusiastic letter to the big publishing house, Doubleday, where his opinion was highly respected, and everything was settled."[8] As far as the market success is concerned, Merton's blurb of praise printed on the anthology's dust jacket proved no less significant. It went as follows:

> This collection of new Polish poetry shows a remarkable vitality. No one could be better qualified than Czesław Miłosz to find and translate the best work of the Polish avant garde, of which he himself is one of the most articulate representatives, and with which he remains in close contact though living in exile. The young Polish poets are writing with total contempt for all political and cultural clichés, independent of ideological imposture, candid, ironic, lucid and sometimes completely shattering. For many of these poets are men who witnessed, and barely escaped, genocide as well as war. One of the most moving poems in the book, at least for me, is Miłosz's own "Poor Christian looks at the Ghetto," written in Warsaw in 1943. The younger poets emerge as the purest and most promising of any group I can think of offhand (except perhaps the Greeks). In the whole collection, Zbigniew Herbert [...] stands out as one of the most important poets of our time in any language.[9]

In his preface to *Postwar Polish Poetry*, Miłosz personally refers to his students' commitment and their contribution to the making of the anthology. He stresses the fact of not being a native speaker of English, which makes him not trust his ear but rely instead on the help and control of those who have spoken English since childhood.

> I wish to thank Mac Goodman, Lawrence Davis, Reuel Wilson[10] and Richard Lourie for the long debates we had over one sentence or, quite often, over one word. Two poems of Slonimski and one of Jastrun ("Remembrance") were given definitive shape by Lawrence Davis. Some poems were translated by Peter Dale Scott with my minor assistance and are marked accordingly.[11]

---

8. Miłosz, "Thomas Merton," in *Ogród nauk*, 189–90.
9. Thomas Merton, in *Postwar Polish Poetry: An Anthology*, ed. Czesław Miłosz (New York: Doubleday, 1965).
10. Mary McCarthy's son.
11. *Postwar Polish Poetry*, vii.

Polish School of Contemporary Poetry

Before *Postwar Polish Poetry* was published, English-speaking readers had only been familiar with the work of Miron Białoszewski and Zbigniew Herbert, printed in *Encounter* in 1958 and 1961, respectively. Miłosz's anthology revolutionized that state of affairs in the sense that it gathered in one book such a great variety of individual poetic voices. Its release marked the date when the term was coined of the Polish school of poetry.[12]

The publication of such work in the United States seemed difficult to accomplish due to the incompatibility of national experience (Americans had never waged war against a foreign aggressor on their own territory), including the poetic experience. "Life *in partibus infidelium* [among the unbelievers] is not a treat, and for the writer it is devastating. There are times when it almost seems to me that I have been beaten. There is this feeling of an undefined audience, and even more than the two languages, these two audiences annihilate each other."[13] Therefore, if an anthology of postwar Polish poetry had a chance at all to come to life on that somewhat virgin territory, it very much depended on the translator's skills and poetic taste, on his selection of young enthusiasts for a team, in this case the seminar members whose first language was English, and—last but not least—on his connections in a renowned publishing house.

Postwar Polish Poetry consists of 90 poems by 21 Polish poets who were living at that time (with the exception of Staff, who had passed away eight years earlier). As a matter of fact, all of them published their poems in Poland after 1956, when censorship was temporarily lifted. The freedom of poetic expression, alongside beautiful phrasing, conditioned the authenticity of the message. However, there were exceptions to that rule. The anthology included a number of war poems or poems written before the war. The exceptions were also poems by emigrant writers, including Czaykowski, Wat and, of course, Miłosz himself. And even if Miłosz did not attach any significance to the place where the particular poet lived and created (as he claimed in his preface), it is rather obvious that in his anthology he gave precedence to national writers above those in exile.

The main section of the volume opens with Leopold Staff's biographical note:

> A gentle old man with a goatee, he was venerated by much younger poets for his passionate interest in their work, his optimism—very necessary at that time—and the poems he sent to underground publications.

---

12. See *Teksty Drugie/Second Texts*, Special Issue English Edition, vol. 1 ("Czesław Miłosz and Polish School of Poetry," 2012).
13. Giedroyc and Miłosz, *Listy*, 77.

> After 1945 Staff profited considerably from his friendships with very young poets, then entering the literary scene, and, being open to their judgments, attained his long-sought ideal: complete simplicity of form. [...] Though he is no longer living, there is no doubt as to his place among the poets of today.[14]

Staff was therefore a poet capable of repelling the war of generations in Polish poetry, absorbing as much from the young as he himself could give them in return. One should notice that in addition to the poems constituting the anthology, the notes on the poets, as composed by Miłosz, are of paramount importance. This is primarily because the strictly biographical data is substituted by other poetry-related facts. Excluding the poems and compiling the biographical notes, we should obtain something like "the history of Polish poetry between 1956 and 1965"—an offbeat piece of text, revelatory of Miłosz's fascinating, willful foresight, as the note on Stanisław Grochowiak shows: "At thirty he won a respectable position in Warsaw which may endanger his future development as a poet."[15] One of the most engaging biographical notes is that of Tadeusz Różewicz, quoted here *in extenso*:

> Różewicz's poetry stems from traumatic war experiences. He served in the guerrilla Home Army and his first poems published immediately after the war are short, nearly stenographic notes of horror, disgust, and derision of human values. Long before anybody in Poland had heard of Samuel Beckett, Różewicz's imagination created equally desperate landscapes. Since he hated art as an offence of human suffering, he invented his own type of anti-poem, stripped of "devices" such as metre, rhyme, and even, most often, of metaphors, and limited to the simplest words. His scorn for "art" is quite programmatic, with all the contradictions such an attitude involves. He is a nihilistic humanitarian, constantly searching for a way out of his negation which is mitigated only by pity; his tenderness bursts out only when he writes on little things of everyday life. He was unsuccessful in his attempts to find solace in an ideology. His poems written between 1949 and 1956, when he tried to sound positive and optimistic, fell often into what he had avoided before and has avoided since, sentimentality. It seems that his tragedy is to deny the values which are affirmed by his revolt. It is not by chance that I have mentioned Beckett. Różewicz is the author of a few plays which exemplify the Polish "theatre of the absurd." The target of his attacks is the precarious normality

---

14. *Postwar Polish Poetry*, 3.
15. Ibid., 133.

undermined by chaos and violence; and the title of one of his plays is, significantly enough, "The Witnesses, or Our Little Stabilization." The impact of his "naked" poetry upon the younger writers has been universally recognized. He lives in Gliwice, an industrial town of Silesia.[16]

The Right of the Living

Miłosz's anthology of Polish poets appeared in February 1965, which he mentions in a letter to Giedroyc, using the occasion to also ask for a review. Besides, Miłosz expresses his need to explain, in a separate text, the reasons why he decided to promote these particular poets, and not some others.[17] His letter meets with no response from the editor. Writing again in April of the same year, Miłosz cannot restrain his irritation and gives an ultimatum to Giedroyc: "Either you force Kot [Jeleński] to review my anthology *Postwar Polish Poetry*, or I'll have to do it myself, for who else? Czerniawski, that miserable scribe, turns out to be our writer in exile only because there aren't any others."[18] Eventually, Giedroyc thanks his friend for sending the book, but his manner is somewhat cool and curt, if not reluctant. "I've only just received your anthology. I think it would be a good idea to also send it to Vujičić in Yugoslavia."[19] Full stop. It may be a good book, but for Yugoslavs! They are not familiar with recent Polish history; they will not realize the deliberate omissions in the selection of authors. A few months later, however, Giedroyc mitigates his initial attitude: "When it comes to your anthology, it would certainly be good if you translated one of its American reviews, or found someone there who would like to do it."[20] But Miłosz already has a different plan. "Well, fine then," he thinks to himself. "My anthology is one of the bestselling books in Berkeley bookstores, though it's hard to say whether it means anything or not on a nationwide scale."[21] In another letter he adds: "I'm going

---

16. Ibid., 61.
17. Giedroyc and Miłosz, *Listy*, 86.
18. Ibid., 95. The editor of Giedroyc and Miłosz's volume of letters is mistaken in his annotation (96), in which he suggests that Adam Czerniawski's review was actually written and published in 1965 in the fourth issue of *Kultura*, while, in fact, Czerniawski's text titled "Poeta sam" [The Poet Alone] is not about Miłosz's anthology but Jan Brzękowski's collection of poems, *Science Fiction* (Londyn: Oficyna Poetów i Malarzy, 1964).
19. Ibid., 97.
20. Ibid., 101. Twenty years later, when the second, expanded edition of *Postwar Polish Poetry* was published—and Miłosz had already won the Nobel Prize—a review appeared by Reuel K. Wilson, one of Miłosz's co-translators for the anthology ("Review of *Postwar Polish Poetry*," *World Literature Today* 58, no. 2 (1984)).
21. Ibid., 102. Here, once again, the editor's footnote leads us astray. Milica Kirkoff's review "Dwie antologie poezji polskiej w Jugosławii" [Two Anthologies of Polish Poetry

to translate Polish poets for Penguin, London; basing on my anthology, they regard me as the best in this field."[22] *Postwar Polish Poetry* had only two superficial reviews at that time, written by Miłosz's friends.[23] Why was it never given proper attention in *Kultura* if Miłosz cooperated with the magazine?[24] The answer can be found in his preface to the anthology. In it, Miłosz explains that the poems included are by poets who are *living*. His criterion is therefore rather peculiar: to publish poems only by those poets who managed to survive the war, the occupation, the Warsaw Uprising, namely, those who have shown their ability to survive, a skill so much appreciated by Miłosz. Thus, the editor mobilizes the living against the dead, which is why the volume could not include poets such as Andrzej Trzebiński, K. K. Baczyński, Józef Czechowicz or Lucjan Szenwald.

> I wish to explain in a few words why and how I made this anthology. The underlying motive, as I see it, was my distrust of a poetry which indulges in negation and in a sterile anger at the world. Man confronted with mechanisms beyond his control is a loser until he learns that what seemed to crush him was, in fact, a necessary trial to open a new dimension and to prepare his mind to cope with unheard-of circumstances. This, in my opinion, is what has happened in contemporary Polish poetry. A historical steam-roller has gone several times through a country whose geographical location, between Germany and Russia, is not particularly enviable. Yet the poet emerges perhaps more energetic, better prepared to assume tasks assigned to him by the human condition, than is his Western colleague.[25]

My answer would be: bullshit, stop pulling our legs. *Postwar Polish Poetry* allowed Miłosz to somehow overlook those poets, most of them his friends, who had died in the Uprising (Baczyński), at the front (Szenwald), of a bomb

---

in Yugoslavia] does not relate to Miłosz's *Postwar Polish Poetry*, but two other anthologies: Peter Vujičić's *Savremena Poljska poezija*, and *Poljska Lirika dvajsetego stoletja* edited by Ryszard Matuszewski.
22. Ibid., 106.
23. At least this is to the best of my knowledge. Jadwiga Zwolska Sell, "Review," *Polish Review* 10, no. 3 (1965), and Babette Deutch, "To Survive Is to Sing," *Book Review* (May 9, 1965).
24. Certainly the two mentions of Miłosz's anthology in *Kultura* (nos. 7–8 (1965): 213–15) are not to be regarded as reviews. Both of them—one penned by Babette Deutch, the other by Maureen Sullivan—can at most be called useful blurbs. It is no surprise, then, why they passed unnoticed.
25. *Postwar Polish Poetry*, v.

(Czechowicz), with mouths plastered up during the execution (Trzebiński). Who was that anthology made for, then? The American critics failed to notice it; the students would rather listen to Aleksander Wat's Russian anecdotes; Giedroyc refused it and preferred to leave it unsaid. It appears, therefore, that the anthology was not made "for someone" but "against someone"—against the poets who had been killed undeservedly or had died prematurely, against whom the editor might have held a grudge. Having lived through the occupation, yet not carried away by patriotic emotion, Miłosz might have felt a prick of conscience, a sense of guilt caused by the fact that he himself had not fulfilled—or only partially fulfilled—the duty that for those other poets was something obvious and self-explanatory.

Chapter 11

THE CHILD OF WAR (FRIEDRICH NIETZSCHE, KRZYSZTOF MICHALSKI)

And Zarathustra stopped and considered. At length he said sadly.
"*Everything* has become smaller!"
"Everywhere I see lower doors: anyone like *me* can still pass through them, but—he has to stoop!"[1]

Ethics and aesthetics are one.[2]

I

The Flame of Eternity by Krzysztof Michalski is a book that I devoured alternately with great pleasure and growing irritation. Congrats! Here's an opportunity to read about Nietzsche, so I won't be fussy, I thought. A sea of nonsense devoted to this author, the ideologization of his thought, patronizing attitude of professional philosophers who live in the tombs of their own speculations—all this puts one in a mood to reach for anything (a book, a lecture, a broadcast) that departs from such trends. In this sense *The Flame of Eternity* is not confined by the crowd of Nietzschean acolytes. Quite the contrary, it shines against their background, it absorbs rather well. Then what is the reason for my irritation? The same: a careful reading of *The Flame of Eternity*, a discovery that it is not free (especially its final section) of longueurs and repetitions, that, while nearly Nietzschean at times, the language tends to get bogged down in "descriptions of nature" that are hard to skim, though.

In the first part of the following chapter, I would like to take a closer look at the "arguments" included in the *Flame* and then, in the second part, to somewhat "criticize" them. As for the "descriptions of nature," particularly the passages that look like something straight out of a textbook on existentialism

---

1. Friedrich Nietzsche, *Thus Spoke Zarathustra*, trans. R. J. Hollingdale (London: Penguin Books, 2003), 187.
2. Ludwig Wittgenstein, *Tractatus Logico-Philosophicus*, trans. Charles Kay Ogden (New York: Harcourt, Brace, 1922), 88.

(apparently Sartre's slogan "existence precedes essence" has just swapped the owner), I will simply skip them.

Nihilism

It is not a state of inner exhaustion, or an individual's "mental" emptiness. Nihilism is above all an event, but not one that can be grasped and explained historically. It is a situation when the highest values inexplicably lose their value. But what is this thing that loses its value? What is a value itself? Well, it is all that which signifies the chaos of phenomena with law and order. Let me illustrate it: in the times when people such as the Shakespearean Hotspur lived, the idea of honor was given priority over health or one's will to live. Honor was not a handy word to be placed on battle flags. It was not yet another slogan drawing the nosy masses toward the barricades (for a better view). Nor was it a "sublime" word that a "moral blackmailer" would turn to, whether he was a politician or an old auntie whose childhood days went by blissfully in the Kresy. In the world of Earl Hotspur, honor was the overwhelming force that kept the world of phenomena on a tight rein of organization, order and systematic approach. It was inherent in reality and in people. Being itself a value, it derived its power from "outside," from the value that is even higher, or indeed the highest—from God. In a world where God lived, people loved, died, held offices on "someone's" behalf; they acted in the name of other, mostly "external" (I suppose I cannot say "imposed") values: homeland, honor, Christ. But God died. It has turned out that the foundation upon which man used to build his life is quicksand, and that his perfectly built house is in fact a house of cards. Nihilism is thus a situation when God's death is brought to light, which is further followed by the disintegration of values that are like cooled-down stars—still shining here and there, although long gone (Heidegger's metaphor).

Therefore, nihilism is not yet another stereotype that we develop about the nature of our experiences. Nor is it a historical "event" like the Uhlans' charge at Somosierra: it has no date of birth and no author. Nihilism is a process, or shall we call it an "occurrence" (*Ereignis*), that is, something that we cannot escape, something that is our own destiny, written in the cooled-down stars.

How to get away from this oppression? Is there a way? Yes, there is—it is in the

> "revaluation of values" [...] possible only if it is a possibility of your life or mine. It is not an intellectual operation. Philosophy can cure the world's sickness and point the way out of crisis only insofar as the "life" in the phrase "philosophy of life" is not just the object but the subject as

well—only insofar as a "life philosophy" is itself life and not just a theory of life. Which also means that one cannot first understand it in order to apply it to life later. Here, the action of understanding and the action of application cannot be separated from one another.[3]

Therefore, it is not the case that a value like honor has faded or lost its effect. Rather, it is ourselves who are not able to adopt it and acknowledge as a value. There is no room for it in ourselves anymore because "the *need* for values in their former shape and in their previous place"[4] has been uprooted from us. We have reached the point when it is no longer possible to organize our lives (unless we want to lapse into some shocking naivety or "bad faith" according to the rules that are dead). Growing out of that is the postulate to create life anew—a new life, based on brand-new values that are "evaluations of how and to what extent something is valuable for the life."[5] Revaluation is not only about revealing the helplessness of the past values but also about "putting" new, *real* values into the world. Understanding is always identified with acting. It is not relativism—a belief that there exists a multitude of tantamount, equally real truths—but an attempt at forcing one's own axiological stance: related to my own power, truth is indeed a process of shaping the world by the rules that I can impose on it, as a child does, chopping thistles, breaking the shrubs, creating a reality that is totally new and unique.

Epictetus argued[6] that the beginning of all philosophy is a consciousness of our own weakness. Nonsense, replies Nietzsche. The beginning of all philosophy is a consciousness of our own strength.

Child

The finest pages of the *Flame* are devoted to the figure of the child whom Michalski simply—and clearly—"envies." He "envies" the child, as well as he "envies" the cows, their ignorance that per se nullifies any record, rationality, self-knowledge. He "envies" the child all its lightness in dealing with time for he sees in this carefree manner the lost dimension of humanity. "When I look at a child, I become aware that that happiness of the grazing herd, the happiness

---

3. Krzysztof Michalski, *The Flame of Eternity: An Interpretation of Nietzsche's Thought*, trans. Benjamin Paloff (Princeton: Princeton University Press, 2012), 10–11.
4. Martin Heidegger, *Nietzsche*, vol. II, trans. David Farrell Krell (San Francisco, CA: Harper & Row, 1982), 6.
5. Michalski, *The Flame of Eternity*, 11.
6. Epictetus, *The Works of Epictetus: Consisting of His Discourses, in Four Books, the Enchiridion, and Fragments*, trans. Thomas Wentworth Higginson (Boston: Little, Brown, 1865), 124.

of forgetting the world, is also something close to me, something my own, something that I once had and then lost, perhaps of necessity, and certainly irretrievably."[7] The child is innocent, the child is beautiful. It lives in a "garden" that is overlooked by time. The child does not remember that it did something "wrong" last Tuesday because the idea of guilt presupposes memory that the child does not possess. It does not have a history; it does not know the concept of either a past moment or a future moment. The child reduces its existence to the activity experienced at this particular moment: peeing under the tree, scribbling with chalk, scuffling for a swing. "This is why in child's play each move is the first, each move is the beginning and the end at the same time."[8]

Adults arrange their lives in a certain sequence of events: yesterday—birthday; today—headache; the day after tomorrow—weekend. They can assign sense to their biographies (usually by means of the Sabbath). The rationalization of events and the memory of them constitute a highly moral act that is driven by self-examination and examination of others. The child is incapable of it, does not remember anything—of neither itself nor others. Its existence is located beyond morality, beyond good and evil. One might say that the child experiences reality beyond time, that the quality of this experience is ahistorical. But even a grown-up is not always a camel and he, too, tastes happiness at times. When? Whenever he forgets about the humps on his back and starts kicking like a puppy. It turns out that life requires a certain dose of ignorance or—in Nietzsche's words—"affirmative memory," which means that we should absorb only as much from life as we *want*. To achieve it we need strength and energy derived from the intensity of happiness that binds what has passed with what is to come into one moment to which we will say "yes."

> It is the force of my life, and thus it makes no sense to speak of it as removed from my life. It is a force that cannot be measured from outside, the way one can measure the physical strength of a person or animal. […] I rely only on the capacity of my life to assimilate, on its *force*. There are differences […] that cannot be overcome through mutual understanding, differences whose overcoming signifies domination or subordination.[9]

We put an excess of energy into *every* situation. An immoralism of a kind, some spontaneity, irresponsibility, forgetting about the storm, about Italian cuisine

---

7. Michalski, *The Flame of Eternity*, 17.
8. Ibid., 18.
9. Ibid., 30–31.

or another person—these are the things we should learn from children; this is what we should adopt from them. A historical life is a life of automata. It is just as predictable as it is easy to design. It leaves no room for coincidence. Every moment is domesticated. The child's behavior alone reveals the fundamental discontinuity of existence: the child tears it up into pieces, which it then cannot—and does not want to—put them all together again. And it was only the child who was given the fate of the Phoenix that struggles every day to pull out its own happiness from underneath this pile of past moments burnt to ashes.

War

It serves the purpose of defining a hierarchy of values. We can learn what they are capable of, how strong they are. War is a total war in the sense it is not limited by any external boundaries, rules or conventions. It is precisely the latter that values originate in. "In this context, *war* is another way of describing differences in the face of which our reason is helpless."[10] One must not identify it with evil, because any form of valuation introduces an external measure, that is, it imposes an *a priori* judgment about what is good and what is bad. Meanwhile, war is always a war over values. It is a situation the result of which is difficult to predict:

> All of our values, are comprehensible only in the context of *war*, only when we uncover their function in the confrontation between my world and that other ("at war"), which waits around every corner. Only when we confront our concepts and our values with something that is radically different from them will we know what they are worth.[11]

War is thus an existential "test," an examination of what we really know about ourselves and whether we have possessed the required amount of civics knowledge to pass it. Thanks to it we learn something certain about ourselves and the world, namely, we learn how strong we are while defining and creating—both ourselves and others.

War is a precarious situation, a radically unpredictable one, something like Pascal's wager in which you either gain everything or lose everything. This is so because, as the poet says, "What we fight is so small! / What struggles with us is so great!" It is precisely this disproportion (and not the war itself) that we sense and that strikes terror into our hearts, fuels our anxiety, keeps us

---

10. Ibid., 81.
11. Ibid., 49–50.

awake at night. What fights with us and what seems to be unyielding to our resolutions is chance, a "sky chance," something alien, not mine, incomprehensible, which wrecks the balance of gains and losses. That is how I understand Michalski's point when he writes: "Only then, when my life will not surrender to the rules I encounter—actually, to any rules at all (because, constantly overcoming itself, it must go on creating them anew)—only then *will I manage to create something that surpasses me*, only then will I become a place where a new form of the world can come to light."[12]

War is not evil. In the end, it depends on us. A fight can be beautiful, just as a difference between two people can be beautiful. But one might just as well sow misery and total destruction. Its source is always "the other"—someone other than myself, someone who introduces into my world the difference that gives rise to existential anxiety. "The other" may turn out to be a woman ("some fucking Jane"), a Gypsy, a Jew, a Catholic or a faggot—take your pick. Each one of them, in any order, can become an easy target, a whipping boy (girl), "the evil one," whose ultimate elimination is both desirable and just. There is only one way, claims Michalski, to avoid the trap of total destruction: to begin with yourself. What does it mean?

I am always "good" in my own eyes. This expresses self-affirmation that we need in order to live. However, the fact that I am "good" does not imply that others are "evil." It is just that they are worse than me—they know less or they are weaker, or less pretty. My self-acceptance does not stem from a comparison with others, but is a spontaneous effort to constitute a criterion (an idea) that others have to meet if they want to be good—as good as me.

> *Good*, in this usage, is, as we see, a designation applied not to others but to myself; it is a positive, not a negative, determination. Accordingly, one who is *good* in this sense is also necessarily active, not passive: he sets the standard of *goodness* that he has accepted himself; he does not need to let someone else do it for him.[13]

It may be said that whenever we begin with ourselves, each time we do not pose a threat to others—or, more precisely, the only threat they are under is they will be worse than us, but not evil. And thus war turns into an agon, a bloody duel becomes an emulation, an opportunity to manifest one's health, swordplay for show. Therefore, an agon proves the efficiency of my organism—it is neither anger nor a desire to lay into others (who are better than me). Then how does evil permeate into the world to constitute, along with good, a moral

---

12. Ibid., 58.
13. Ibid., 37.

difference. *Unde malum?* It stems from the temptation to invert the scale of values so that "the good" suddenly turn out to be bad egoists, while "the evil" (scil. worse than "the good") turn out to be those who love their neighbor, create the world anew, according to the law that guarantees "eternal peace," love (ἀγάπη) and stillness. That is how the worse ones are trying to become good, yet in a perverse way, namely, by changing the rules of the game, constituting *morality* that changes the meaning of deeds to date. And soon the good ones cease to command respect and instead become the object of desire for the hungry prey, the aggressive mob. The final, universal triumph, without historical precedent, turns out to be the triumph of the "slave" (Hegel), the victory of "the last man" (Nietzsche), the win of "the shoemakers" (Witkacy).

In the passages devoted to "the last man," Michalski brings back my old obsessions[14] when (after Nietzsche) he spins a tale of "the man" recreated anew in his maximum culminations—a flawless one, without deficiencies or any pathology. "The last man" is a picture of vigor, a proof of immortality because—like animals—he never dies (i.e., he *does not know* that he will die). He finds his happiness in "drugs," and modern civilization supplies him with an abundance of these—be it Prozac, a beer garden or entertainment defined even more broadly. "He does not love, if love means risking everything one has, if it is a fire in which all virtue and all reason, every happiness known till now, are lost (though he gladly loves if love is just pleasure, without pain)."[15] He shuns differences and divisions; he is satisfied with any form of compromise and simplification. He himself is an ideal of perfection and consistency, while at the same time he imposes the standards of his own upon his antecedents: he is better than them, meaning, he is *good* in the extramoral sense of the word. Finally, it is within him, and not within the knights of the round table, that history finds its bloodless end. In this way, by means of a well-gnawed bone, we form a view on human nature.

Transformation

There is a moving scene in *King Lear*—a transformation of man into superman. The Earl of Gloucester is defending Lear against a pack of his wicked daughters and gets severely punished by them. He has his eyes gouged out and is then disinherited and banished. On his "way of the cross" he is joined by his elder son, Edgar, hiding from the world behind a beggarly cloak of madness. It is

---

14. Which I expressed in my book titled *Ontologia sukcesu. Esej przy filozofii Alexandre'a Kojève'a* [Ontology of Success. An Essay on the Philosophy of Alexandre Kojève] (Gdańsk: słowo/obraz terytoria, 2006).
15. Michalski, *The Flame of Eternity*, 158.

him who is to carry his blind father toward the edge of the world through the grim lands of Britain. The old man remembers a precipice that now he would like to use as his "Tarpeian rock" to throw off its top the tortured remnants of his own humanity. As they finally reach the hill, Gloucester makes sure for this one last time whether he really stands at the very top and whether the fall will be fatal. He orders Edgar to carefully describe the place that will soon see him crashing to the ground together with the truth about this world. He wants to take one last look at life with the eyes of the "beggar," making him paint before his senile eyes the images hitherto unknown to him. They are at once beautiful and fearsome. Edgar tells him about the birds flying *under* his feet, about a weary gatherer of samphire who reaches for his daily ration, climbing dangerously high, or about the sea, with its murmur inaudible from the cliff. But the old man rejects the truth of these images as for him they are not distorted enough!

> O you mighty gods!
> *He kneels.*
> This world I renounce, and in your sights
> Shake patiently my great affliction off:
> If I could bear it longer and not fall
> To quarrel with your great opposeless wills,
> My snuff and loathed part of nature should
> Burn itself out.

The verge of the precipice where Edgar has led the blind old man is—as with all things touched by nihilism—nearly half a meter deep. Gloucester does not realize that and therefore he falls head down dozens of miles, though, according to human measurements, his jump might be compared to sliding down a chair. "But have I fall'n, or no?" he asks with disbelief. Let us ask the same question: has Gloucester really fallen? Well, yes and no. He fell down a hillock, but he *rose as a man who survived a fall*. What is more, his jump has also changed Edgar who was standing nearby. Toward the end of this scene, the latter acts as midwife for the *survivor*, briefly speaking—for the "arch" or "super-humanity."

> *Edgar.* Give me your arm.
> Up, so. How is 't? Feel you your legs? You stand.
> *Gloucester.* Too well, too well.
> *Edgar.* This is above all strangeness.
> Upon the crown o' th' cliff, what thing was that

Which parted from you?
Gloucester. A poor unfortunate beggar.

On that summit Gloucester has left both himself and the "beggar," who, being his own alienation—not merely the son he disowned but also the symbol for misery, madness, pain and the old, past world—brought him to the edge of humanity by pushing him into the abyss. One can use Nietzsche's terminology here to say that while on the verge of the precipice, Gloucester parted with the beings limited by the values of *that* world, irreversibly dead and gone: "the last man" and "the higher man" ("beggar"). It is only from the perspective of this vale he has crashed into that he can now see with his eye sockets how—at the very end—he is *above* human form. The shock experienced by the old blind earl bears all the hallmarks of a religious *nominosum*—when a man is visited by the sacred. Edgar understood it perfectly well, consistently guiding his *father* into a new life. For where values are no longer in force, where they are no longer the organizing force, one is at a loss as to who is whose father, who is the son and who leads whom through life.

> Therefore, thou happy father,
> Think that the clearest gods, who make them honors
> Of men's impossibilities, have preserved thee.[16]

The superhuman metamorphosis above all affected Gloucester. The moment he rises from the bottom, where he has slid down, is a moment when he learns "that the abyss belongs to the heights. To overcome outrage is not to put it out of action but to acknowledge its necessity."[17] This knowledge enables him to become an overman, to rise over man, both over his "higher" and his "last" form. Gloucester's transformation, like any other critical situation, is accompanied by pain and uncertainty, for its result is not known in advance. To rise over man and to endure this superhuman condition—these two things, being separate after all, do not always go hand in hand. But it is already too late for the Shakespearean old men (their sun long set); therefore, Gloucester and Lear die in a human way. The Nietzschean experiment proved to be too difficult, too dangerous.

---

16. William Shakespeare, *The Tragedy of King Lear* (New York: New American Library, 1963), 147–49.
17. Heidegger, *Nietzsche*, 60.

Death

It arrives from the future. Or to be more precise: the impetus with which the future invades the present can destroy what is human. It is a radical exteriority that we cannot say anything definite about. In this respect, any form of anticipation is a futile effort, and prophecy is just a clown's gesture. "The future," claims Levinas, one of the authors cited by Michalski, "is what is in no way grasped. The exteriority of the future is totally different from spatial exteriority precisely through the fact that the future is absolutely surprising."[18] There is no future for the instant that I am experiencing right now; there can be only a "future now." It is relatively easy to design, and the conditions for its emergence can be easily specified. The "future now" is a guarantee of life's continuity, enables planning life as well as taming it. Thanks to it, we do not fear the future, for we imagine our future life to be simply an extension of the current existence. Meanwhile, the future comes (as in the old adage) as a bolt from the blue.

> When one deprives the present of all anticipation, the future loses all co-naturalness with it. The future is not buried in the bowels of a preexistent eternity, where we would come to lay hold of it. It is absolutely other and new. And it is thus that one can understand the very reality of time, the absolute impossibility of finding in the present the equivalent of the future, the lack of any hold upon the future.[19]

Michalski's starting point is this: man is "sick with death." His existence is underlain with uncertainty, threatened by the Apocalypse ("future"). It slips through his fingers, and in this sense, it flees. One can try to deceive time in many ways—by means of studying, shopping, kicking the ball—but the end remains inevitable, invariably bloody. "And therefore never send to know for whom the *bell* tolls; It tolls for *thee*" (to recall one of the most celebrated lines in the seventeenth-century metaphysical poetry).[20] There is no point in waiting for the Apocalypse that is yet to come (with the convenience of home delivery), because the Apocalypse happens every day: the bell tolls the end of every hour, knocking it out of its state of bliss and oblivion. It weans the living from life just like a baby is weaned from breast milk (to evoke a line from Różewicz). For the future—and not the "future now"—is as related to

---

18. Emmanuel Levinas, *Time and the Other*, trans. Richard A. Cohen (Pittsburgh, PA: Duquesne University Press, 1987), 76.
19. Ibid., 80.
20. John Donne, "Devotions upon Emergent Occasions" (XVII. Meditation), in *The Works of John Donne* (London: John W. Parker, 1839), 575.

the fragility of the human world as it is linked with its radical unpredictability and discontinuity.

Witchcraft is helpless when it comes to taming the future. And so are any other tools—the latest medical inventions or the oldest philosophical arguments. Even if the latter happens to appeal to us, even if at times we yield to Socrates's persuasion (a few moments before his death he still argued that there is nothing to be afraid of, that death is like leaving one apartment for another, a bigger one perhaps or maybe brighter), the child within us is scared of darkness and can never be lulled to sleep. It is pointless, claims Michalski, to act all big in before death, even if one is actually one of the big guys (or, like Socrates, the biggest of them all). One does not play dice with death nor looks death in the eye. But eventually it is not the philosopher who dies, and it is not the God (Christ) either. What dies in them is always the child who—at the very end, in despair—hopefully asks his *father* for help, asking him to hold his hand, if only for a little while longer.

Love

Only love is stronger than death. Love alone can blunt its poisonous sting. But how? In what way? Well, it opens us to eternity. Let us imagine someone who has never loved. How will he ever learn about the irretrievable loss? From the bitterness of life, says Michalski, the bitterness that no kind of sugar icing and no ambrosia can sweeten: "This bitterness is a symptom of being sick with eternity, of the stinging awareness of a wound that will never heal."[21] Its opposite is "totality," the sweetness that comes from love. But what does it mean that it is *stronger than death*? Poetry seems to provide the answer to this question, Michalski points out, "Bolesław Leśmian's poem about a girl who steps out of dream [...] A tiny bit of a page—and he wrote everything I wanted to but so much better than I ever could!"[22] This poem—as does Leśmian's poetry in general—shows death that is not related to physical disintegration, or, at least, not only to it. Its characters live many times and they die many times. The poem "Girl" features brave brothers who are trying to break down the wall beyond which a girl's voice is crying. And they die three times: as brothers, as their shadows and, ultimately, as hammers. What, then, does not die? What is eternal? The love for the voice is eternal, action, common endeavor; the desire is eternal, the desire for love. One dies a couple of times, *ad infinitum*,

---

21. Michalski, *The Flame of Eternity*, 139.
22. Krzysztof Michalski, "Płomień Nietzschego" [The Flame of Nietzsche], interview by Paweł Dybel, *Nowe Książki*, no. 5 (2007): 5.

sometimes before one's very eyes (as it happens in a line from a poem about Don Juan), but one never dies forever.

Like death, love eludes all prediction. It comes from the future, remaining something undeserved; one cannot strive for it or attain it through prayer. Perhaps it is an instance of grace? Certainly a gift. It comes to us always from *the other side*. And like death, love is an "illness" that "doesn't have any particular characteristics; it takes on the characteristics of the people it attacks."[23] Therefore, a beloved one cannot be mistaken for someone else, some stranger, even though the fire of love annihilates all the distinctive features defining who I was before I loved. Like death, it storms into the room, bringing "catastrophe" (from Greek "an overturning"); it is an absolute exteriority unknown in advance. "Shuddering bodies struggling with something inhuman, alien, new, mysterious, desired. The convulsions, the scream. Ecstasy? Agony? Who can tell them apart?"[24] If love is stronger than death, then corpse—that decomposed corporeality—may still shiver with caress. This is what happens in Leśmian's poetry: "Shiver with posthumous love, if its charms are within reach."[25] Eternity, as we read in the *Flame*, enters the world along with love and by means of love. Or, strictly speaking, by means of the body that is—the body, the shadow and then the hammer and the corpse—the vehicle for love (eternity). Eternity is thus unambiguously corporeal in nature. That is why it must hurt.

The body is always "on the way," that is, it can be both a place of disintegration and a place of "transformation." "The body is not a thing, destructible, in which we are enclosed. It is an effort to move out beyond ourselves, beyond what is."[26] On the one hand, it opens us to eternity, the eternity of love; on the other—"alas! alas!"—it relates us to life, to reality that—like a woman—is whimsical and mercurial, prone to disintegration and breakdown.

Truth

According to the classical definition, truth consists in correspondence, in the "congruity" between things and sentences, when we say how things *really* are. Here is its classical formula, beautiful in its simplicity: "To say of what is that it is not, or of what is not that it is, is false, while to say of what is that it

---

23. Rainer Maria Rilke, *The Notebooks of Malte Laurids Brigge*, trans. Stephen Mitchell (New York: Vintage Books, 1990), 62.
24. Michalski, *The Flame of Eternity*, 139.
25. Bolesław Leśmian, "Rok nieistnienia" [The Year of Nonexistence], in *Poezje zebrane* (Toruń: ALGO, 1995). Trans. Renata Senktas.
26. Michalski, *The Flame of Eternity*, 144.

is, and of what is not that it is not, is true." A person who seeks truth strives for stability, wishes to get rid of uncertainty that is the source of suffering and that underlies existential anxiety. He craves for warmth that truth can undoubtedly give, he feeds on its bread, only let life not hurt him so much nor happiness procrastinate on coming. Nietzsche argues that this kind of truth does not exist, and if it existed, it would remain unknowable. Even if we chose to ignore this statement and presupposed that truth is knowable, it would certainly be impossible to express. And besides, *es gibt keine Wahrheit*—man is left to speculations, interpretations, an "army of metaphors." One needs a bit of falsehood and lie in order to live—deception often contributes to a better understanding of life far more than a blind obedience to truth. For life is a game of appearances. There is no truth as such; truth is in the making, unveiling—as a woman unveils—only as much as she wishes to. "It requires the rarest, good chance for the veil of clouds to move for once from the summits, and for the sun to shine on them. We must not only stand at precisely the right place to see this, our very soul itself must have pulled away the veil from its heights." Each time truth is surrounded by an aura of something unrepeatable. It is to be associated with the beauty of the original (truth) but not with its repetition. An aura wafts over beauty, just as the spirit of Providence wafts over man. It appears whenever beauty (truth) fuses with the place and time of its origin as well as its future existence. To put it yet another way, an aura refers to the relationship between beauty (truth) and man—not necessarily with his creator alone but also with the audience, for example, a wide historical audience. Thus understood, the concept of aura relates to the concept of *Jetztzeit*—the time when what has passed is revived and actualized as "present." It is a phenomenon of the imperishable, current past that is constantly renewing itself within a single moment. For Nietzsche, however, the philosopher who contains within himself many contradictions and puzzles that ever accumulate with his work, nothing important happens twice in one's life. In order to carry this important argument to its conclusion, in the last paragraph of *The Joyful Wisdom*, Nietzsche underlines that truth "*unveils itself to us but once,*"[27] that it happens to us very rarely. It is ephemeral, inevitably doomed to its momentary, one-day life. Truth's death is thus inscribed in its birth certificate. Therefore, those maintaining that they enjoy constant communion with the Absolute, the durable, the only truth, are braggarts and bastards.

---

27. Friedrich Nietzsche, *Joyful Wisdom*, trans. Thomas Common (New York: F. Ungar, 1960), 269.

The Eternal Recurrence of the Same

We all remember Julian Tuwim's *Locomotive*, which we both read about and hear it coming.[28] We deal with something similar in the last chapter of *The Flame of Eternity*, devoted to the eternal recurrence of the same. One and the same thought keeps recurring in it, is recycled time and time over in many different ways. The subsequent paragraphs sound alike; they are almost identical. The "arguments" sufficiently and fully developed in the previous chapters are now developed anew. Tuwim's words imitate the toot of a choo-choo, and Michalski seems to achieve the same effect when at the end of his book he writes about the eternal recurrence: everything returns in the act of continuous repetition.

The eternal recurrence of the same is not identical with the toil we associate with self-recreation of life. It is not about autumn being followed by winter, or July being followed by August. Michalski does not linger on these obvious things. For him, the meaning of life consists in a radical discontinuity, *unrepeatability*. The natural repeatability of phenomena has nothing to do with the Nietzschean "thought of thoughts," the thought that liberates the human spirit from the constraints imposed on it by time. What is its sense?

Let us imagine, claims Michalski (after Heidegger), a gate or, better still, a swinging door that leads to the bar. It is the place where the past and the future bump into each other. As a result of this encounter, the *kairos* is born—a timeless moment, one that is worth being reinforced by one's effort. This moment cannot be snapped from a distance; it requires it to participate. It is very difficult to determine how we "enter" it—from the side of the future or the past—because, as with the swinging door, it is impossible to tell whether someone has just used it to come in or go out. What, then, constitutes its past and its future? This we never know. The nature of every instant is that it can be both its own beginning and end—the "future," Apocalypse—getting ready for a leap or this leap's history. Caught in the frame of eternal recurrence of the same things, life turns out to be their becoming, unrestrained frolic of free spirits, children's play. It is through and within their inexhaustible creativity that a certain form of the world comes to light, if only to be negated—at the same time—from the "other" side. And so it moves in circles. The structure of the reality in the making is itself immutable. Hence the impression that everything returns, that things are constantly—"structurally"—the same.

Children, the real "artists of life," do not know the past, do not know what the future is. Their existence is enclosed within this very moment. They

---

28. Julian Tuwim, "The Locomotive," trans. Walter Whipple, http://allpoetry.com/poem/8537691-The-Locomotive-by-Julian-Tuwim.

neither care for it nor try to keep it. For this the way things are: they come to life and pass away *at the same time*; they expire in the motion of becoming; their existence is "momentary" by nature ("torn between the past and the future"). Thinking his "thought of thoughts," Nietzsche did not want to say that, as a result of some strange apocatastasis, the same matters keep returning to the world (these precisely are *unrepeatable* and *do not* return), but that the structure of being itself consists in eternal becoming, in repetition that—at the moment of happiness—kindles the "flame of eternity" within time.

> While wondering whether or not to send out the laundry, I am like an arc stretching from there, from the primal beginning, to its latest realizations in what is before me. Not losing a most everyday train of thought for even a second, I am the Mystery of being and its pride, its malady and torment[29] (this is Gombrowicz on the "eternal recurrence of the same").
>
> "Look at that carriage," one of them said to the other. "Think you it will be going as far as Moscow?" "I think it will," replied his companion. "But not as far as Kazan, eh?" "No, not as far as Kazan."[30]

To sum up: The burden of tradition manifests itself in the fact that one sees things as they are not—from behind the cover of foreign, borrowed concepts and notions. Meanwhile, "our heritage"—as René Char once put it—"is not preceded by any testament"; we are not limited by any verities inherited from our ancestors. The old truth is like Baubo—the old hag, toothless and cackling, that one should stay away from. Each of us should constantly enact ourselves anew and for our own use—one does not need to know who one is; the intuition alone as to where one is heading to will suffice. Let us then create new, momentary, one-off, unrepeatable truths: this is our state of emergency we are doomed to; this is our "Tarpeian rock" that serves the purpose of renewing the "human" condition. Nietzsche-Michalski's aim is not to discredit truth as such. Nietzsche-Michalski explores truth in terms of its quantum of power, its usefulness for life. "So much mistrust, so much philosophy!" he repeats. And the dictum on man's death should be considered in this light. The statement is not a mere provocation; it does not contribute to the repertoire of academic tricks and disarmaments. Rather, it is a necessary need, a superhuman task. Man is something that should be finally surpassed, "overcome" along with his world—a world he yielded to and where he lived. This postulate has nothing

---

29. Witold Gombrowicz, *Diary*, trans. Lillian Vallee (New Haven, CT: Yale University Press, 2012), 435.
30. Nikolai Gogol, *Dead Souls*, trans. D. J. Hogarth (Mineola, NY: Dover, 2003), 5.

to do with the old mania that haunts the dreams of virtually every revolutionary. It contains the "negative anthropology" project that, in turn, is not satisfied with any of the past forms of human reality.

Man's God has to pass away together. And thus two Gods get on board of Charon's boat: the vindictive and preposterous God of the Old Testament, for whom humanity is only a keyboard, and the merciful God of the Christians. Both of them determined the meaning of human life—the meaning that has long been lost though. Therefore, man gets rid of the powerful idols who have been tormenting him for ages. What remains? There remains within him an inextinguishable "religious" desire, a longing for God *whom* (rather than: in whom) one believes. This God has no name—or all things are His names, if we prefer to follow Pseudo-Dionysius the Areopagite. One can try to discover this God in every creature one happens to encounter.

> In a lovely village church. The thin wax candles glowed like red points before the pictures of the saints. […] [S]ome one stepped in behind me, and placed himself near me.

> I did not turn, but had nevertheless a feeling that this man—was Christ. I was overcome by emotion, curiosity, and fright all at once. I controlled myself, and looked at my neighbors. He had a countenance like other people's;—a countenance like any other man's face. […] At last I became uncomfortable, and collected myself. Then it suddenly became clear to me that Christ had really just such a common human face.[31]

II

Gombrowicz

It is by no means a coincidence that my reflections on "the eternal recurrence of the same" include a quote from Witold Gombrowicz's *Diary*. My aim was to show to what extent Michalski's essays are permeated with Gombrowicz's idiom, how much he derives (benefits) from Gombrowicz's prose (not so much the content itself but more of his phrase, manner of expression, his flow of thoughts and associations, his temperament and atmosphere). Let me illustrate it with a couple of examples:

> Existence is like a river—this river, when it encounters obstacles, immediately begins to seek other beds and bursts through whatever it can,

---

31. Ivan Tourgueneff, "Christ," in *Poems in Prose* (Boston: Cupples, Upham, 1883), 94–96.

opening new outlets for itself sometimes in directions it would never have imagined.[32]

Life grows into each of its successive forms and adapts to them, is rooted in them, it nests there—and at the same time it obliterates them, it must abandon them, it must move on.[33]

Do you want to know who you are? Don't ask. Act. Action will delineate and define you. You will find out from your actions. But you must act as an "I," as an individual [...] To be someone is to inquire incessantly about who I am and not to know in advance.[34]

We are who we are dependent on what we do.[35]

These concepts—like all concepts, like everything we know—cannot be divorced from what we do [...] What has happened in this story [e.g. the story of my life] can therefore never be settled completely: there is no one, ultimate answer to the question of the "meaning of life." And if "to understand" means "to find the ultimate answer," then life cannot be understood. [...] the "I" in this context is not a known quantity. How could it be? It's not just that I don't know but that I cannot know completely who I am.[36]

Oh! I am mortally in love with the body! The body I almost my only touchstone. No spirit can redeem corporeal ugliness, and a man physically unattractive will always hail from a race of monsters even though he may be Socrates himself! [...] I take more pride in the fact that I am sensual than in the fact that I am knowledgeable about the Spirit. My passion, my sinfulness and darkness, are more valuable to me than my light. [37]

And here is how Michalski elaborates on the above thought:

The corporeality of human life is expressed in the pain smoldering in each moment—for in every moment of my life, in my every gesture, in my every movement, a child is born in whom the world begins all over again. Every moment of one's life is the birthplace of something that had not been there before. It hurts.[38]

---

32. Gombrowicz, *Diary*, 444.
33. Michalski, *The Flame of Eternity*, 162.
34. Gombrowicz, *Diary*, 411–12.
35. Michalski, *The Flame of Eternity*, 32.
36. Ibid., 100–106.
37. Gombrowicz, *Diary*, 383.
38. Michalski, *The Flame of Eternity*, 146.

The pain of existence (also the physical one), immaturity, puerility, strong perspectivism, the hierarchization of reality according to the quantum of power ("the superior and the inferior"), relentless critique of science (as in the chapter "The Time Is at Hand")—all those motifs were already laid out half a century ago, with equal verve, by the greatest Polish Nietzschean, Witold Gombrowicz. He developed his philosophical creed in dispute with existentialism. He chose to undertake anew only those of its issues that particularly annoyed him, disavowing, for instance, the right of existentialism to determine what is authentic and conducive to life, and what is artificial and out of use (while proving at the same time that degraded forms, all sorts of deformities and pathologies may also be of use). He accused existentialism—and rightly so, I suppose—of the excess of concepts that were to lure the less sophisticated, timid minds into the circle of its influence. Michalski's writing did not originate in a vacuum either. He does not argue—as Gombrowicz does—with the corpse of existentialism (though his wording is no less drastic at times). Instead, he tries to inscribe Nietzsche's thought in the lineage of American pragmatism that has always been interested in the "practical" side of the Nietzschean philosophy.[39]

Pain

The Flame of Eternity does not bring comfort, nor does it promise any easy solution. Quite the contrary. Supposedly it is going to be even harder.

> There can be no illusion that concepts, whatever they are, allow us to relieve the pain of our lives, that they will cure us of our eternity-disease. They won't. They themselves contain traces of this disease. Knowledge is not a treatment for this pain. It affords no real consolation. No logic or dialectic provides an answer to this pain.[40]

Not to mention the fact that at times Michalski's book reads like a handbook for nurses (there is always something that he finds painful). I, on the other hand, am concerned more with something greater than occupying others with my pain. In *The Flame of Eternity*, Michalski points to the circumstances under

---

39. I allude to the pioneering book by Arthur C. Danto, *Nietzsche as Philosopher* (New York: Simon & Shuster, 1965). It should be pointed out here that the Nietzschean pragmatism of Danto (and to some extent also of Michalski) derives as much from the American philosophical tradition as directly from Nietzsche and Heidegger who highlight the inextricable relationship between acting and thinking.
40. Michalski, *The Flame of Eternity*, 148.

which his own pain cuts him off from the outer world. This pain makes him center around himself to such an extent that he is unable to focus on anything else. If it hurts me—he claims—if it hurts so much that I cannot stand it any longer, then what do I care about other people's pain! The utter immersion in his own pain, and thus in his own weakness, his own corporeality, in his "I myself," leads him to the desert of "solipsism," the attitude excluding from one's environment the presence of other people: "for there is no 'outside,'"[41] if I myself bicker with pain and with death. Such a perspective gives rise to antinomies. Does not this mutual, loving "lighting of each other's faces" only intensify and fuel the feeling of uncertainty and pain that inevitably reduces me to my own experience, to myself alone? To what extent, then, does love open us to another person, and to what extent does it compel us to escape for fear of pain that gradually grows—as love keeps growing—more intense within me? Michalski is inconsistent whenever he questions exteriority and at the same time calls for the other. For example, when he wants to *differ beautifully*. On the one hand, he argues, he is "good," because he "overflows," because he affirms the world from the perspective of a superman submerged in his own perfection. Yet, on the other hand, how can he differ (let alone beautifully), having previously negated the possibility of difference as such when he reduced the image of the world to the resultant of forces flowing from *him*? Would not variety and diversity in this strange "solipsistic" world be only an act of arbitrary constitution. And lastly—if he wants to differ beautifully, then why does he reject the very first, that is, the instinctive and physical manifestation of difference by comparing the athletic efforts of "the fitness nuts"[42] to the monastic "fashion" for the emaciation of the body by feeding it on roots and prayers?

Anecdote

But this is all academic baloney, chutzpah and folly, pure fuss in the face of doubts that have been troubling me since I read *The Flame of Eternity* (for the second time). But first—a recollection, a souvenir, a postcard from the "other world." In 1996 I worked on my dissertation on the "death of man" at the Institute for Human Sciences in Vienna. Krzysztof Michalski was its founding father and rector at that time. One June afternoon, and I remember it very clearly, Michalski's secretary called me, saying that the rector would like to meet me after five, downstairs, in the hallway, by the elevator. Having arrived there at the given time, I came upon Darek Gawin, Barry Gilbert

---

41. Ibid., 40.
42. Ibid., 128.

and Alejandro Vallega who had been invited, too. "That may turn out to be not that bad after all," I thought and felt distinctly relieved. We got into his car, which drove us to an outdoor restaurant in Grinzing. Appetizers, a few decanters of young wine emptied, an anecdote. Michalski: "I'm very much into the idea of intrigue, playing with people. They can be bought, sold, exchanged, in brief, they can be played with. It is a question of price, tactics, approach. In fact, my administration of the Institute comes down to this. One can get everything—except for the things one can't afford. But there are still people who can't be bought for yet another reason—they don't understand the game itself, its rules or rates. *They would prefer not to*." (A voice from the audience) "Who are they?" Rector: "I'll enumerate their names for you: Cardinal König, Professor Ricoeur, Father Tischner. To wit: a couple of days ago I received a letter from Paul Ricoeur, in which he asked me if he could come to Castel Gandolfo if he had not prepared his paper in due advance.—Sir, I answered, shall we send a plane for you? Gentlemen! It was Paul Ricoeur!" Eventually the evening became more and more "Polish," with the anecdote seeming more and more Greek to the Americans (they didn't get a thing) while Darek and I kept indulging ourselves. Rector: "Late 1970s. Warsaw. I'm walking down Krakowskie Przedmieście when I bump into Dzidek Jankowski. And he goes: listen, Wolniewicz informed on me, he wrote I didn't like the Soviet Union. Man...me, of all people? I mean, I'm the one that doesn't like the Soviet Union?!" On my way to the toilet Michalski says to me: "What, it's got colder?" Me: "Your tone was so entertaining that I guess I didn't notice." Michalski: "Yeah, it has got colder." At the end of our meeting he turned to Darek Gawin and me, and said, in Polish: "Gentlemen, we have to bring this fucking university down, and I have a way." He waved and drove off.

There is no point pretending one does not know who wrote this book, that one is not aware of its author's creative as well as causative possibilities. *The Flame of Eternity* should be read twice: first as "an interpretation of Nietzsche's thought" and then as a kind of *autobiography* where "the facts of life" are unimportant, inessential, for they may be always guessed or pictured. However, with Michalski's books in general, they need not be detached from the person, from the reality they originated in, where they were conceived—these two things are strongly related. Krzysztof Michalski was an excellent writer, a wonderful teacher, rector of one of the most important institutions on the map of philosophical life in Europe (it's not puff but facts). He was also—or maybe above all—a child who played with people because they move, because he delighted in poking them with a stick, as if some of them were half-dead moles, brimstone or cabbage butterflies. Traditional ethics,

Michalski echoes Nietzsche, is no longer possible, because the principles (i.e., "values") it has been based on to date have lost their legitimacy, their binding force. Still in Kant's times everything had a price *or* a dignity. "Whatever has a price—Kant argues—can be replaced by something else as its equivalent; on the other hand, whatever is above all price, and therefore admits of no equivalent, has a dignity."[43] Today everything has its price, and at the same time everyone is stripped bare of dignity ("values"). The code of ethics must therefore be of a temporary nature. Like the road traffic law, it is in force and effect in order for us not to kill one another. Thus reduced to a mere procedure, ethics becomes law—the ability to resolve practical problems. There is no room in it for all this spiritual ado: "the purity of conscience," "the imperative of not hurting others" or "the responsibility for the other" (responsibility tends to be identified with one's reliability in business). Proceduralism is not to Michalski's liking; he is unwilling to accept this solution. Instead, he suggests something else, namely, a sort of *aestheticization* of ethics. If unquestionable differences exist between us, he claims, then let us at least try to differ *beautifully*. As expressed by Michalski, ethics—along with responsibility—remains a question of taste and arbitrary decision, a "will to power." It is not the ethics of submissiveness, but of decision: "This is what I want!" This was once lectured on at the Institute for Human Sciences by a professor of moral philosophy "paid off" by Michalski; it was done openly and without beating about the bush (as indeed one does not know whether it is a description of social reality or part of its critique). "The development of inequalities is closely related to the detachment of certain individuals from the common run of mankind and to the legitimation of their right to distinguish themselves from others."[44] In other words, the greater the *formal* equality of opportunities guaranteed by the law, the deeper the *actual* stratification and diversification of people, which in fact is hard to deal with and which cannot be changed.

On the descriptive level, *The Flame of Eternity* is a fascinating book. Reading it can be compared to looking up at the Sistine Chapel ceiling. It induces in us the "superhuman" effort in self-creation from scratch, beginning with first principles—that is for sure. On the postulative level, however—and I am

---

43. Immanuel Kant, *Grounding for the Metaphysics of Morals: On a Supposed Right to Lie because of Philanthropic Concerns*, trans. James W. Ellington (Indianapolis: Hackett, 1993), 40.
44. Pierre Rosanvallon, "Rethinking Equality in an Age of Inequalities" (Jan Patočka Memorial Lecture), *IWM Post*, no. 108 (September–December 2011): 5.

writing this with caution—the *Flame* is as daring and dangerous as fire. It constitutes an additional smokescreen for "the children of war" who cause us to veer off course, who start the day—like Gide's Lafcadio—with tossing an old man out of a train window, simply because it suits their taste or whim at the moment. "Eeny, meeny, miny, moe, catch a tiger by the toe."[45]

---

45. Michalski, *The Flame of Eternity*, 18.

Chapter 12

PLENTY COUPS AND THE END OF THE WORLD (JONATHAN LEAR)

> By dreaming, man trains himself for life.
>
> Friedrich Nietzsche

I

Jonathan Lear is a philosopher, professor at the Committee on Social Thought at the University of Chicago, and a practicing psychoanalyst. That last information seems of paramount importance when it comes to his *Radical Hope* that I am going to discuss here, for the book responds to three fundamental questions: (1) how to live in a world that has suddenly lost all meaning; (2) is hope still possible in such a world; and, if so, (3) in what language should one try to express it? I would say that Lear's *Radical Hope* is a kind of first-aid textbook after the collapse of the world we know, or at least this the impression I get from it.

But Lear addresses an even more basic and general question: what happens to the people whose culture vanishes unexpectedly, when everything they were used to becomes annihilated? To illustrate this, he chooses the example of North American Indian tribe—the Crows. At the turn of the twentieth century, most Indian tribes were confronted by two technical inventions, the power of which they could not oppose: American Winchester and "firewater." The former killed three-quarters of the Indians; the latter depraved the remaining rest.[1] Lear's research grounds on an oral account of the Crow leader, which was written down by Frank B. Linderman. Plenty Coups (which is how the

---

1. See Carl Schmitt's sarcastic footnote in *The Concept of the Political* (trans. George Schwab [Chicago: University of Chicago Press, 1996], 54–55), in which he deliberates on the possible conditions for extermination of unpolitical nations.

    Specific peoples are "proscribed by nature itself," e.g. the Indians, because they eat human flesh. And in fact the Indians of North America were then exterminated. As civilization progresses and morality rises, even less harmless things than devouring human flesh could perhaps qualify as deserving to be outlawed in such a manner. Maybe one day it will be enough if a people were unable to pay its debts.

chief was called) expressed the thought that served as a starting point for Lear's story: "But when the buffalo went away the hearts of my people fell to the ground, and they could not lift them up again. After this nothing happened."[2] What does it mean that nothing happened?—asks Lear. After all, Plenty Coup was an exceptionally long-lived and vigorous person. Having retired as a warrior, he took to farming, made a success of it, received awards and, what is more, his share in the reconciliation between the "savages" and the US government was much appreciated, acknowledged and honored. So in what sense "nothing happened"? In order to understand this, one has to go back a 9-year-old Plenty Coups's dream-visions that permanently shaped his mind. In his first dream, Plenty Coups dreamed of how he would manage after his older brother's death. His second dream (a nightmare rather) was much more weird: the little boy saw the specter of the Apocalypse that would wipe out the Crow tribe in the future. It was also in this case that the dream-vision was accompanied by some practical advice on how to reduce the force with which the inevitable was slowly invading the life of his nation. Dreams, Lear argues, can let us in to reality through the back door, or a back staircase, leading us directly to some perplexing and often inexplicable situations. It so happens that dreams influence decision-making, sometimes sabotaging our decisions and thus solidifying the moral basis much more than tradition can do, for tradition always takes a roundabout way. "Why do you compare the inner commandment to a dream? Does it seem senseless as a dream, incoherent, inevitable, unique, making you happy or frightening you equally without cause, not wholly communicable, but demanding to be communicated?"[3]

II

Plenty Coups was a man who knew the cultural change to his cost. Before he became the leader, as a young boy he had bravely defended the coup-stick marking the boundary that no one was allowed to pass. In the reality of the Crows, where religion intertwined with a fight for the death, the planting of a coup-stick meant defining a territory where no one except the Crows had the right to enter. Therefore, the planting itself had both a psychological and a military aspect—it shook the morale of the enemy. It was also believed that one could suffer a fate much worse than death or defeat, namely, a life of shame, being stigmatized as a hopeless loser who did not defend his coups

---

2. Jonathan Lear, *Radical Hope: Ethics in the Face of Cultural Devastation* (Cambridge: Harvard University Press, 2006), 2.
3. Franz Kafka, *The Blue Octavo Notebooks*, trans. Ernst Kaiser and Eithne Wilkins (Cambridge, MA: Exact Change, 1991), 45.

and exposed his tribe to destruction. And vice versa: a warrior demonstrating his coups, successfully defending a coup-stick stuck in the ground, was greatly respected by his fellow tribesmen. If he happened to be young, he could choose a wife for himself without even waiting for his coming of age; his wife, in turn, could walk ahead of him, carrying his shield and the like privileges. Yet another way to "count coup" was to strike the enemy with a coup-stick without hurting him or killing him immediately. For the aim of "counting coups" was not to directly eliminate the enemy but to create a situation that would make him realize that he was about to die. The agon between the feuding tribes was then par excellence Kojèvean: what was fought for was pure prestige, recognition, not elimination, but forcing the rival to recognize the winner. On the other hand, considering the same act in more general terms, it should be added that what the warrior defined in battle was the living space for the whole community. Moreover, since a coup-stick separated life from death, one had to protect it even at the cost of one's own life. A warrior testified with his life the value of the stick stuck in the ground, thus verifying also the concept of courage, so essential for North American Indian culture. Courage, as we read in the last chapter of Lear's book, is a virtue, because it is the best way of affirming a basic fact about us, namely, that we are finite erotic creatures. By saying "*finite*," Lear means to communicate a set of limitations to which our human nature is subjected. We are not omnipotent, he says, nor are we omniscient; our ability to create is limited; the same is the case with our ability to get what we want; our beliefs may turn out to be false; even the concepts that we use to describe the world are vulnerable and prone to deformation. But Lear follows Plato in his concept of the erotic nature of the human condition. All that man lacks as a result of his human finitude makes him reach out to the world longing for it, desiring and seducing it and, finally, yearning for what he considers (rather mistakenly) to be valuable, beautiful and good. However, could a warrior of the Crow tribe (or any other tribe) perform a similar act of planting a stick in the ground in a reservation created for him? Would he experience the same feeling of lack that called him to fight for recognition? It was soon to turn out that in a world devoid of freedom and naturalness, there was no room for dignity and courage. In the reservation, a stick remained a stick, and no one would ever fight for it or think of defending it. So Plenty Coups led his tribe from the world in which stealing the enemy's horse was a reason for glory, to the world in which the same act was qualified as a common crime. In other words, the end of the culture of rivalry began with domestication of the element, taming of the "wind," destroying the buffalo and criminalizing the behavior that used to bring fame and honor. Those who were moved to the new reality lived in total confusion. One might say that the concepts that had so far cemented the Indian culture and contributed to a meaningful whole were disintegrating in their presence, before their eyes. The devastation that affected the reality of the Indian tribes resembles in so many ways the modern culture eroded by nihilism. This can be seen on the example of Heidegger's category of temporality applied by Lear in his analysis of the decline of concepts characteristic of North American Indian culture. Temporality, the understanding of time as manifested in specific forms of culture, is clearly datable. If time is always the time "when this or that" has already happened, one may easily imagine the "end" of such time, or the moment at which "this or that" is no longer happening. When the buffalo went away, the Crows "just lived," to quote Two Leggings. According to Lear, that peculiar "end of time" might happen at any moment, literally, to anyone. No reality proves sufficiently immune to defend itself against the destructive effect of nihilism, which is like acid that dissolves everything. Thinking in an "impoverished time" turns into thoughtlessness, university into a factory, vibrant agglomerations suddenly empty out and die, work and struggle gradually lose meaning, turning into idle rest and unemployment. The way out of the existential impasse—and I find it one of the most beautiful intuitions worded in the book—can be found by a poet who will grant a completely new meaning to the devastation of his tribe. What Lear has in mind here is someone

> who could take up the Crow past and—rather than use it for nostalgia or ersatz mimesis—project it into vibrant new ways for the Crow to live and to be. Here by "poet" I mean the broadest sense of a creative maker of meaningful space. The possibility for such a poet is precisely the possibility for the creation of a new field of possibilities. No one is in a position to rule out that possibility.[4]

For the poet usually draws from the reserves saved for more difficult times. Without him, the nation lives its life without reflection, in complete emptiness, detached from its own memory. The poet's vocation, then, is to wake his people from indolence in which they have found themselves—through no fault of their own—and to stir the drowsy remnants of tribal consciousness.

III

It is interesting to see how the limits of cognition were expanded by the Indian community. The elders encouraged the younger male members of the tribe to go off into the mountains, or into the woods, and dream. Depending on what

---

4. Lear, *Radical Hope*, 49.

they dreamed, their dream-visions were then subject to powerful interpretations; so the boys would dream and the elders would explain those dreams. It was believed that the young were endowed with a mediumistic ability, that through them some images spoke that were born on the edge of two worlds, natural and supernatural. The boys dreamed what they could not think, and it was Plenty Coups who was to dream the Crows' future.

> I saw the Four Winds gathering to strike the forest, and held my breath. Pity was hot in my heart for the beautiful trees. I felt pity for all things that lived in the forest, but was powerless to stand with them against the Four Winds that together were making war. I shielded my own face with my arm when they charged! I heard the Thunders calling out in the storm, saw beautiful trees twist like blades of grass and fall in tangled piles where the forest had been. Bending low I heard the Four Winds rush past me as though they were not yet satisfied, and then I looked at the destruction they had left behind them. Only one tree, tall and straight, was left standing where the great forest had stood. The Four Winds that always make war alone had this time struck together, riding down every tree in the forest but *one*. Standing there alone among its dead tribesmen, I thought it looked sad. 'What does this mean?' I whispered in my dream.[5]

Plenty Coups's dream, recollected and rediscovered, helped him find a solution to the situation that his tribe faced. When the rules of the game change and we have no influence over it—he argued, trying to convince his fellow tribesmen—we too must change ourselves, otherwise we will die. Therefore, it is good to imitate (as in a dream) the behavior of a chickadee that listens to others and knows how to learn from them. This would entail a new definition of the idea of courage, so that it no longer means defending of coup-sticks planted in the ground, but a great, heroic attempt to assimilate the new culture and adapt to it. Of course, it does not make much sense anyway (the buffalo are gone, and along with them the souls of the Indians, their courage), but it allows biological survival. It was supposed to be a means of surviving their own death. At least that much.

Plato wrote in the *Laches* (198bc) that things that we naturally fear are yet to come in all their indeterminacy. If this is true, then the Crow Indians were stripped of yet another human quality, because recreating the environment that they used to inhabit also meant that their fear of the unknown was tamed.

---

5. Ibid., 129–30.

This way we have reached the point of confrontation that took place between Plenty Coups and Sitting Bull, the chief of the Sioux nation. Visited by the idea of saving all Indian tribes from the plague of the white man, Sitting Bull declared war against the US government. And he lost it, just like he lost a way of life that he could not defend. How does Plenty Coup fare against this background? One might accuse him (and not that falsely) of conformism, allying with the stronger, or realism based on a cold calculation of both his own and his enemy's chances. However, the novelty of Lear's concept lies elsewhere. Lear follows the voice of Plenty Coups's dream in which, regardless of the specter of the Apocalypse, the idea of *radical hope* was revealed to him. What kind of hope is it and what does its radicalism mean?

We deal with radical hope in its most absurd form—as in the myth of the sacrifice of Isaac—when God urges one of the parents to suspend the ethical duty of guardianship of his or her child in the name of some principle that goes beyond ethics, transcends this world. The hope here is based on the belief that we are able to preserve old ways of life under radically different conditions, though such intention itself might seem quite absurd. This faith is complemented with the conviction that good can appear even in a world where there is no room for it, and that good itself is unfathomable. It turns out that good is of an irreducible structure that allows it to last, even if the traditional ways of framing it have atrophied. Therefore, one should act "in the name" of the highest value, engage *practically* on its "side" (I use quotation marks here, for in a world infected with nihilism there are no "names" or clearly defined "sides"), although it escapes the current concepts. Only a hurry-scurry action, blind but committed, will—"perhaps"—make it possible to resuscitate the signs of old life, restore its meaning and faith in the tribal resurrection. Thus, radical hope is born in the circumstances when we expect a happy ending but cannot tell where it should come from. Its radicalism lies in the fact that a culture in crisis heads for a successful solution that *is not yet there* and does so in the person of its leading representatives: poets, statesmen, haunted prophets. This hope has nothing to do with the cheap optimism of social ideologies, for the rescue may or may not come. In a sense, it creates a new type of bravery, one that takes risks in a situation when nobody knows what to do, when every choice might prove tragic. It is a frail kind of bravery, rooted in the ruins of the past world and the awareness of failure. Hence, radical hope differs from ordinary hope in that it is an empty one, stripped of its substance, weak and vague, unfocused, a hope "for nothing." All this makes it radical and thus directed toward a future good that goes beyond the current ability to understand what that good could possibly be. What, in turn, distinguishes it from optimism is—let me repeat—the fact that it cannot be reduced to awaiting anything specific, for example, a practical or effective solution to some case. Radical hope requires a new type of courage, as it fuels our uncertainty and prepares us to confront an "unknowable" situation. It is utterly irrational, supported by no incontrovertible evidence.

IV

It turns out that the end of the world can be "redone" many times. As many as there are worlds that shall end. I would risk saying that Jonathan Lear's *Radical Hope* is yet another version of the "end of history," brilliantly retold and rediscovered (its characteristic feature being the incredible vividness of image and exuberant narration). The book tells the story of not only the disappearance of traditions, the erosion of certain modes of behavior, but also the disappearance of a possible basis for them; we can observe *ad oculos* the destruction of a particular cultural formation. Therefore, I see how the story might appeal to the imagination of readers who are specially sensitized to the context of historical cataclysms in which our history abounded. But also those inclined to the so-called historical politics, as it seems that Plenty Coups was its first great supporter. Now that the buffalo are out, the identity of the tribe needs to be built anew, basing on the new values that are propagated in the new world. How? By building reservations, breeding new buffalo, teaching people to hunt and dance through stories of how people used to hunt and dance in the olden days. Lear's book is heartening as it resurrects the forgotten language of hope, the fulfillment of which is to come from the hazy future, from the undefined "outside." It is a narrative about a small nation subjected to planned extermination, which survived the annihilation because in the person of Plenty Coups they found both Piłsudski and Mickiewicz.

Besides, *Radical Hope* is nice (reminiscent of pictures from Fiedler's *Little Bison*) and very true.

Chapter 13

THEY REFUGEES (HANNAH ARENDT)

In accordance with the law the death sentence was announced to Cincinnatus C. in a whisper.[1]

I remember a conversation with Debord in which Guy said: "You know, I'm not a philosopher. I am a strategist." The opposite is true for me. When I hear the question: "What should be done, what actions should be taken?" I reply: "I don't know. I am not a strategist, but a philosopher." And then I hear: "It's just an excuse. It's all because you are a great pessimist." And then I say that everything that supports understanding is not pessimistic. A being that understands the essence of things cannot be pessimistic. For me, pessimism means only one thing: not wanting to see.[2]

Agamben knows how to formulate and average a lot of important things. And if at times he seems to wander off the subject, unnecessarily and unrestrainedly piling up successive thresholds of understanding, it is always the unclear language that is to blame. The thought itself is frightfully, glaringly clear. It is just a few motifs taken after Benjamin, Arendt, Schmitt or Foucault and developed, thought out to the end "as a warning." If they carry a prophecy, what is it about? Man? His time? The world in which he is made to live? The near future? Or does it, rather, tell us more about what happened, what has already taken place? Finally, the most important question is: who is it that Agamben is addressing? Man? Or does he formulate his thought in the form of an epitaph after man, so to speak, over his grave? If so, who needs it? Who shall sing this prophecy and who will care?

---

1. Vladimir Nabokov, *Invitation to a Beheading*, trans. Dmitri Nabokov (New York: Putnam's Sons, 1959), 11.
2. Giorgio Agamben, "Kapitalizm jest religią, w której nic nie należy do ludzi" [Capitalism Is a Religion in Which Nothing Belongs to People], interview by Maciej Nowicki, *Europa* 11, a supplement to *Dziennik* (March 15, 2008): 4.

Bios and *zoe*

For Foucault, the study of past events—Agamben observes—generally resembles the play of shadow that the present casts over the past; the shadow reaches back to the seventeenth century at the latest. The shadow that Agamben's work casts over the past, however, seems to be much longer. Agamben himself admits that he likes to create at dusk, when shadows dominate, when things are enveloped in darkness. In his case, the shadow reaches back to very distant events; it gets to the source of the unacknowledged contents, some basic distinctions, like that between *bios* and *zoe*.[3]

The distinction between *bios* and *zoe* is of paramount importance to classical philosophy. And Agamben also surrounds it with a specific halo, regarding recognition of the duality of life as the founding act of humanity, the establishment of a "political" man. Although *both* these terms mean life, they point to its Janus-like nature. *Zoe* is an ordinary, animalistic will to continue, inherent in all living beings, and manifested in the pursuit of self-preservation. *Bios*, in turn, is a strictly defined form of life, the multitude of its forms, including customs, religiousness, law, politics, art or science. That is, practically any activity that goes beyond self-preservation, beyond the will to survive. If a given political community highlights the importance of the *quality* of existence, if it stresses the stabilization of its cultural and political forms, then we deal with the peak of human creative powers, as was the case in Pericles's Athens, Republican Rome or Christianity. However, the moment *zoe* enters the space of politics brings about a "catastrophe" (Greek καταστροφή, revolt, reversal), a change in the meanings of basic categories used to describe and understand *human* life. And so on the threshold of modernity, along with the Great French Revolution, in the center of political and social interest, there suddenly appears bare life in the form of an invasion of poverty, privacy and body. The colonization of the world by the burning "social question"[4] that demands a quick solution and causes irrevocable consequences. Politics falls prey to biopower, the activity whose aim is to rule over life—*zoe*—by means of legal and political categories as well as technological tools defining the technical conditions for the possibility of what is to be done. Thus understood, biopower decides about the difference between bare life and death, drawing and arbitrarily shifting the demarcation line that separates reality from nothingness.

---

3. Giorgio Agamben, "Der Papst ist ein weltlicher Priester," *Literaturen*, no. 6 (2005): 58. Agamben makes his own genealogy here, disregarding, I think, certain facts. Or else what to do with Foucault's *The History of Sexuality* or *The Hermeneutics of the Subject* that contains his 1981/82 lectures from Collège de France, in which he travels to the world of ancient Greeks.
4. Hannah Arendt, *On Revolution* (London: Penguin Books, 1990), 59–114.

Biopower embraces the human body; it takes control of it even more by penetrating into life than by the threat of putting it to death. From now on, it is no longer about living beautifully, with dignity and majesty. By all appearance, the era of creating intransgressible artistic and political works is gone forever. Today, no one writes great treatises; no one makes music to praise new worlds; one does not feel the need to contribute a new cathedral to the existing ones. Reality shrinks and becomes simplified. Only bare, trivial, private life advances in value, of which Agamben says that can be killed, scraped out, raped or removed in any other way, but cannot be sacrificed.[5] Bare life, therefore, is devoid of any dignity, which is understandable to the point that only *bios*—the source of morality, social norms, religion and also their substance—can give dignity to such life. What happens before our eyes is a transformation of the political sphere into a homogeneous area of bare life. This heralds the birth of a new totalitarianism. Both in democracy, where life is worshiped in its most trivial aspects, and in totalitarianism, where only the ability to survive matters, it is life that is claimed to be the leading actor; everything revolves around it. There is nothing more precious than life. And where has man got to? In what part of the planet should one look for him? Well, man was ousted and replaced by life, *zoe*, that—in a way—took over his place. Man left to the void of gelatinous existence, man indistinguishable from it, overlapping with partial, defective life, is *homo sacer*—the area of an unbridled element set free, or the result of an amorphization of the political space that smoothly changes from totalitarian oppression to democracy and back, excluding any other political forms along the way, possibly due to their anachronism and incompatibility with life (from monarchy to the Greek politeia). On the one hand, we have various types of totalitarianism—communism, Nazism, fascism, Maoism and the like—with an unleashed machine of death that they developed and,

---

5. Giorgio Agamben, *Homo Sacer. Sovereign Power and Bare Life*, trans. Daniel Heller-Roazen (Stanford: Stanford University Press, 1998), 12. The term *homo sacer* comes from Sextus Pompeius Festus, Roman grammarian who maintained that:

   the sacred man is the one whom the people have judged on account of a crime. It is not permitted to sacrifice this man, yet he who kills him will not be condemned for homicide; in the first tribunitian law, in fact, it is noted that "if someone kills the one who is sacred according to the plebiscite, it will not be considered homicide." This is why it is customary for a bad or impure man to be called sacred.

   Sextus Pompeius Festus, *De verborum significatio*, quoted after Agamben, *Homo Sacer*, 47. At the same time it is interesting to notice how the phrase "sacred man" was used in a non-Christian culture. It referred to man to whom neither human nor divine law applied, and not to man of special moral qualifications or having direct contact with God. Generally speaking, a "sacred man" is an outlaw, an outlaw, hence *sacer*, but not a *sanctus*.

on the other hand, the inhuman hedonism of the zoomorphic homo sapiens living in democracy, one that lacks inner purpose or any restraint. Under such conditions, in the absence of people who were swept away from the political scene by *zoe*, it seems natural and reasonable to proclaim a state of exception in order to "find man" (or create him) and eliminate the threat to "higher values." The decision to declare it is independent of the prevailing legal order because, being external to it, it has the power to suspend it.

> Instead the decisive fact is that, together with the process by which the exception everywhere becomes the rule, the realm of bare life—which is originally situated at the margins of the political order—gradually begins to coincide with the political realm, and, exclusion and inclusion, outside and inside, *bios* and *zoē*, right and fact, enter into a zone of irreducible indistinction. At once excluding bare life from and capturing it within the political order, the state of exception actually constituted, in its very separateness, the hidden foundation on which the entire political system rested. When its borders begin to be blurred, the bare life that dwelt there frees itself in the city and becomes both subject and object of the conflicts of the political order, the one place for both the organization of State power and emancipation from it.[6]

I think these rather Aesopian sentences require some explanation.

State of Exception

The exception consists in excluding certain facts, phenomena or behaviors from the general norm. In other words, the exception becomes incorporated into law as that which excludes it and is *eo ipso* outside of it, outside the law. With one reservation, namely, the exception is not so much outside the law but, rather, belongs to it as an exclusive inclusion, *esclusione inclusiva*. In other words, "state of exception" means a biopolitization of bare life, not a single event of authoritative character but a specific way in which the masses exist and organize themselves.[7] In the case of the "state of exception," we are dealing with a permanent situation, not a one-off or temporary one. It is a kind of blurred "political" structure, a framework within which "people" can rearrange their existence according to laws that either still apply, even if they do not mean anything anymore, or coincide with life and cease to be laws.

---

6. Ibid., 12–13.
7. This is why I choose to place the term in inverted commas, which by no means makes it less oppressive.

That is to say, a situation in which "pure form of law as 'being in force without significance' appears for the first time in modernity."[8] What is symptomatic of this process is the lack of distinction between the inner side of law and the matter to which it relates as well as—parallelly—the obscure boundary between what is private and what is public. Losing its normative substance, law begins to interfere with life and ceases to be that which is different from it. Legal norms are not applicable to the world, because they are elusive and invisible. In the "state of exception," each situation can be assessed one way or another. Judgments are given ad hoc on the basis of convenient interpretations of inevitably ambiguous facts. And since things can be "one way or another," actions are deprived of a relevant legal qualification: it is not clear whether something is legal or not, because there is no law anymore, because law coincides with a given fact. Therefore, any behavior can be counted as a transgression against the enigmatic "law," whereas an undoubtedly criminal behavior can be considered normal. At the same time, it is not necessary to make new laws. It is enough to shift the old legal norms into the field of exception. In a "state of suspension," when one does not know what is good and what is bad, what is legal and what is not, any foul mean would get away, any crime is permitted. According to Agamben, "In our age, the state of exception comes more and more to the foreground as the fundamental political structure and ultimately begins to become the rule. When our age tried to grant the unrealizable a permanent and visible localization, the result was the concentration camp."[9] Let us repeat: the situations provoked by the "state of exception" seem paradoxical, for it is impossible to distinguish between being against the law and acting in accordance with the law.

In order to better explain it, let us use an illustration. Imagine a refugee camp and a refugee who goes outside the gate without a required permit. This man does not break the law any more than the sentry does, who, by killing him or her, only enforces the law—the law of the "state of exception," suspending the validity of the hitherto prevailing norms.

> The stateless person, without right to residence and without the right to work, had of course constantly to transgress the law. He was liable to jail sentences without ever committing a crime. More than that, the entire hierarchy of values which pertain in civilized countries was reversed in his case. Since he was the anomaly for whom the general law did not provide, it was better for him to become an anomaly for which it did provide, that of the criminal. The best criterion by which to decide whether

---

8. Agamben, *Homo Sacer*, 35.
9. Ibid., 19.

someone has been forced outside the pale of the law is to ask if he would benefit by committing a crime. If a small burglary is likely to improve his legal position, at least temporarily, one may be sure he has been deprived of human rights.[10]

Agamben expresses a similar thought even more precisely: in the camp—the *ultima thule* of the "last man"—the line separating crime from normal behavior, life from death, is a matter of legal formula, but before that, it depends on a political decision. Let us consider the otherwise representative status of beings called "neomorts," that is, people who have suffered an accident or illness and are in a coma. What about them? Who decides about their existence if they cannot decide for themselves? Family? Its rights in this respect are limited by the right to life, which is absolute, categorical and fundamental. If not family, then who? The meaning of the difference between life and death is always determined by biopower. Today, death is considered to be the death of the brain—the only organ that is not transplanted—which means that a metaphysical and existential hypothesis is formulated based on technological premises. If so, then what will death be tomorrow, if its scientific, biopolitical definition changes? Time will tell.

A History Lesson from the Perspective of a Refugee

The refugee problem, which became as acute in the second decade of the twenty-first century as the "social question" was in the nineteenth century, is in the heart of Agamben's most important book. In the chapter on "Biopolitics and the Rights of Man," he offers the reader a short history lesson. Immediately after the First World War, Europeans faced a disturbingly large refugee movement, triggered by the emergence of national minorities on the world stage, which, in turn, were brought into being under agreements and treaties between states. As it happened, Eastern Europe turned out to be a special place for minorities. Every now and then new states were born, or reborn from the rubble, and a peaceful cohabitation of many nations living within common borders was imposed on them. It did not work well. Treaties concluded far from the reach of ordinary people obliged them to assimilate, often painfully, by adopting the laws and customs of the majority who inhabited a given territory. Those who could not accept it had to leave. In this way, one and a half million Belarusians and Ukrainians, half a million Bulgarians, seven hundred thousand Armenians, one million Greeks and hundreds of thousands of Germans changed their homes for other homes.

---

10. Hannah Arendt, *The Origins of Totalitarianism* (New York: Harcourt Brace Jovanovich, 1973), 286.

Refugees who formed a national minority in national states reported, so to speak, the need for double legal protection: on the part of the state they lived in and on the part of international institutions guarding the implementation of their right to exist. The rights to communicate in one's own language, to remain in one's own cultural circle and to perform religious activities specific to the religion(s) of minorities were all constantly jeopardized and protected without conviction. An additional complication arose from the fact that nothing indicated that this state was a temporary one. In brief, only people who were citizens of a given country could rely on legal protection, while those who declared a different nationality, who applied for a culture other than the one dominating in a given territory, were deprived of such protection. The practice of sovereign states and international arrangements thus generated successive categories of unwanted people pushed to the margin of the state or meeting their end outside of it, in "no-man's land." In 1915, France became the first country to massively strip of passports its naturalized citizens from countries with which it was at war. Belgium followed in its footsteps in 1922 and Italy in 1926. The governments of both of these countries took away identity documents from people who turned out to be "unworthy" of their citizenship. The Nuremberg Race Laws of September 1935 only crowned the course that Europe took at that time.[11] The process of denationalizing its citizens and ostracizing new citizens was illustrated in Franz Kafka's novel, *The Castle*. "But one should bear in mind at the same time," claims Hannah Arendt, commenting on the fate of refugees, "that there was hardly a country left on the Continent that did not pass between the two wars some new legislation which, even if it did not use this right [i.e., hostile to refugees] extensively, was always phrased to allow for getting rid of a great number of its inhabitants at any opportune moment."[12]

The idealists of the past called for fundamental and inalienable rights that protected minorities on equal terms with rightful citizens of developed countries. Today it is demanded by political realists and even decision-makers. But the means of realizing this utopia—the utopia of making the rights and aspirations of the majority equal with the rights and aspirations of the minority—always remains the same: it is a refugee camp, the new address of *displaced persons*. It is in such conditions that these people start their new life—subject to legal regulations created for exceptional circumstances, the shape of which they did not negotiate. Human rights, the last instance they may resort to, are more like an appeal to conscience and have no effect whatsoever on statutory law in majority territory. The ineffectiveness of these laws and their

---

11. Agamben, *Homo Sacer*, 99.
12. Arendt, *The Origins of Totalitarianism*, 278–79.

pitiful morality have almost become proverbial. "The comity of European peoples went to pieces when, and because, it allowed its weakest member to be excluded and persecuted."[13] It quickly turned out that refugees cannot be thrown out of their place just like that. Indeed, it was still possible to refuse to let them in, as was the case with refugees trying to get to the New World; however, if they managed to cross the border, the authorities would launch the procedure of naturalizing the refugees, or carry out the difficult task of repatriation (the difficulty was on the fact that some of the countries from which the refugees came ceased to exist).

A number of uncomfortable questions can be asked at this point: why in today's political and legal reality the so-called human and civil rights have ceased to protect anyone? Have they ever protected those who referred to them? Why is the power of these laws incomparably lesser than the power of the positive law in force in a given country? I think that the answers to these questions should be sought in the distinction between *bios* and *zoe*, mentioned early in this chapter. The life that is protected by human rights cannot be the subject of any rights due to its trivial, amorphous nature. On the other hand, a free man is undoubtedly such a subject—a citizen aware of his or her own freedom and rights. Combining these two, human rights and citizens' rights, is an attempt to marry fire with water; it is a risky synthesis of two heterogeneous elements.

> If refugees [...] represent such a disquieting element in the order of the modern nation-state, this is above all because by breaking the continuity between man and citizen, *nativity* and *nationality*, they put the originary fiction of modern sovereignty in crisis. Bringing to light the difference between birth and nation, the refugee causes the secret presupposition of the political domain—bare life—to appear for an instant within that domain.[14]

However, Agamben seems to ignore the rather obvious fact that refugees themselves often drag behind them a specific *bios*, that they did not emerge out of nowhere, that they were born in a specific time and place, that their social and cultural existence cannot be seen as fiction or nothingness. In other words, a refugee, while explicitly demanding absolute protection of life, which cannot by any means be denied to him, implicitly postulates that his *bios* should be

---

13. Hannah Arendt, "We Refugees," in *The Jewish Writings* (New York: Schocken Books, 2007), lxiii.
14. Agamben, *Homo Sacer*, 77.

equally protected, that is, all those habits, prejudices, culture and language that make him different.

> The separation between humanitarianism and politics that we are experiencing today is the extreme phase of the separation of the rights of man from the rights of the citizen, in the final analysis, however, humanitarian organizations—which today are more and more supported by international commissions—can only grasp human life in the figure of bare or sacred life, and therefore, despite themselves, maintain a secret solidarity with the very powers they ought to fight.[15]

This is because the European, post-Enlightenment modernity cannot—it is not able to—incorporate into its own bloodstream those elements that in its eyes are considered pre-Enlightenment, "barbaric" remnants that deserve "hospitalization" or rejection.

Agamben's prophetic deliberations, present in most of his works from the *Homo Sacer* series,[16] as well as his insight and deliberate lack of "procedural caution" in formulating accusations against modernity, break many stereotypes that are fairly commonly harbored in relation to political reality. His words are powerful, yet grow weak when applauded by the somewhat hysterical left-wing intellectuals. They could serve as a genuine prophecy, were they not used as a whip, and if the author himself refrained from commenting on what he wrote. Therefore, I will follow up Agamben's lead to further discuss the "refugee issue." I will also nuance the stance he adopted on the issue when writing *Homo Sacer* as well as his famous essay on refugees,[17] enriching them with new facts, new illustrations and sinister forebodings.

A Lesson in the Present from the Perspective of an Autochthon

The more enlightened, unprejudiced demographers have long warned against the threat of masses of people moving toward the affluent Europe.

---

15. Ibid., 78.
16. The series comprises *Homo Sacer: Sovereign Power and Bare Life* (1995), *State of Exception. Homo Sacer II, 1* (2003), *The Sacrament of Language: An Archaeology of the Oath. Homo Sacer II, 3* (2008), *The Kingdom and the Glory: For a Theological Genealogy of Economy and Government. Homo Sacer II, 4* (2011), *Remnants of Auschwitz: The Witness and the Archive. Homo Sacer III* (1998).
17. Giorgio Agamben, "We Refugees," trans. M. Rocke, *Symposium* 49, no. 2 (1995), 114–19.

The migration of peoples who we are dealing with today (in 2014 and 2015) was therefore something easy to anticipate, but instead was completely ignored by politicians preoccupied with observing the current polls. And what's wrong about some people wanting to live in a better world? Is it really necessary to stand in the way of their dreams? After all, in the recent past—as some German politicians tend to remind us—Poles also chose to emigrate and were hosted by generous German, English or French hosts. So why are they not able to repay by welcoming thousands of Mohammedans to their country? The point is that Poles, Lithuanians, Latvians, just like in every European nation, manifest—let me put it this way—a certain ease of assimilating the European axiology and customs; they have the ability to melt into the newly adopted nation, which, on the other hand, is not very praiseworthy. The Mohammedan newcomers neither know how nor want to do this. Living in Europe, they assimilate only the material level of being while rejecting its religious emptiness with contempt. Spiritually immersed in a religion untouched by the ideas of enlightenment, a religion that never had its Luther, they pose a serious challenge to common, secularized sense. By definition, they do not respect the values of the secular state, regarding it as an impermanent and contingent existence, and the land as a gift from Allah. Many factors reinforce Muslim proselytism in Europe. The most important of them is political correctness—a disease that the Western world, stripped of values, is afflicted by. Another factor is the bankrupt ideology of multiculturalism, celebrating its posthumous triumph. Also of significance for the pro-immigration policy of European countries are the calculations of German social engineers who see the masses of people flowing into Europe as a solution to the crisis of an aging, childless society. Finally, it is important to note that the current ruling class are former hippies, smoking pot with just anybody, loving anyone who turns up—this one today, that one tomorrow. There is also the memory of the crimes of the long colonial policy and of something as embarrassing as the everlasting domination of Christianity in Europe.

The autochthons know that the abovementioned reasons for social openness and consent to otherness are all nonsense. Where does this shameful lack of political will come from, they ask, on the part of European politicians who could find many ways to help Mohammedans solve problems in their own countries? Why is the failure of the assimilation of the third generation of Muslim immigrants, from which European jihadists originate, not taken into account? We are not saying, the autochthons admit, that all Mohammedans are terrorists; we claim that the overwhelming majority of terrorists are Mohammedans.

Dziekański Case

Robert Dziekański, a Polish construction worker, arrived in Canada on October 13, 2007, with immigration in mind. While at the airport, he was overwhelmed and stopped by the problems completing customs formalities and, in consequence, spent many hours there. He did not speak English, and no one was able to support him. His mother, who was supposed to pick him up at the airport, told her son to wait at the baggage claim area, where she was not allowed to enter. Informed by airport staff that there was no Dziekanski on the passenger list, she returned home thinking her son had mistakenly boarded another flight. At that time, Dziekański, extremely exhausted, hungry, unable to communicate with anyone and in any language, used a chair to force the door separating the customs clearing area from the arrivals hall. Airport staff called the police. Four police officers took part in arresting Dziekański, who did not resist. The handcuffed man was electrocuted many times and died as a result.

Another scene, from the summer of 2015, this time at the Austrian–Italian border. Masses of swarthy immigrants in dire straits. Exhausted, furious, rushing forward. They shout something, want something, but no one knows exactly what. Both sides cannot communicate on any matter. Language barrier stands in the way. There is a growing nervousness on both sides. Immigrants try to swing a coach with a group of "normal" tourists on the side of the road. Eventually, they throw excrement at the coach and spit on it. Then the luggage compartments are plundered. The bus continues its journey, smeared with feces, scratched, with broken windows. The witness of this event noted that there were virtually no women among the immigrants, and no children. The vast majority, he writes on his blog, were young, aggressive men. Finally, the Austrian border guard gives a consent notice that they can cross the border, but none of the immigrants understands this message. At the same time, each of them continues to fight for the right to cross the border. They are given the permission, but do not understand the message. They return to Italy.[18]

And one more image, covered with a patina, of the Paris suburbs inhabited by ethnic minorities: Clichy-sous-Bois, Sevran, Neuilly-sur-Marne, Bondy and many others. Thousands of private cars are burned, many malls and restaurants are burned. Fire destroys and paralyzes public transport. Naturalized descendants

---

18. Many people drew my attention to the uncertain source of this information. The point is that I do not care about facts so much, just like—I dare say—Agamben. I am more interested in images (like the one above) with which ordinary people feed their imagination. And I always stress it. I leave the determination of facts to the police.

of immigrants take to the streets after two of them, fleeing the police, die electrocuted. There is a series of regular battles between the police and the immigrant community. *The New York Times* of November 5, 2005, reports that those involved in the fighting are mostly young Muslims of African or North African descent. In some places, the authorities impose a curfew. A similar riot will take place in London six years later, after the forces of order have shot dead a Black resident of Tottenham, a neighborhood inhabited by a colored minority. From time to time, houses for asylum-seekers burn in Germany. In 2015, an Aruban man, Mitch Henriquez, dies at a police station in the Hague as a result of "brain hypoxia." The news does not make its way to the mainstream media, and so no riots follow this time. Finally, an Iraqi Mohammedan, Rafik Y., stabs a Berlin policewoman, then dies of gunshots that come from a police patrol.

I have noticed many more similar reports on the events at the EU borders, as well as on the problematic neighborhood of Europeans and ethnic minorities living in Europe, in various media; the above are just a few selected examples. Who prepares these reports, for what purpose and with what intention? Finally, what ground do these media reports fall on, of Mohammedans storming the European *limes*? It does not matter. As Agamben puts it, "In our age all citizens can be said, in a specific but extremely real sense, to appear virtually as *homines sacri*."[19] Welcome to the brave new world.

Apocalypse

The worst is yet to come. It certainly cannot be the case that Muslim immigrants will be regarded as racially inferior. It's out of the question, we live in different times. Nor can it be the case that they will take over some professions, that they will exclude Europeans from important areas of social life, that they will purchase tracts or invest capital for their own profit that they will then transfer abroad. Nobody would believe it. If I do not want Mohammedans in Europe, if I am afraid of their presence in the Old Continent, it is so because I am afraid of their fate; it is for fear not of them but for them. History tends to repeat itself, and not in the least as a farce. In short, they will die here, be eliminated, trampled on, pressed into European soil, because the conditions for the possibility of Shoah have not been eradicated, as can be read in the writings of Benjamin,[20] Arendt,[21]

---

19. Agamben, *Homo Sacer*, 66. See also 68.
20. Walter Benjamin, "Theses on the Philosophy of History" (also known as "On the Concept of History"), in *Illuminations*, trans. Harry Zohn (New York: Schocken Books, 1968).
21. Here, I mostly refer to *The Origins of Totalitarianism* and the category of "radical evil."

Adorno,[22] Marcuse,[23] Bauman,[24] Nowosielski,[25] Jonas,[26] Améry,[27] Rymkiewicz[28] or Besançon.[29] The work of destruction can always repeat itself in a new form, in fact at any moment.[30]

Let's switch to another subject. The year 1996 marked the height of the panic caused by Creutzfeldt-Jakob disease. Hundreds of thousands of cows were burned in just a few months. The killing operation was carried out efficiently and effectively. I call those terrible events—exaggeratedly and inadequately, I hope—"exercises in Holocaust," or a burnt offering to the god of technology. Suffice it to say that they proved that if something is possible, it will be performed, sooner or later. So does it mean that the Holocaust—the

---

22. Theodor W. Adorno, "Late Capitalism or Industrial Society?", in *Modern German Sociology*, ed. V. Meja, D. Misgeld and N. Stehr (New York: Columbia University Press, 1987). See also *Dialectic of Enlightenment* in which the authors analyze the circumstances of the birth of modern totalitarianism from the spirit of the enlightened mind. Max Horkheimer and Theodor W. Adorno, *Dialectic of Enlightenment: Philosophical Fragments*, trans. Edmund Jephcott (Bloomington, IN: Stanford University Press, 2002).
23. Herbert Marcuse, "The New Forms of Control," in *One-Dimensional Man* (Boston: Beacon Press, 1964).
24. Zygmunt Bauman, *Modernity and the Holocaust* (Cambridge, MA: Polity Press, 1989).
25. Jerzy Nowosielski, *Mój Chrystus: Rozmowy z Jerzym Nowosielskim* [My Christ. Conversations with Jerzy Nowosielski] (Białystok: ŁUK, 1993).
26. Hans Jonas, "The Concept of God after Auschwitz: A Jewish Voice," *Journal of Religion* 67, no. 1 (January 1987): 9.
27. Jean Améry, *At the Mind's Limits: Contemplations by a Survivor of Auschwitz and Its Realities*, trans. Sidney and Stella P. Rosenfeld (Bloomington: Indiana University Press, 1980).
28. Jarosław M. Rymkiewicz, *The Final Station. Umschlagplatz*, trans. Nina Taylor (New York: Farrar, Strauss and Giroux, 1994).
29. Alain Besançon, *A Century of Horrors: Communism, Nazism, and the Uniqueness of the Shoah*, trans. Ralph C. Hancock and Nathaniel H. Hancock (Wilmington: ISI Books, 2007).
30. From time to time I expressed my concern at various international conferences. In general, my sinister formulations and worries about the fate of the Mohammedans were neither understood nor well received. At that time, I was overwhelmed by the question of what must happen for this inevitable, as I imagined, Shoah to take place at all. More terrorist attacks against helpless people? Israel's assertive politics? Today I know: "they" must come here. They have to get to Europe to deactivate *nomos*; they would prefer not to. For it all began here, and here it will end. See also Giorgio Agamben, "Bartleby, or On Contingency," in *Potentialities. Collected Essays on Philosophy*, trans. Daniel Heller-Roazen (Stanford: Stanford University Press, 1999); Piotr Nowak, "United States and Europe—Their 'Elective Affinities' from the Perspective of the Trojan Ass," in *Where Europe Is Going: Leadership–Ideas–Values*, ed. H. Taborska (Pułtusk: Akademia Humanistyczna im. Aleksandra Gieysztora, 2007); Piotr Nowak, "Carl Schmitt and His Critic," in *Modernity and What Has Been Lost: Considerations on the Legacy of Leo Strauss*, ed. P. Armada (South Bend, IN: St. Augustine's Press, 2010).

Shoah—has to happen again only because, in technical terms, it is an easy task to carry out? No, not only because of that. There is one more reason, a more important one.

The German philosopher and legal theorist Carl Schmitt noted that all political categories constituting the foundation of the modern world are secularized theological concepts. The state of exception that suspends law corresponds to the theological concept of a miracle, positive law—to the Scripture, partisans have replaced dissenters; an act of grace is what used to be the forgiveness of sins; and the present outlawing is the former excommunication. And so on, and so forth. But the point is that a similar translation of concepts can also be successfully done the other way around. If so, let us ask what our secularized modern age is in strictly theological terms. Well, it is a short, pre-apocalyptic period during which (as the Scriptures say) the planet is ruled by the Antichrist. He is no one special. The Antichrist is not a person equipped with scorched wings, limping on his left leg, and clothed in a bright yellow checkered pattern. Antichrist is the time we live in; it is a specific aura of the decline of all important values, a radical overestimation of humanity. Our age embodies the purest opposite of Christ's teaching. Love is replaced by indifferent philanthropy; faith—by reason; religion—by science; the eschatological dimension of death—by the ideas of longevity and good health. Sovereignty is defined by the possibility of suspending law, which means nothing anymore, even if it is still in force.[31] In such conditions, humanity learns to live beyond good and evil—beyond any values that turn out to be a field of constant negotiation. It also learns how to do without God, and indeed it succeeds. Today, God is replaced by "the highest values," be they the right to life, money or security. In the twentieth century, the most ominous century in history, those who could not understand it and accept it were religious Jews (it is a pleonasm, as there are no nonreligious Jews). In this sense, the racist theory of the superiority of the Aryan race over others was only a screen, a pretext for the Holocaust. Its real cause was the unenlightened religiousness of the chosen peoples, which presented a challenge to the Enlightenment model of civilization. Not that the road to Shoah was something absolutely impossible, impossible to comprehend or anticipate. Under specific conditions, the impossible became the road that had to be followed by those to whom religion appeared as a matter of life or death. "The disappearance of the Jews was instrumental in bringing about the world of perfection. The absence of Jews was precisely

---

31. Agamben writes about the messianic character of the deactivated law in his *The Time That Remains: A Commentary on the Letter to the Romans*, trans. Patricia Dailey (Stanford: Stanford University Press, 2005).

the difference between that world and the imperfect world here and now."[32] The Jews, however, were not *sacrificed* on the altar of modern era. They died because their *bios* did not fit; it did not dissolve in *zoe*—the basic value that flatters the civilization of enlightened Europeans. Being chosen, they "stuck out" of life; they did not coincide with it, did not assimilate.

By questioning the Jewish *bios*, Jews were stripped of their *zoe*; the possibility of killing and being killed was actualized.[33] Jews—the *homines sacri* of the modern era—were not sentenced to death for their alleged crimes, nor were they sacrificed (which "god" should accept such offering?). They were removed "as lice," as bare, defenseless life, being denied even the right to be anyone's opponent. The Jewish existence turned out to be worthless, "unworthy of being lived."[34] These words need to be shouted out very emphatically and loudly: Mohammedans living in the pre-Enlightenment faith will have to, like the Jews 70 years ago, either perish because of that faith or dissolve their own particular substance in the mass of several hundred million secularized Europeans; they will have to die because it is possible. It is the dictate of reality. The decision about the Shoah is a decision independent of the legal order, and therefore it can be taken. It would be hard to consider it as a consequence of anti-Semitism or anti-Muslimism that, in turn, results from bad passions and resentment. They have always been, they are, they always will be. Progress is a matter of technology or science, not morality. In this sense, low feelings on the one hand and the Holocaust on the other are two separate cosmoses, two nonintersecting spheres: human and devilish. Reason in the hands of the devil is only an instrument—a dumb, passive tool that man uses as he wishes. The murderous machinery does not work by its own momentum and routine. The capacity to commit mass murder can be used not only because it has been developed.[35] It is a temptation that is hard to resist.

Map

I look over the map of New York that Staś has lent me. He has been there, so I must ask him how he would visualize a great extermination in Manhattan.

---

32. Bauman, *Modernity and the Holocaust*, 76.
33. Agamben, *Homo Sacer*, 68. There is something of a historical perversion in the fact that those dying in the concentration camps who maintained themselves in a strange state of suspension between life and death were called Muselmänner (sg. Muselmann).
34. Ibid., 80–81.
35. This is a polemical in relation to the theses of Zygmunt Bauman, for whom the settlement of the Holocaust consists in the settlement of instrumental reason. Bauman, *Modernity and the Holocaust*, 98.

Where are the railroad lines? A siding could start at Pennsylvania Station and end somewhere on the edge of Central Park. Unless the siding started from Central Park? But then it would have to bypass the Pan Am Building—to get a full picture I may have to go there after all. The sentry would be at intersection of Sixty-third Street and Central Park West. The Befehlsstelle would be positioned in the vicinity of Columbus Circle, where Gulf & Western is. Central Park would be enclosed by a red-brick wall three meters high, topped by another meter of barbed wire. A vast Umschlagplatz is proportion to the city. At the point where West Drive cuts through Transverse Road (someone who visited New York told me one can drive right through the park from Central Park West to Fifth Avenue) there would be a wooden gate with a sign: "No entry under penalty of death." This is where the last selection would take place. I can't say what language the sign would be in. Time will tell. Someone may protest that the idea of a siding at Pennsylvania Station, of an Umschlagplatz in Central Park, of blockades around the houses in Greenwich Village, is tasteless or frankly obscene. That someone is an idiot. For only an idiot could think that what began on July 22, 1942, in the area of Niska Street, and Stawki Street is over. The extermination came to a halt. But we who live near Umschlagplatz know it is not the end. Our century can still go on for a long time. Living on the edge of Umschlagplatz we can be sure of only one thing. We wait on the corner of Dzika Street and Stawki Street for the next episode. For there will be a sequel, there is absolutely no doubt about that.[36]

Slaughter

The slaughter will begin when Mohammedans stop being somewhat abstract and exotic people and change to some omnipresent, intrusive others—with their chalats, payots, foreign Word and perplexing speech. When the inhabitants of Europe become convinced that the unwanted strangers—tenants and peddlers—pose a real threat to them, then the sleeping demons will wake up. Such phenomena as tolerance, human rights and the idea of *dignitas hominis* will be laughed at in the face of extreme otherness. First, the Europeans will imprison Mohammedans in internment camps, within the newly built stadiums that have already served such purposes more than once, and then murder them using the same technical means as the Canadian police used to murder the Polish, pre-Enlightenment immigrant. For today we are all Canadian policemen, supported by the media that gradually dehumanize the image of Mohammedans, deadening or lulling our sensitivity to the harm of

---

36. Rymkiewicz, *The Final Station*, 84–85.

others; we are inspired by the chaotic, corruptible and inexplicable decisions of European politicians. If the refugee issue is not quickly resolved by political means, it will be resolved by policemen and philanthropists. And the latter will exchange their soul for just everything. With our blessing. Only then will come the time for expiation, sprinkling ashes on our heads, a pilgrimage to Canossa or a memorial museum of murdered European Mohammedans—in this respect we can still learn from the Germans. In their vocabulary, the word "Holocaust" has long been smoothly rephrased as "expired," as if it refers to expired cheeses or yoghurts.[37] We dealt with it, the Germans seem to be saying; the rest will be overgrown with grass, covered by snow. Soon we too will deal with the masses of immigrants. They will be overgrown with grass, covered by snow.

> However this war may end, we have won the war against you; none of you will be left to bear witness, but even if some of you survive, the world would not believe him.

There will perhaps be suspicions, discussions, research by historians, but there will be no certainties, because we will destroy the evidence together with you. And even if some proof should remain and some of you survive, people will say that the events you describe are too monstrous to be believed: they will say that they are the exaggerations of the Allied propaganda and will believe us, who will deny everything, and not you. We will be the ones to dictate the history of Lagers.[38]

Final Note

Agamben's books, which invariably arouse cognitive anxiety, cannot be passed unnoticed. They have their place on the pedestal of contemporary humanities, and there is no point in questioning that, just like there is no reason to revise the position of their author. His books diagnose—with great clarity—the degeneration of European reason, the phenomena that is so hard to define. At the same time, in his deliberations, Agamben flinches from adopting the theological-political perspective (his work on St. Paul only simulates the

---

37. The premature, collective amnesia of the Germans is backed by—even if against the author's intentions—virtually all of W. G. Sebald's books that contribute to the relativization of German responsibility for the Shoah. If human history is a chain of catastrophic events, history from 70 years ago is only one of its many links.
38. This imaginary statement by an SS officer opens Primo Levi's *The Drowned and the Saved*, trans. Raymond Rosenthal (New York: Simon & Schuster Paperbacks, 1988), 1.

problem). Rightly so or not? He himself admits that his relationship with theology is somewhat harsh. It is similar to that between blotting paper and ink. The blotting paper absorbs the ink so aggressively that was up to it; it would drink the ink to the last drop. "Same with theology. I absorbed it, but in such a way that theology is gone. All its ink has soaked in me."[39] This chapter is therefore not a correction of Agamben's position. Rather, it is an attempt to drive Agamben's political philosophy back toward the inexhaustible source of theology.

---

39. Agamben, *Der Papst ist ein weltlicher Priester*, 58.

Chapter 14

THE REMAINDER OF CHRISTIANITY (VASILY ROZANOV, GIORGIO AGAMBEN, MARTIN HEIDEGGER)

Religion, there, in the grave—well, that's obvious; here, where escape from the grave begins—through children, through giving birth—there is only sin and a wallowing through the ocean of "Satanic miasma." Satan—life. God—death.[1]

The Empty Promise

I call to You through the darkness of the ages,
I tell You, O Creator,
That we are deceived, that we weep, like children,
As we search: where is our Father?[2]

Why do we ever talk about God? Why do we want to listen about Him so eagerly and in amazement? Because it is impossible to stay silent about God, it is impossible to abstract from the elementary human relations with what remains hidden, what is obscured by darkness and oblivion. Why do we call that which is hidden and forgotten God? I do not know. You can try some other way.

Two thousand years have passed since God's death on the Cross, and the promises He made have remained unfulfilled. Considered from this perspective, whether eventually they will be fulfilled today, the day after tomorrow, in a week's time or in the next two thousand years' time is clearly irrelevant. For two millennia, people have waited for those promises to be fulfilled, and they died disappointed.

---

1. Vasily Rozanov, *Metafizika Khristianstva* [Metaphysics of Christianity] (Moscow: AST, 2000), 71.
2. Konstantin Balmont, "Zachem?" [Why?]. https://slova.org.ru/balmont/zachemgospod/. Trans. Renata Senktas.

We seem to know why Job waited for God—he wished for solace and deliverance from the earthly oppression. But why are we waiting for God? Why are we not satisfied with secular consolation, this tremendous amount of goods that we are supplied with? Because we are convinced, as was Job, that no matter what affluence we enjoy, the suffering that we experience exceeds our sins. If we wait for God, then, it is primarily because we expect him to be righteous, to settle the score. God's promises concern the *flesh*; they concern *this* earth, which is why man expects their immediate fulfillment. For the body is related to the present moment, not to the future. The future of the body lies in its old age and death; it is impossible not to know it. The body neither wants to wait, nor it can wait—it needs God, with His consolation, *hic et nunc*, without delay, right now.

In the world today, no one mocks God, and no one beats Him either. He is simply not talked about; we are simply incapable of taking the content of the Scriptures seriously. Christians, like gay people and transvestites, are an unpopular minority (and I do not mean those Sunday troglodytes who massively populate little village churches while also filling them with vapors of the spirits). "It is, of course, the defeat of the faithful, the defeat of faith, but above all, it is the defeat of God who reveals Himself in the pages of the Bible as that who gives life and saves. The failure of salvation is the failure of God Himself."[3] If the man of today turns to new gods—those suggested to him by popular culture—if he advocates a separate "system of values," then it is not only his fault; the same amount of "fault" may be ascribed to God. In any case, unable to understand the reasons for God's delayed second coming, we have all become victims of His omission. Something went wrong. Perhaps we are dealing with a God who is weak, a powerless God, one who lacked the strength to return. Is it a good God? If so, then it is not a comprehensible God (though the Scriptures say that He is). If He is good and comprehensible, then He is not omnipotent. And if He is good and omnipotent, then He is unintelligible. Meanwhile, "a completely hidden God is not an acceptable concept by Jewish norms. But he would have to be precisely that if together with being good he were conceived as all powerful."[4] Omnipotence along with justice ("vengeance is mine, I will repay") are not God's attributes. Quite the contrary, success, and hence a certain degree of power, is shared in by those who have turned their back on Him. Whereas God himself is a weak God, a God who deserves help.

---

3. Sergio Quinzio, *La sconfitta di Dio*, translated from the Polish edition: *Przegrana Boga* (Kraków: Homini, 2008), 41.
4. Hans Jonas, "The Concept of God after Auschwitz: A Jewish Voice," *Journal of Religion* 67, no. 1 (January 1987): 9.

The Specter of God

> If your voice were heard clearly even for a moment,
> I would have been happy in the brightness of the day,
> But life, love and death—all are terrifying, obscure,
> All are inescapable for me.[5]

Hans Jonas, a philosopher who combines Kabbalistic Jewish thought with Schelling's philosophy, puts it very clearly: God set out on a journey. He embarked on an adventure that was extremely uncertain, risky and dangerous, for both Himself and His creation, the adventure of becoming in time and space. He took to the road to reveal Himself to Himself, as if to regain Himself at the end of the development of His divine nature. Therefore, in a sense, God's nature is historical, but not as Hegel wanted it. For Hegel, the actions of the Absolute must be "cunning," strictly rational, "planned," whereas what we are left with is the trouble of discovering them. The God that Jonas reflects on is a mysterious God, coming from the abyss of undifferentiation. He is a God of chaos and incoherence to whom Schelling refers when he writes that "the forces of that [i.e., primeval] consuming fire still slumber in life, only pacified and, so to speak, exorcised by that *word* by which the one became the all."[6] On the other hand, for Quentin Meillassoux—a contemporary French philosopher of the so-called speculative realists circle—the "divine chaos" is becoming spectral. It is like a vision of the future that appears to present man. But what does it mean?

A specter is that which remains after a dead person who is unable to leave this world, usually of a person who died of terrible death or who came to an "untimely" end (these words are self-explanatory to the inhabitants of the Muranów neighborhood in Warsaw). "Essential spectres are the dead who will always refuse to 'pass over', who obstinately cast off their shroud to declare to the living, in spite of all evidence, that they still belong amongst them."[7] It turns out that it is not only the living who need help; it is also the dead, the remainder of those who refuse to leave. But how to excuse a God, asks Meillassoux, who let "terrible deaths" take place, thus taking away eternal peace from those who died them? What does mercy mean to Him? What is the requirement of martyrdom or the testimony of faith? Who is that God that acknowledges his own existence through human suffering? "You say that in

---

5. Balmont, "Zachem?"
6. Friedrich Wilhelm Joseph Schelling, *The Ages of the World*, trans. Jason M. Wirth (Albany: State University of New York Press, 2000), 49.
7. Quentin Meillassoux, "Spectral Dilemma," trans. Robin Mackay, *Collapse* IV (December 2012): 262.

the dazzling presence of such a God, I will grasp the infinitely loving nature of his attitude to his creatures?"[8] Similar dilemmas and questions constitute the aporia that Meillassoux refers to as "the spectral dilemma." Therefore, those who died an odious death have a chance to erase that stigma only through the act of raising from the dead, which is still unattainable, though. Those who consider this kind of discourse to be trickery need to be reminded that, whether we like it or not, we are all bound by the fundamental imperative of St. Luke's Gospel, proclaiming that we owe our fathers life and that we should do our best to infuse life back into them, to give back what we acquired from our ancestors, and shift the center of our commitment to the cemetery. Here I am posing the questions of resurrection and miracle, which I would rather not reduce to the statistical-psychological dimension (what to do with a hundred billion newly resurrected zombies?). However, this intuition, which relates back to Fedorov, would have to be complemented—to follow Meillassoux— with an atheistic thought about the nonexistence of God who otherwise would have to allow also a terrible death in his economy of salvation. Such a God should be refused existence. Therefore, if God is possible, then it is only "in an objective future sense (where I maintain that God could really come about in the future). At stake is the unknotting of the atheo-religious link between God and necessity (God must or must not exist) and its reattachment to the virtual (God could exist)."[9]

The God who emerges from the future is not a present God. More precisely, throughout the human time he is an *absent* God. In order to *create* such God, to arrange his coming, one would need science, technology, power. This is why we are trying to take matters into our own hands and to slightly prompt the "messianic" "parousia" (hence the Large Hadron Collider, technobiology, Fedorov's lightning rod aerostat and other interesting inventions). However, strength, power, *kraft* belong not to man but to the devil. Therefore, man does not so much create God, but favors (or not, as he may be not in the least concerned) the divine emergence. All he can do about it is to be even more vigilant, for example, to stand at the gate through which the Messiah is to enter the world.[10] But today none of us is attentive or patient enough to devote even a second of our precious time to the divine epiphany. Thus, the Absolute can reveal itself by some miracle, by chance, as something *ex definitione* uncontrolled. This is hard to imagine, since our daily experience teaches us only about what was and what is. It does not—and if it does, it is only to a limited

---

8. Ibid., 265.
9. Ibid., 269.
10. Walter Benjamin, "Theses on the Philosophy of History," in *Illuminations*, trans. Harry Zohn (New York: Schocken Books, 1968), 264.

extent—influence our recognition of the future. The God we know from Meillassoux's work as one coming from the future will come from the direction of chaos and within it. Such a God will destroy all permanence, all law. His name is not therefore "I am that I am." It needs to be read according to the rules of Hebrew grammar as "I will be what I will be." "From this point on, God must be thought as the *contingent*, but eternally possible, *effect of a Chaos unsubordinated to any law.*"[11]

The premonition that God, like death, emerges from the future is nothing new to Christian apocalypticists. Let us maybe put it this way: it is not God who is to come to us, but it is us who are to come to Him. His first name, then, would certainly be "death," which—to follow Schelling again—is a great affirmative force. For death is the withdrawing God, just like God in the *Book of Genesis* is the creating God. Therefore, the Parousia will be something terrifying for this world, because it will come as violence—radical violence. What is radical violence? Radical violence means death; it is the day of the Last Judgment. On the Judgement Day, the divinity of God, claims Schelling, is "the devouring ferocity of purity that a person is able to approach only with an equal purity. Since all Being goes up in it as if in flames, it is necessarily unapproachable to anyone still embroiled in Being,"[12] limited by the crust, that human clay that encases him. It is clear that the resurrection in the flesh can only take place in a *transfigured body*, that our empirical casing must be incinerated. A new body, a new earth, must be reborn from the ashes and, more precisely, from that which remains.

Ten Words

You are great, O Lord, but your world is unwelcoming,
Like all that is great, it is silent,
And for thousands of centuries, unheeded, unanswered,
My anguished cry resounds: Why? Why?[13]

In the six chapters of *The Time That Remains*,[14] Giorgio Agamben analyzes the first ten words of St. Paul's Epistle to the Romans, assigning one day of the week (a workday, excluding "Sunday," the Sabbath) to each word or a group of words.

---

11. Meillassoux, "Spectral Dilemma," 274.
12. Schelling, *The Ages of the World*, 25.
13. Balmont, "Zachem?"
14. Giorgio Agamben, *The Time That Remains: A Commentary on the Letter to the Romans*, trans. Patricia Dailey (Stanford: Stanford University Press, 2005).

When analyzing the phrase *Paulos doulos christos Iēsou* on Monday, Agamben wonders, inter alia, why Saulos ("grand") changes his regal name to Paulos ("small, insignificant, low-ranking"). In his opinion, replacing *sigma* with the letter *pi* should be perceived as an act of self-deprecation, humility, modesty. The same holds true of the second word in the phrase, *doulos* ("servant," "slave"). *Christos Iēsou*, on the other hand, does not mean a proper name, as we usually see it. Rather, it is descriptive of the figure who came into the world as the Messiah, the liberator of the enslaved, the belittled.

The Epistles of St. Paul were written in Greek by a member of the Judeo-Hellenic community where the Septuagint—the Old Testament translated into Greek—was used on a daily basis. It was strange Greek, peculiar, breaking the grammatical rules of Standard Greek, or—to be more precise—it was the language spoken by the minority who opposed the use of Hebrew in everyday life, because they considered it a holy language. In this sense, Paul's letters constitute a kind of pragmatic message; they remain part of his mission, and one should not read them otherwise.

On Tuesday, Agamben focuses his attention on the word κλητός (*klētos* "calling, being called"). God calls Paul on a mission, appoints him to accomplish a particular task, which is tantamount to cancelling any other calling. Whether you are an efficient bailiff, a beautiful woman or a gentleman, one day it just ceases to matter. And even if it still mattered, one would have to question the value of it and leave, abandon oneself. Because on Tuesday one dies to the old world in order to be reborn in a new life, as if outside the calendar. This is the birth of freedom from this world, and freedom toward God. If a Christian lives in this world, he or she must live in it briefly and by chance. "Because he is not anything in himself, man can only be if he acts *as if* he were different from what he is (or what he is not)."[15] Apart from the doctrinally existential interpretation, what can be also read from these lines is the ontological impotence of man who is nobody in a world characterized by ephemerality and impermanence. However, even when he finally abandons this world, he will continue being nobody, for he has just rejected everything and set off—"being called"—to seek himself and God. ("The messianic announcement means that these walls have come down, that a division no longer exists between men, or between men and God."[16])

Agamben speaks of ἀφωρισμένος ("separation") on Wednesday. It turns out that St. Paul was separated from the world in at least three ways. First of all, as I have already mentioned, it was due to the Greek speech used in

---

15. Ibid., 37.
16. Ibid., 44.

order not to profane the holy Hebrew, or, to put it another way, due to the "oral Torah" that was different from the "written law" dictated to Jews by God. Then, he was also separated from his worldly past and, more importantly, from the community of the chosen people, for he claimed that the resurrection was universal and not regional in its character, that is, not strictly Jewish. If it were to apply only to the Jews, it would contradict the teaching of Jesus—it would no longer carry a universal meaning. This raises a series of troublesome questions: who was elected after all? What is election about, and what does being elected oblige one to? Finally, how can one be sure of one's election, and is circumcision sufficient evidence and mark of it? "What is the exact relation between the supposed universality of the postevental truth (that is, what is inferred from Christ's resurrection) and the evental site, which is, indubitably, the nation bound together by the Old Testament?" asks the French philosopher Alain Badiou, and goes on to answer: "What Paul must be given exclusive credit for establishing is that the fidelity to such an event exists only through the termination of communitarian particularisms and the determination of a subject-of-truth who indistinguishes the One and the for-all."[17] The event of the resurrection does not have to lead to the universalism of some new fashion similar to, say, modern human rights. On the contrary, it is a principle that abolishes *all* distinctions.

By virtue of the resurrection, man is separated from all that "remains," a "remainder" that is not so much worth remembering as it cannot be forgotten. It is this "squandering that we bear within ourselves"[18] and that cannot be possibly spent. The effort of anamnesis—remembering the forgotten—thus leads to a specific form of memory that consists in bringing back the memory of the real life; not its content, but its meaning. Therefore, one should push aside all that constitutes the so-called content of life, except for the "remainder" that is unforgettable. "At the same time, the ἀναμένειν [waiting] is an obstinate waiting before God."[19] Only such a man is indestructible, then, who has forever retained the meaning of his deeds, stripped of their accidental worldly content, who did not renounce them, nor he concealed their meaning not only from himself but even from God. "But if man is that which may be *infinitely* destroyed, this also means that something other than this destruction, and within this destruction, remains, and that man is this remnant."[20]

---

17. Alain Badiou, *Saint Paul: The Foundation of Universalism*, trans. Ray Brassier (Stanford: Stanford University Press, 2003), 22, 108.
18. Agamben, *The Time That Remains*, 40.
19. Martin Heidegger, *The Phenomenology of Religious Life*, trans. Matthias Fritsch and Jennifer Anna Gosetti-Ferencei (Bloomington: Indiana University Press, 2004), 83.
20. Agamben, *The Time That Remains*, 53.

On Thursday, Agamben continues what was set down on Wednesday. He begins his reflections by describing the condition of the messenger (απόστολος). The messenger is certainly not a prophet, because he is not prophesying or announcing the coming of the Messiah. Rather, he informs the not-so-diligent observers of contemporary events that the Messiah, our Lord, has come. Prophesying is a kind of power that struggles with forces that go against prophecy. The apostolate is different. It is more of a physical toil, labor, effort to share the "good news" with others. Jesus Christ will not come to us, for He has already come, which is a message for the less perceptive. According to the Scripture, "time" will come to an end when the "remnant," namely, "not non-Jews," understand it, that is, all those who question or do not contemplate the messianism of Jesus the Messiah. For Παρουσία is by no means the Second Coming of the Person, His yet another *entre*. It is παράουσία, "being close to man," here and now and the hour of our death. Amen.

What does it mean?

Time can be understood in two ways. Its chronological understanding enables us to grasp the sequence of historical events. For example, we know that the Battle of Lenino was preceded by the great war with the Teutonic Knights, and that both of these events were preceded—to stick to the martial arts—by the bloody clashes of Roman gladiators at the Colosseum. Besides the chronological perception of the flow of time, there is also the kairotic experience. Καιρός, which is somehow placed within χρόνος, fills each of the succeeding moments—or at least it does so potentially—opening it to a timeless eternity. Καιρός is an "occasion," an "opportunity," a "now-time," a time to summarize, to gather all time and therefore the entire individual history in a single moment; it is the essence of the anamnesis and at the same time the moment of departing toward death, which—should it occur—is the one and only encounter with God, the Parousia proper, the Second Coming. This moment is, to use Agamben's phrase, "time within time," an examination of conscience that we eventually submit to both ourselves and God. It is the decisive moment when "we will have to settle our debts [...] first and foremost with the past. This obviously does not imply attachment or nostalgia; quite the opposite, for the recapitulation of the past is also a summary judgement pronounced on it."[21] One that cannot arrive at the meaning of one's own life dies "the second death," as we read in the Scripture. "For every image of the past that is not recognized by the present as one of its own concerns threatens to disappear irretrievably."[22] Thus, the messianic time, the time to settle debts with one's own life, is the time that—as it were—needs time to come to an

---

21. Ibid., 78.
22. Ibid., 141.

end, in which "all things are recapitulated in him."²³ This moment is for us a good occasion—one of a kind and it seems an unrepeatable one—to learn the meaning of the story we tell ourselves and God. Chronological time makes it difficult to reach the end thus understood, because it lasts—as we seem to believe—forever. It is only *kairos* that gathers an entire life in a brief moment, in a chance, a jump, a short flash. Or, to follow Kafka, in a sentence parable containing everything that is needed:

> My grandfather used to say: "Life is astoundingly short." To me, looking back over it, life seems so foreshortened that I scarcely understand, for instance, how a young man can decide to ride over to the next village without being afraid that—not to mention accidents—even the span of a normal happy life may fall short of the time needed for such a journey.²⁴

Friday is the most tragic day in Agamben's calendar. It introduces a state of emergency in which action is "deactivated." If the visible world ends, says Agamben, it does not end suddenly—the world, like individual human existence, dies out gradually. The "stop and crash" does not intrude the world through sudden action; quite the contrary, it comes nearer as a result of the world *growing weak*, as in the case of the builders of the Tower of Babel, who were suddenly deceived by the language of pragmatics, touched by the crisis of action. Let us go into details.

Δύναμις in Aristotle's language—and this is exactly the language Agamben uses on Friday—corresponds to the category of potentiality and power. Power becomes powerful, and potentiality is realized only when both are complemented by ἐνέργεια. This term in Greek means "the principle of actuality and operativity,"²⁵ while in the language of Christians it corresponds to faith, for it is faith that signifies the causative principle in Christianity, that which releases potentiality from itself. (Otherwise, the wine would remain wine, and not the blood of Christ.) Therefore, the "good news"—εὐαγγέλιον—draws its power from the faith of the one who preaches it—first from Paul's faith, then from the faith of the whole church. Everything that is born to the world is thus necessarily accompanied by faith. And vice versa—lack of faith deactivates the world inoperative, makes its movement futile. Apocalypse, the end of the world known to us, will come "on the legs of doves" (Nietzsche). The world will end without fireworks, running out of its time in a series of idle

---

23. Ibid., 75.
24. Franz Kafka, "The Next Village," in *Collected Stories*, trans. Willa and Edwin Muir (New York: Knopf, 1993), 182.
25. Agamben, *The Time That Remains*, 90.

behaviors—weakness, powerlessness, ineffectiveness. At the very end, it turns out that weakness turns into power—the power that paralyzes the power of the temporal world. Messianic δύναμις acts without acting; it does not impact the current order in a simplified, "Machiavellian" way; it does not destroy the law that is its warranty, but "overpowers" it, so that it cannot be executed. "The messianic is not the destruction but the deactivation of the law, rendering the law inexecutable."[26] This messianic suspension of law in favor of a "lawless exception" is what the declaration of a state of exception would mean at the end of time. Indeed, this is the indirect evidence of the Messiah's presence in this world—when what I do in my life has no more effect, when all that I tamper with ceases to make any sense. Therefore, on Saturday, the last day of Agamben's calendar, it is best to say one's prayers, if it is not the law but one faith that may help save the soul. We feel it with the fibers of our nerves. Except we do not really know whether we should believe in what Jesus believed, or whether we should believe in Jesus as a product and message of Christianity, which, of course, is not the same.

> How these two religions, the religion of Christ and the Christian religion, can exist in Christ in one and the same person, is inconceivable. [...] The former, the religion of Christ, is contained in the evangelists quite differently from the Christian religion. The religion of Christ is therein contained in the clearest and most lucid language. On the other hand, the Christian religion is so uncertain and ambiguous, that there is scarcely a single passage which, in the history of the world, has been interpreted in the same way by two men.[27]

There is one certain thing in all this confusion: the author of *The Epistle* to the Romans did not know the living Jesus, Jesus in the flesh and blood. He knew the risen Christ; therefore, he has nothing to tell about His life. He eulogizes the resurrection, another dimension of life that is at the very antipodes of human existence, as seen from the perspective of the "tyranny of values." He is an advocate of faith in the impossible, the weak, in what is laughable or deserves a brutal attack.

The Remainder of the Aroma

> Lord, O Lord, hear me, I weep, I yearn,
> I pray to you in the evening twilight.

---

26. Ibid., 98.
27. Ibid., 125.

Why did you give me a soul not of this earth—
Then bind me to the earth?[28]

"Does God exist?" "Does a human being have a soul?" "What day is supposed to be Doomsday?" "Do unbaptized babies really go straight to Hell?" These are the questions that all of us have asked at different stages of our lives (and especially in childhood). Today, however, I am struck by the ungodliness of such questions, in other words, by how much idolatry of fundamental questions they might carry, which is the risk inherent in any speculative theology or speculative reflection on God. For what is theology? Its essence is summarized in St. Anselm's saying: *credo ut intelligiam*, "I believe so that I may understand." Meanwhile, the theology that tries to understand ceases to be "theo"-logy, reflection on God, and becomes philosophy. Or, to refer to Martin Heidegger, it becomes onto-theology, reflection on the nature of being and its becoming. Therefore, a living faith must break away from theology thus understood; it must part with reason. The tendency to an exalted expression of oneself through singing and prayer lies in the essence of faith, for no one in his or her right mind will suddenly begin to pray or sing Lord; no reasonable person will ever believe in God. And so the question that interests me is not whether theology is possible but whether we need it to believe. Personally, I think we do not. While describing God's nature, theologians have no choice but to use human language and anthropomorphic images that—rather ineffectively—are meant to contradict the anthropomorphic idea of God. This leads nowhere. Faith does not even need the object of faith; faith is sufficient for itself.

However, a sensible person might inquire how to love someone who is said to have died (*Gott ist Tot*—Nietzsche)? How to love a dead God? There is a phenomenal scene in Vasily Rozanov's *Temnyi Lik* (Dark Countenance). Rozanov gazes from behind the pillar on a woman crying on the steps of the reliquary. As the woman walks away, Rozanov kneels down and kisses her tears. His behavior betrays traces of Russian exaggeration; however, Rozanov quickly disabuses us of a mistake. Indeed, he says, you cannot love God, but how not to love that crazy love for God that squeezes tears out of your eyes? Man praying is a holy man.

In happiness, writes Rozanov, man is a pagan, and in hardship a Christian. When we are affected by death, lameness, illness, failure, betrayal, our good Lord comes to mind—the source of life and joy. Now, I do not quite understand it: why does misfortune bring to mind a *good* God? God as a horseshoe hung over the door, a consolation, a happy pill? I cannot understand it fully.

---

28. Balmont, "Zachem?"

I believe Rozanov himself could not understand it either, if in the sad, "sublunary" Christ he saw the disturbing face of Antichrist.[29]

In the present days, the death of God has become a kind of philosophical banality. Meanwhile, *in truth*, God died. He died on Friday and his death is evidenced by relics. The relics are for those who believe in relics; for the rest, it is just sham. After a person's death, "soul" departs, and reason "separates" from him or her, most often in the form of the artifacts it has left behind. What is left is a corpse, a dead, decaying body. Yorick's skull. The existence of relics shatters that gloomy picture. Relics are the trace of Christ in the tomb; they are *news from the next world*. They communicate with us through their aroma. Let me quote from Rozanov:

> Is there a soul in them [i.e., in the relics]? No one claims that. And life? Even fewer seem to be sure. So what is in them? Memory, remnant. No one doubts that the relics are actually flesh, corporeal remnant, without any *soul or spirituality*: *the lifeless* remainder is holy. This is what "holiness" means—to die. [...] To die—it means to attain holiness.[30]

So death is holy. To die is to achieve holiness, to cross the threshold. Seen from the perspective of one's attachment to life, death is evil; from the perspective of faith, death is a transition to a holy state. Now, what does theology have to do with this? Theological or philosophical concepts seem to die out. What remains is the night, pitch-dark.

Coda

Describing the conditions of religious experience in his commentary on *The Epistle to the Galatians*, Martin Heidegger first of all distinguishes between the "I" and the "not-I," whose duality and internal interweaving are a constitutive feature of consciousness—in this case, the religious consciousness of Paul the Apostle. He maintains that one should first reflect the specific character of this universal pronoun, to show the "I" in its complexity and multilayeredness— the "I" that *is* (exists) just as much as it *has* the "not-I." This means that the "I" not only exists but also has something that certainly does not belong to it, yet is contained in it (something like a spoon in a soup is not soup). On the other

---

29. I devoted more space to this issue in *Ontologia sukcesu: Esej przy filozofii Alexandre'a Kojève'a* [Ontology of Success: An Essay on the Philosophy of Alexandre Kojève] (Gdańsk: słowo/obraz terytoria, 2006).
30. Rozanov, *Metafizika Khristianstva*, 71. For more on the sacred remnant ("relics"), see the last chapter of an excellent book by Glenn W. Most, *Doubting Thomas* (Cambridge: Harvard University Press, 2005).

hand, the "not-I" is only *in itself* and has nothing that could belong to it. The "I" is therefore always involved in the "situation" (which it *has*); it observes everything from a strictly defined perspective (which is *its* own perspective). In this sense, "the relation of the people before Paul to him is how *he* has them."[31] Let us now talk about who Satan is to Paul? Does he also "have" him, just like he "has" other people? In the Old Testament the word means "enemy" or "adversary in a war," one who fights that which God wants. Speculations over the *existence* of Satan are then completely empty—he "is" wherever the realization of God's Work faces obstacles. Therefore, one should not ask whether Satan, Antichrist, the devil and all the devilish temptations exist or not, but to what extent all of us "have" them, how the Apostle "has" them. I "have" the devil in me, as everyone else "has" him, who has not yet settled one's relations with the world; as the Apostle "had" him, for whom the empirical existence was a source of anxiety, spurred by a restless inner element. Therefore, Antichrist-enemy-Satan is not one's hallucination or figment, nor is it one's *hysterica passio*. Certainly, he is not anyone in particular; he is not some personal being. "Antichrist"—and quotation marks are crucial here—is our own situation in the context of the *Homo sapiens* species commonly turned into bestiality. Everyone keeps him inside, allowing for further loosening of the human form, for making bestial the only world we have. "Antichrist," then, is no stranger; it is ourselves in the state of fundamental instability. It is the situation that we find ourselves in and consent to. People who are not religiously inclined might easily call it "Leviathan," but for Christians it will be the reality of "Antichrist." It is not that "Antichrist" "is"; it is that one "has" him and carries him around, like a splinter in one's finger, or a piece of broken glass that irritates a nonhealing, infected sore. It is a shadow that eludes language, or the reverse; thanks to that language, it becomes a description of the trivial, brutish reality of the "last men." Let me just remind you that this is exactly how Ivan Karamazov is "caught" by the "devil" who suddenly gets into his eye. There is something that starts bothering him—or is it just a blade of grass? The problem is that he "has nothing" stuck in his eye, nothing visible at least, and yet there is something in it that cannot be removed in any way.

"Not mystical absorption and special exertion," Heidegger goes on to say, "rather withstanding the weakness of life is decisive. Life for Paul is not a mere flow of events; it *is* only insofar as he *has* it."[32] Life makes sense only as much as one is able to absorb all that is radically alien, not mine. And thus also (or above all) God. The Parousia—or Apocalypse, as these two names signify the same event—depends on myself, on the situation I found myself in; "the question of

---

31. Heidegger, *The Phenomenology of Religious Life*, 65.
32. Ibid., 70.

the When leads back to my comportment."³³ Those who remain deaf to the thought of the Parousia—Apocalypse—have "not" ever "had" themselves and will never "have." At the most they "are" or have already "been." And "the ruin hits them in such a way that they cannot flee from it. They cannot save themselves, because they do not have themselves, because they have forgotten their own self, because they do not have themselves in the clarity of authentic knowledge. Thus they cannot grab hold of and save themselves."³⁴ It turns out that the coming of God can be overlooked—one might oversleep or just miss it, just like one might oversleep or miss one's own salvation, for both depend to some extent on us, that is, more on the situation in which we find ourselves than on a particularly quick perception. The Parousia, just like Apocalypse, is one of the dimensions of human life (yet the most basic and important one) and "depends upon how I live."³⁵ Then Heidegger adds: "Whether one is a true Christian is decided by that fact that one recognizes the Antichrist. [...] With the arrival of the Antichrist, each must decide."³⁶ Ἀπολλύμενοι, and so "the rejected" by God, or those "in the state of becoming rejected," because "the *participium praesentis* instead of *participium perfecti* emphasizes the enactment that is still in process," are unable to embrace the horror of their own situation, namely, the fact that they risk "*absolute annihilation.*"³⁷ St. Paul the Apostle does not speak of damnation and tortures of hell—this is a much later "interpolation." He clearly states the danger of annihilation, the danger of nothingness, when "all who stand outside the Christian context of becoming are without guidance as to the question of the dead."³⁸ For "the rejected," whom Nietzsche calls "the last men," the day of the Lord will come suddenly, "as a thief in the night." It will come as a thief because it will bring them ruin. Those who have settled down comfortably in this world and do not want to lose anything will consider the meeting with God as a scandal, an unlawful interference in their private lives. "For the wise the day does not come (like the thief in the night)—not suddenly and inescapably."³⁹ To those who live in permanent grief, in their "misery," meeting with God shall bring true liberation and expected relief. For all, however, both "the rejected" and "he called", the Parousia will come as the Apocalypse, as death, since God reveals Himself only there, where man perishes—this is the essence of Christ's death and

---

33. Ibid., 73.
34. Ibid., 72.
35. Ibid., 75.
36. Ibid., 78.
37. Ibid., 80.
38. Ibid., 81.
39. Ibid., 107.

Resurrection. If "death [...] is an immediate transition to community with Christ,"[40] then the Parousia must inevitably be associated with it. There was no thought back in those days that would break into people's everyday world more boldly, turning their beliefs upside down.

The question remains: how to know the "deception of the Antichrist." *Sola fide*, by believing. But not believing in "him" (that he *is* the Antichrist), but through faith in Christ and His Resurrection. Only such faith will enable us to acknowledge our own defeat against the background of the world around us, the world of "successful people", will make us experience chaos and misery—"the greatest misery." But faith alone will not suffice. It needs to be complemented with a separate decision, for you can believe in anything, but not in everything you *want* to believe. Hence, it is only *decision* that will allow us to believe in a situation that is totally absurd: "that through faith, the deception of the Antichrist will be recognized as deception."[41]

Christianity constitutes the only religion in which is inscribed the inevitability of a historic, *worldly* defeat. For two thousand years, Christianity governed the material side of human life through institutions, with the Pope being also Caesar. Today, the visible Church has gone bankrupt—it has not survived its own death, nor has it survived the death of God. It speaks through the voices of contemporary apocalypticists, such as Rozanov, Schmitt, Heidegger, Kojève, Quinzio, Meillassoux or Agamben, prophesying the end of the world that is basically impossible to live in any longer, in which nothing works as it should. Apocalypse, the end of human time, is the end of human history, the end of man's faith and freedom. Because freedom makes sense only in a situation of choice. Where choice is made impossible, any action undertaken in order to overcome this unbearable situation becomes paralyzed—it ceases to be an action; it deactivates itself. Lack of faith only exacerbates the state of collective apathy; it reduces human spirituality to a flat clockface on which the evil spirit of history indicates the noon, the time of madmen after they have lost God.[42] What is left is a "remainder," a "memento," relics, their salutary aroma—expression of the last grace.

---

40. Ibid., 106.
41. Ibid., 82.
42. See also Friedrich Nietzsche, *The Gay Science* (aphorism no. 125), trans. Josefine Nauckhoff (Cambridge: Cambridge University Press, 2001), 119–20.

BIBLIOGRAPHY

Acosta, Uriel. *A Specimen of a Human Life*. New York: Bergman, 1967.
Adorno, Theodor W. "Late Capitalism or Industrial Society?" In *Modern German Sociology*, edited by V. Meja, D. Misgeld and N. Stehr. New York: Columbia University Press, 1987.
Agamben, Giorgio. "Bartleby, or On Contingency." In *Potentialities. Collected Essays on Philosophy*. Trans. Daniel Heller-Roazen. Stanford: Stanford University Press, 1999.
Agamben, Giorgio. "Kapitalizm jest religią, w której nic nie należy do ludzi" [Capitalism Is a Religion in Which Nothing Belongs to People]. Interview by Maciej Nowicki. *Europa* 11, a supplement to *Dziennik* (March 15, 2008).
Agamben, Giorgio. "Der Papst ist ein weltlicher Priester." Interview by Abu Bakr Rieger. *Literaturen*, no. 6 (2005).
Agamben, Giorgio. *Homo Sacer. Sovereign Power and Bare Life*. Trans. Daniel Heller-Roazen. Stanford: Stanford University Press, 1998.
Agamben, Giorgio. *The Time That Remains: A Commentary on the Letter to the Romans*. Trans. Patricia Dailey. Stanford: Stanford University Press, 2005.
Agamben, Giorgio. "We Refugees." Trans. M. Rocke. *Symposium* 49, no. 2 (1995).
Aleichem, Sholem. *Tevye the Dairyman and Motl the Cantor's Son*. Trans. Aliza Shevrin. London: Penguin, 2009.
Améry, Jean. *At the Mind's Limits: Contemplations by a Survivor of Auschwitz and Its Realities*. Trans. Sidney and Stella P. Rosenfeld. Bloomington: Indiana University Press, 1980.
Améry, Jean. *On Aging: Revolt and Resignation*. Trans. John D. Barlow. Bloomington: Indiana University Press, 1994.
Apokryfy Nowego Testamentu: Ewangelie apokryficzne [The Apocrypha of the New Testament. Apocryphal Gospels], vol. 1. Ed. Marek Starowieyski. Kraków: Wydawnictwo WAM, 2003.
Arendt, Hannah. *The Jewish Writings*. New York: Schocken Books, 2007.
Arendt, Hannah. *On Revolution*. London: Penguin Books, 1990.
Arendt, Hannah. *The Origins of Totalitarianism*. New York: Harcourt Brace Jovanovich, 1973.
Arendt, Hannah. *Wykłady o filozofii politycznej Kanta*. Trans. Rafał Kuczyński and Marcin Moskalewicz. Warszawa: Fundacja Augusta hr. Cieszkowskiego, 2012.
Atwood, Margaret. "Introduction." In *The Cambridge Guide to Literature in English*, edited by Ian Ousby. Cambridge: Cambridge University Press, 1988.
Auden, W. H. *The Dyer's Hand and Other Essays*. London: Faber and Faber, 1963.
Auden, W. H. "Spain." In *Selected Poems*. New York: Vintage, 2007.
Auden, W. H. "Two Sides to a Thorny Problem. Exploring below Surface of Shakespeare's 'Merchant.'" In *Prose (1949–1955)*, vol. III. Ed. Edward Mendelson. London: Faber and Faber, 2008.
Babich, Babette. "Ad Jacob Taubes." *New Nietzsche Studies*, nos. 3–4 (2008).

Baczyński, Krzysztof Kamil. *White Magic and Other Poems*. Trans. Bill Johnston. Los Angeles, CA: Green Integer, 2006.
Badiou, Alain. *Saint Paul: The Foundation of Universalism*. Trans. Ray Brassier. Stanford: Stanford University Press, 2003.
Balmont, Konstantin. "Zachem?" [Why?]. https://slova.org.ru/balmont/zachemgospod/.
Bauman, Zygmunt. *Modernity and the Holocaust*. Cambridge, MA: Polity Press, 2008.
Benjamin, Walter. "Theses on the Philosophy of History" (also known as "On the Concept of History"). In *Illuminations*. Trans. Harry Zohn. New York: Schocken Books, 1968.
Benn, Gottfried. "The Doctor." In *Selected Poems and Prose*. Trans. David Paisey. Manchester: Carcanet Press, 2013.
Besançon, Alain. *A Century of Horrors: Communism, Nazism, and the Uniqueness of the Shoah*. Trans. Ralph C. Hancock and Nathaniel H. Hancock. Wilmington: ISI Books, 2007.
Bloom, Allan, and Harry V. Jaffa. *Shakespeare's Politics*. New York: Basic Books, 1964.
Brzękowski, Jan. *Science Fiction*. Londyn: Oficyna Poetów i Malarzy, 1964.
Buber, Martin. *Two Types of Faith*. Trans. Norman P. Goldhawk. Syracuse: Syracuse University Press, 2003.
Burgess, Anthony. *Flame into Being: The Life and Work of D. H. Lawrence*. New York: Arbor House, 1985.
Cavafy, C. P. "One of Their Gods." In *Collected Poems*. Trans. Edmund Keeley and Philip Sherrard. Princeton: Princeton University Press, 1992.
Céline, Louis-Ferdinand. *Journey to the End of the Night*. Trans. Ralph Manheim. New York: New Directions, 2006.
Cioran, Emil. *The Temptation to Exist*. Trans. Richard Howard. New York: Arcade, 2012.
The Complete Works of D. H. Lawrence. Parts Edition. Delphi Classics, 2015, e-book.
Czerwiński, Marcin. "Krzysztof." In *Żołnierz, poeta, czasu kurz... Wspomnienia o K.K. Baczyńskim* [Soldier, Poet, the Dust of Time... Memories of K. K. Baczyński], edited by Zenon Wasilewski. Kraków: Wydawnictwo Literackie, 1979.
Danto, Arthur C. *Nietzsche as Philosopher*. New York: Simon & Shuster, 1965.
Deleuze, Gilles. "Nietzsche and St. Paul, Lawrence and John of Patmos." In *Essays Critical and Clinical*. Trans. Daniel W. Smith and Michael A. Greco. London: Verso, 1998.
Deleuze, Gilles, and Felix Guattari. *What Is Philosophy?* Trans. Hugh Tomlison and Graham Burchell. New York: Columbia University Press, 1994.
Descartes, René. "Meditations on First Philosophy." Trans. Elizabeth S. Haldane. In *The Philosophical Works of Descartes*. Cambridge: Cambridge University Press, 1911.
Deutch, Babette. "To Survive Is to Sing." *Book Review* (May 9, 1965).
Döblin, Alfred. *Journey to Poland*. Trans. Joachim Neugroschel. New York: Paragon House, 1991.
Donne, John. "Devotions upon Emergent Occasions" (XVII. Meditation). In *The Works of John Donne*. London: John W. Parker, 1839.
Dowley, Tim (ed.). *Introduction to the History of Christianity*. Minneapolis, MN: Fortress Press, 2013, e-book.
Epictetus. *The Works of Epictetus: Consisting of His Discourses, in Four Books, the Enchiridion, and Fragments*. Trans. Thomas Wentworth Higginson. Boston: Little, Brown, 1865.
Franklin, Ruth. *A Thousand Darknesses: Lies and Truth in Holocaust Fiction*. Oxford: Oxford University Press, 2010.
Freud, Sigmund. "Negation." In *The Standard Edition of the Complete Psychological Works of Sigmund Freud, Volume XIX (1923–25): The Ego and the Id and Other Works*. London: Hogarth Press, 1964.

Freud, Sigmund. "New Introductory Lectures on Psycho-Analysis." In *The Standard Edition of the Complete Psychological Works of Sigmund Freud, Volume XXII (1932–36): New Introductory Lectures on Psycho-Analysis and Other Works*. London: Hogarth Press, 1964.
Fučík, Julius. *V zemi, kde zítra již znamená včera*. Praha: Karel Borecký, 1932.
Giedroyc, Jerzy, and Czesław Miłosz. *Listy 1964–1972* [Letters]. Ed. Marek Kornat. Warszawa: Czytelnik, 2011.
Girard, René. *Things Hidden since the Foundation of the World*. Trans. Stephen Bann and Michael Metteer. London: Continuum, 2003.
Girard, René. *A Theatre of Envy: William Shakespeare*. New York: Oxford University Press, 1991.
Girard, René, with Pierpaolo Antonello and João Cezar de Castro Rocha. *Evolution and Conversion: Dialogues on the Origins of Culture*. London: Bloomsbury, 2017.
Gogol, Nikolai. *Dead Souls*. Trans. D. J. Hogarth. Mineola, NY: Dover, 2003.
Gold, J. R. "Jacob Taubes: 'Apocalypse from Below.'" *Telos* 134 (2006).
Gombrowicz, Witold. *Bacacay*. Trans. Bill Johnston. New York: Archipelago Books, 2004, e-book.
Gombrowicz, Witold. *Diary*. Trans. Lillian Vallee. New Haven, CT: Yale University Press, 2012.
Gorecki, J. [real name Aleksander Kamiński]. *Stones for the Rampart: The Story of Two Lads in the Polish Underground Movement*. London: Polish Boy Scouts' and Girl Guides' Association, 1945.
Hage, Volker. *Zeugen der Zerstörung: Die Literaten und der Luftkrieg. Essays und Gespräche*. Frankfurt am Main: S. Fischer, 2003.
Heidegger, Martin. *Being and Time*. Trans. Joan Stambaugh. Albany: State University of New York Press, 1996.
Heidegger, Martin. *Nietzsche*, vol. II. Trans. David Farrell Krell. San Francisco, CA: Harper & Row, 1982.
Heidegger, Martin. *The Phenomenology of Religious Life*. Trans. Matthias Fritsch and Jennifer Anna Gosetti-Ferencei. Bloomington: Indiana University Press, 2004.
Heine, Heinrich. *O Polsce* [On Poland]. In *Dzieła wybrane: Utwory prozą* [Collected Prose Works]. Warszawa: Państwowy Instytut Wydawniczy, 1956.
Hobbes, Thomas. *Leviathan*. Ed. Marshall Missner. New York: Routledge, 2016, e-book.
The Holy Bible: Containing the Old and New Testaments. Oxford: Oxford University Press, 1901.
Horkheimer, Max, and Theodor W. Adorno. *Dialectic of Enlightenment: Philosophical Fragments*. Trans. Edmund Jephcott. Bloomington, IN: Stanford University Press, 2002.
Hortmann, Wilhelm. *Shakespeare on the German Stage: the Twentieth Century*. Cambridge: Cambridge University Press, 1988.
Iwaszkiewicz, Jarosław. "A śpieszył się z pisaniem…" [And He Hurried Writing…]. In *Żołnierz, poeta, czasu kurz… Wspomnienia o K.K. Baczyńskim* [Soldier, Poet, the Dust of Time… Memories of K. K. Baczyński), edited by Zenon Wasilewski. Kraków: Wydawnictwo Literackie, 1979.
Jankélévitch, Vladimir. *To, co nieuchronne*. Trans. Mateusz Kwaterko. Warszawa: Państwowy Instytut Wydawniczy, 2005.
Januszewski, Tadeusz (ed.). *Rozmowy z Tuwimem* [Conversations with Tuwim]. Warszawa: Wydawnictwo Naukowe Semper, 1994.
Jaspers, Karl. *Nietzsche and Christianity*. Trans. E. B. Ashton. Chicago: Henry Regnery, 1961.
Johnson, Paul. *A History of Christianity*. New York: Touchstone, 2014, e-book.

Jonas, Hans. "The Concept of God after Auschwitz: A Jewish Voice." *Journal of Religion* 67, no. 1 (January 1987).
Kafka, Franz. *The Blue Octavo Notebooks*. Trans. Ernst Kaiser and Eithne Wilkins. Cambridge, MA: Exact Change, 1991.
Kafka, Franz. "The Next Village." In *Collected Stories*. Trans. Willa and Edwin Muir. New York: Knopf, 1993.
Kamieńska, Anna. "Ostatnie wcielenie 'Króla Ducha.' " In *Od Leśmiana: Najpiękniejsze wiersze polskie* [From Leśmian: The Most Beautiful Polish Poems]. Warszawa: Iskry, 1974.
Kant, Immanuel. *Critique of Pure Reason*. Trans. J. M. D. Meiklejohn. London: Henry G. Bohn, 1855.
Kant, Immanuel. *Grounding for the Metaphysics of Morals: On a Supposed Right to Lie because of Philanthropic Concerns*. Trans. James W. Ellington. Indianapolis: Hackett, 1993.
Keble, J. "Sun of My Soul." *Hymns to the Living God*, no. 329 (1820), https://hymnary.org/text/sun_of_my_soul_thou_savior.
Keener, Craig S. *Komentarz historyczno-kulturowy do Nowego Testamentu*. Trans. into Polish by Zbigniew Kościuk. Warszawa: Vocatio, 2000.
Kmita-Piorunowa, Aniela. "Zaczęło się od *Listu do Jana Bugaja*." In *Kazimierz Wyka*, edited by Henryk Markiewicz and Andrzej Fiut. Kraków, 1978.
Kołakowski, Leszek. *Czas ciekawy, czas niespokojny. Część I*. Interview by Zbigniew Mentzel. Kraków: Znak, 2007.
Kołakowski, Leszek. "Klęska i kariera Uriela da Costy" [The Defeat and Career of Uriel da Costa]. In *Wizerunek własny żywota* [Exemplar Humanae Vitae], edited by Uriel Acosta. Warszawa: Państwowy Instytut Wydawniczy, 1960.
Kołakowski, Leszek. *Tales from the Kingdom of Lailonia and the Key to Heaven*. Trans. Salvator Attanasio. Chicago: University of Chicago Press, 1989.
König, Franz, and Ernst Ludwig Ehrlich. *Żydzi i chrześcijanie jedną mają przyszłość* [Jews and Christians Share One Future]. Interview by Bernhard Moosbrugger. Trans. Dominika Motak. Kraków: Wydawnictwo Znak, 2001.
Kundera, Milan. *The Curtain: An Essay in Seven Parts*. Trans. Linda Asher. New York: Harper Perennial, 2008, e-book.
Larkin, Philip. "Annus Mirabilis." In *Collected Poems*. London: Marvell Press & Faber and Faber, 1990.
Lawrence, D. H. "And Oh—That the Man I Am Might Cease to Be." In *The Complete Poems of D. H. Lawrence*. Ware: Wordsworth Editions, 2002.
Lawrence, D. H. *Apocalypse*. Hamburg: Albatross, 1932.
Lawrence, D. H. "Introduction." In *Apocalypse and the Writings on Revelation*, edited by Mara Kalnins. Cambridge: Cambridge University Press, 2002.
Lawrence, D. H. "Introduction to *The Dragon of the Apocalypse* by Frederick Carter." In *Apocalypse: And the Writings on Revelation*. Cambridge: Cambridge University Press, 1980, e-book.
Lawrence, D. H. *Introductions and Reviews*. Ed. N. H. Reeve and J. Worthen. Cambridge: Cambridge University Press, 2005.
Lawrence, D. H. *Lady Chatterley's Lover*. Cambridge: Cambridge University Press, 2002.
Lawrence, D. H. *The Letters of D. H. Lawrence*. Ed. Aldous Huxley. New York: Viking Press, 1932.
Lawrence, D. H. *The Selected Letters of D. H. Lawrence*. Ed. James T. Boulton. Cambridge: Cambridge University Press, 1997.

Lear, Jonathan. *Radical Hope: Ethics in the Face of Cultural Devastation*. Cambridge: Harvard University Press, 2006.

Lebovic, Nitzan. "The Jerusalem School: The Theopolitical Hour." *New German Critique* 105, no. 3 (2008).

Leśmian, Bolesław. "Rok nieistnienia" [The Year of Nonexistence]. In *Poezje zebrane*. Toruń: Algo, 1995.

Letters: Summer 1926: Pasternak, Tsvetayeva, Rilke. Trans. Margaret Wettlin and Walter Arndt. San Diego, CA: Harcourt Brace Jovanovich, 1985.

The Letters of Jacob Burckhardt. Trans. Alexander Dru. London: Routledge & Kegan Paul, 1955.

Levi, Primo. *The Drowned and the Saved*. Trans. Raymond Rosenthal. New York: Simon & Schuster Paperbacks, 1988.

Levi, Primo. *If This Is a Man: The Truce*. Trans. S. Woolf. London: Abacus, 2013, e-book.

Levinas, Emmanuel. *Time and the Other*. Trans. Richard A. Cohen. Pittsburgh, PA: Duquesne University Press, 1987.

Liiceanu, Gabriel. *The Păltiniş Diary: A Paideic Model in Humanist Culture*. Trans. James Christian Brown. Budapest: Central European University Press, 1999.

Longfellow, H. W. "The Spanish Jew's Tale. The Legend of Rabbi Ben Levi." In *The Poetical Works of Longfellow*. London: Henry Frowde, 1906.

Lustiger, Jean-Marie. *The Promise*. Trans. Rebecca Howell Balinski, Msgr. Richard Malone and Jean Duchesne. Grand Rapids: William B. Eerdmans, 2007.

Mackiewicz, Józef. *Fakty i ludzie* [Facts and People]. Warszawa: Oficyna Liberałów, 1988.

Mackiewicz, Józef. *Fakty, przyroda i ludzie* [Facts, Nature and People]. Londyn: Kontra, 1984.

Marcuse, Herbert. "The New Forms of Control." In *One-Dimensional Man*. Boston: Beacon Press, 1964.

Meillassoux, Quentin. "Spectral Dilemma." Trans. Robin Mackay. *Collapse* IV (December 2012).

Michalski, Krzysztof. *The Flame of Eternity: An Interpretation of Nietzsche's Thought*. Trans. Benjamin Paloff. Princeton: Princeton University Press, 2012.

Michalski, Krzysztof. "Płomień Nietzschego" [The Flame of Nietzsche]. Interview by Paweł Dybel. *Nowe Książki*, no. 5 (2007).

Miłosz, Czesław. "Against Incomprehensible Poetry." In *To Begin Where I Am: Selected Essays*. Trans. Bogdana Carpenter and Madeline G. Levine. New York: Farrar, Straus & Giroux, 2002.

Miłosz, Czesław. *Czesława Miłosza autoportret przekorny* [Czesław Miłosz's Willful Self-Portrait]. Interviews by Aleksander Fiut. Kraków: Wydawnictwo Literackie, 1988.

Miłosz, Czesław. *Miłosz's ABC's*. Trans. Madeline G. Levine. New York: Farrar, Straus & Giroux, 2001.

Miłosz, Czesław. *Ogród nauk* [The Garden of Science]. Lublin: Norbertinum, 1991.

Miłosz, Czesław (ed.). *Postwar Polish Poetry: An Anthology*. New York: Doubleday, 1965.

Miłosz, Czesław. *A Treatise on Poetry*. Trans. by author and Robert Hass. New York: Ecco Press, 2001.

Most, Glenn W. *Doubting Thomas*. Cambridge: Harvard University Press, 2005.

Nabokov, Vladimir. "Excerpts from Memories." In *W. H. Auden: A Tribute*, edited by Stephen Spender. New York: Macmillan, 1975.

Nabokov, Vladimir. *Invitation to a Beheading*. Trans. Dmitri Nabokov. New York: Putnam's Sons, 1959.

Nancy, Jean-Luc. *Corpus.* Trans. Richard A. Rand. New York: Fordham University Press, 2008.
Nietzsche, Friedrich. *The Antichrist.* Trans. H. L. Mencken. Mineola: Dover, 2018.
Nietzsche, Friedrich. *Daybreak: Thoughts on the Prejudices of Morality* (§ 68). Trans. R. J. Hollingdale. Cambridge: Cambridge University Press, 1997.
Nietzsche, Friedrich. *The Gay Science* (aphorism no. 125). Trans. Josefine Nauckhoff. Cambridge: Cambridge University Press, 2001.
Nietzsche, Friedrich. *Joyful Wisdom.* Trans. Thomas Common. New York: F. Ungar, 1960.
Nietzsche, Friedrich. *Thus Spoke Zarathustra: A Book for Everyone and No One.* Trans. R. J. Hollingdale. London: Penguin Books, 2003.
Norwid, Cyprian Kamil. "Pascha." In *Pisma wierszem i prozą.* Warszawa: Państwowy Instytut Wydawniczy, 1970.
Nowak, Piotr. "Carl Schmitt and His Critic." In *Modernity and What Has Been Lost: Considerations on the Legacy of Leo Strauss,* edited by P. Armada. South Bend, IN: St. Augustine's Press, 2010.
Nowak, Piotr. *Ontologia sukcesu: Esej przy filozofii Alexandre'a Kojève'a* [Ontology of Success: An Essay on the Philosophy of Alexandre Kojève]. Gdańsk: słowo/obraz terytoria, 2006.
Nowak, Piotr. "United States and Europe—Their 'Elective Affinities' from the Perspective of the Trojan Ass." In *Where Europe Is Going: Leadership–Ideas–Values,* edited by H. Taborska. Pułtusk: Akademia Humanistyczna im. Aleksandra Gieysztora, 2007.
Nowosielski, Jerzy. *Mój Chrystus: Rozmowy z Jerzym Nowosielskim* [My Christ. Conversations with Jerzy Nowosielski]. Białystok: ŁUK, 1993.
Nowosielski, Jerzy. "O Judaszu i tajemnicy cierpienia" [Judas and the Mystery of Suffering]. Interview by Zbigniew Podgórzec. In *Rozmowy z Jerzym Nowosielskim* [Conversations with Jerzy Nowosielski]. Kraków: Znak, 2014.
Peterson, Erik. "Christ as *Imperator.*" In *Theological Tractates.* Trans. Michael J. Hollerich. Stanford: Stanford University Press, 2011.
Phoenix: The Posthumous Papers of D. H. Lawrence. Ed. E. D. McDonald. New York: Penguin Books, 1936.
Phoenix II: Uncollected, Unpublished and Other Prose Works by D. H. Lawrence. Ed. W. Roberts and H. T. Moore. New York: Viking Press, 1968.
Piętak, Stanisław. "Jeden z bohaterów" [One of the Heros]. In *Żołnierz, poeta, czasu kurz... Wspomnienia o K.K. Baczyńskim* [Soldier, Poet, the Dust of Time... Memories of K. K. Baczyński), edited by Zenon Wasilewski. Kraków: Wydawnictwo Literackie, 1979.
Pismo Święte Starego i Nowego Testamentu: Nowy Testament. Ed. Michał Peter and Marian Wolniewicz. Poznań: Księgarnia św. Wojciecha, 1975.
Przybyszewski, Stanisław. *The Synagogue of Satan.* Trans. Joe Bandel. Bandel Books Online, 2012. E-book.
Quinzio, Sergio. *Hebrajskie korzenie nowożytności.* Trans. Maciej Bielawski. Kraków: Homini, 2005.
Quinzio, Sergio. *Przegrana Boga.* Trans. Maciej Bielawski. Kraków: Homini, 2008.
Rilke, Rainer Maria. *The Notebooks of Malte Laurids Brigge.* Trans. Stephen Mitchell. New York: Vintage Books, 1990.
Roby, Henry John. *Roman Private Law in the Times of Cicero and of the Antonines,* vol. II. Cambridge: Cambridge University Press, 1902.
Roetzer, Florian (ed.). *Denken, das an der Zeit ist.* Frankfurt am Main: Suhrkamp, 1987.
Rosanvallon, Pierre. "Rethinking Equality in an Age of Inequalities" (Jan Patočka Memorial Lecture). *IWM Post,* no. 108 (September–December 2011).

Rosenzweig, Franz. *The Star of Redemption*. Trans. B. E. Galli. Madison: University of Wisconsin Press, 2005.
Roth, Joseph. *The Wandering Jews*. Trans. Michael Hofmann. New York: W.W. Norton, 2000.
Roth, Joseph. *Żydzi na tułaczce*. Trans. Małgorzata Łukasiewicz. Kraków-Budapeszt: Austeria, 2017.
Rozanov, Vasily. *The Apocalypse of Our Time and Other Writings*. Trans. Robert Payne and Nikita Romanoff. New York: Praeger, 1977.
Rozanov, Vasily. *Metafizika Khristianstva* [Metaphysics of Christianity]. Moscow: AST, 2000.
Rozanow, Wasilij. "Magiczna stronica u Gogola" [Gogol's Magic Page]. *Kronos*, no. 3 (2013).
Rozanow, Wasilij. "O radości przebaczania" [The Joy of Forgiving]. In *Przez śmierć* [By Death]. Trans. Piotr Nowak. Warszawa: Fundacja Augusta Hrabiego Cieszkowskiego, 2017.
Różewicz, Tadeusz. "Włosek poety" [The Hair of the Poet]. In *Uśmiechy*. Wrocław: Wydawnictwo Dolnośląskie, 2000.
Rudolph, Kurt. *Gnosis. The Nature & History of Gnosticism*. Trans. R. McL. Wilson. Edinburgh: T&T Clark, 1998.
Russell, Bertrand. *Portraits from Memory and Other Essays*. New York: Simon and Schuster, 1956.
Rymkiewicz, Jarosław M. *The Final Station. Umschlagplatz*. Trans. Nina Taylor. New York: Farrar, Strauss and Giroux, 1994.
Rymkiewicz, Jarosław Marek. *Kinderszenen*. Warszawa: Sic!, 2008.
Schelling, Friedrich Wilhelm Joseph. *The Ages of the World*. Trans. Jason M. Wirth. Albany: State University of New York Press, 2000.
Schivelbusch, Wolfgang. *The Culture of Defeat: On National Trauma, Mourning, and Recovery*. Trans. Jefferson Chase. London: Picador, 2004.
Schmitt, Carl. *The Concept of the Political*. Trans. George Schwab. Chicago: University of Chicago Press, 1996.
Schmitt, Carl. "Four Passages from Letters of Carl Schmitt to Armin Mohler." In *To Carl Schmitt: Letters and Reflections*, edited by Jacob Taubes. Trans. Keith Tribe. New York: Columbia University Press, 2013.
Schmitt, Carl. "The *Großraum* Order of International Law with a Ban on Intervention for Spatially Foreign Powers: A Contribution to the Concept of Reich in International Law (1939–1941)." In *Writings on War*. Trans. Timothy Nunan. Cambridge, MA: Polity, 2011.
Schmitt, Carl. *The Nomos of the Earth in the International Law of Jus Publicum Europaeum*. Trans. G. L. Ulmen. New York: Telos Press, 2006.
Schmitt, Carl. *The Tyranny of Values*. Trans. Simona Draghici (1959). https://www.counter-currents.com/2014/07/the-tyranny-of-values-1959/.
Schulz, Bruno. *Sanatorium under the Sign of the Hourglass*. Trans. Celina Wieniewska. New York: Walker, 1978.
Sebald, W. G. "An Attempt at Restitution. A Memory of a German City." Trans. Anthea Bell. *New Yorker* (December 20 and 27, 2004).
Sebald, W. G. *The Emigrants*. Trans. Michael Hulse. New York: New Directions, 1996.
Sebald, W. G. *On the Natural History of Destruction*. Trans. Anthea Bell. New York: Random House, 2003, e-book.
Sedakova, Olga. "Nieudana epifania: dwie chrześcijańskie powieści—*Idiota* and *Doktor Żywago*" [An Unsuccessful Epiphany: Two Christian Novels—*The Idiot* and *Doctor Zhivago*]. *Kronos*, no. 1 (2014).
Shakespeare, William. "The Merchant of Venice" (1596). In *Complete Works*. Ed. Jonathan Bate and Eric Rasmussen. London: Macmillan, 2007.
Shakespeare, William. *The Tragedy of King Lear*. New York: New American Library, 1963.

Simic, Charles. "Conspiracy of Silence." *New York Review of Books* (February 27, 2003).
Słonimski, Antoni. "Elegy of Jewish Towns." In *Stranger in Our Midst: Images of the Jew in Polish Literature*, edited by Harold B. Segel. Ithaca, NY: Cornell University Press, 1996.
Słonimski, Antoni. *Gwałt na Melpomenie*. Warszawa: Wydawnictwa Artystyczne i Filmowe, 1982.
Snyder, Timothy. *Bloodlands: Europe between Hitler and Stalin*. New York: Basic Books, 2010.
Stern, James. "The Indispensable Presence." In *W. H. Auden: A Tribute*, edited by Stephen Spender. New York: Macmillan, 1975.
Stirling, Brents. "Introduction." In *William Shakespeare's The Merchant of Venice*. Ed. Brents Stirling. Baltimore, MD: Penguin, 1959.
Strand, Mark. "Error." In *Man and Camel*. New York: Alfred A. Knopf, 2006.
Szymborska, Wisława. "Atlantis." In *Poems New and Collected*. Trans. Stanisław Barańczak and Clare Cavanagh. San Diego: Harcourt, 1998.
Taubes, Jacob. "Carl Schmitt: Apocalyptic Prophet of the Counterrevolution." In *To Carl Schmitt: Letters and Reflections*. Trans. Keith Tribe. New York: Columbia University Press, 2013.
Taubes, Jacob. "Das stählerne Gehäuse und der Exodus daraus oder Ein Streit um Marcion, einst und jetzt." In *Vom Kult zur Kultur: Bausteine zu einer Kritik der historischen Vernunft: Gesammelte Aufsätze zur Religions- und Geistesgeschichte*. München: Wilhelm Fink Verlag, 1996.
Taubes, Jacob. *Occidental Eschatology*. Trans. David Ratmoko. Stanford: Stanford University Press, 2009.
Taubes, Jacob. *The Political Theology of Paul*. Trans. Dana Hollander. Stanford, CA: Stanford University Press, 2004.
Taubes, Susan. *Divorcing*. New York: Random House, 1969.
Teksty Drugie / Second Texts, Special Issue English Edition, vol. 1 ("Czesław Miłosz and Polish School of Poetry," 2012).
Terpstra, M. "'God's Love for His Enemies': Jacob Taubes' Conversation with Carl Schmitt on Paul." *International Journal in Philosophy and Theology* 70 (2009).
Tolstoy, Leo. *The Complete Works of Count Tolstoy: War and Peace*. Trans. Leo Wiener. New York: AMS Press, 1968.
Topornicki, Karol [real name Tadeusz Gajcy]. "Poezja o nucie dostojnej" [A Dignified Poetry]. *Sztuka i Naród*, no. 5 (1942).
Tourgueneff, Ivan. "Christ." In *Poems in Prose*. Boston: Cupples, Upham, 1883.
Trznadel, Jacek. *Hańba domowa: Rozmowy z pisarzami* [Home Shame. Conversations with Writers]. Paryż: Instytut Literacki, 1986.
Tuwim, Julian. "The Locomotive." Trans. Walter Whipple. http://allpoetry.com/poem/8537691-The-Locomotive-by-Julian-Tuwim.
Vallejo, César. "No One Lives in the House Anymore…" In *The Complete Posthumous Poetry*. Trans. Clayton Eshleman and J. R. Barcia. Berkeley: University of California Press, 1980.
Vonnegut, Kurt. *Slaughterhouse-Five or the Children's Crusade: A Duty-Dance with Death*. New York: Delacorte Press, 1969.
Wilson, Reul K. "Review of *Postwar Polish Poetry*." *World Literature Today* 58, no. 2 (1984).
Wittgenstein, Ludwig. *Tractatus Logico-Philosophicus*. Trans. Charles Kay Ogden. New York: Harcourt, Brace, 1922.
Woroszylski, Wiktor. "Lustro" [Mirror]. In *Lustro; Dziennik internowania; Tutaj*. Londyn: Aneks, 1984.

"Wywiady z pisarzami pochodzenia żydowskiego. Rozmowa z Julianem Tuwimem" [Interviews with Writers of Jewish Origin. A Conversation with Julian Tuwim]. *Dziennik Warszawski* (February 6–7, 1927).

Zabierowski, Stefan. "Legendotwórczy charakter biografii Krzysztofa Kamila Baczyńskiego" [The Legendary Nature of Krzysztof Kamil Baczyński's Biography]. *Prace Polonistyczne* XLIII (1987).

Zagórski, Jerzy. "Śmierć Słowackiego" [Słowacki's Death]. In *Żołnierz, poeta, czasu kurz… Wspomnienia o K.K. Baczyńskim* [Soldier, Poet, the Dust of Time… Memories of K. K. Baczyński), edited by Zenon Wasilewski. Kraków: Wydawnictwo Literackie, 1979.

Zwolska Sell, Jadwiga. "Review." *Polish Review* 10, no. 3 (1965).

INDEX OF PERSONS

Abraham 2, 8, 29
Acosta, Uriel 30–32
Adam 5
Adonis 55
Adorno, Theodor W. x–xi, 184–85
Agamben, Giorgio 173–75, 177–81, 183–87, 189–90, 195–200, 205
Ahab (*Moby Dick*) 61
Aldington, Richard 37, 39
Aleichem, Sholem 29
Alexander, the Great 46
Améry, Jean 99–108, 116–17, 185
Andruszkiewicz, Marta 36
Anselm, St. 201
Antonello, Pierpaolo 5, 18
Antonio (*The Merchant of Venice*) 27–28, 33–34
Arendt, Hannah 27, 33, 64, 101, 112, 129, 173–74, 178–80, 184
Aristarchus of Samos 77
Aristotle 199
Atwood, Margaret 41
Auden, W. H. 26, 28, 33–34, 112, 121
Augustine, St. 4, 7

Baal Shem Tov of Medzhybizh 83
Babich, Babette 64, 68–69
Bach, Johann Sebastian 99
Bachmann, Ingeborg 69
Baczyńska, Stefania 128
Baczyński, Krzysztof Kamil (pen name Jan Bugaj) xi, 123–25, 127–31, 140
Baczyński, Stanisław 125
Badiou, Alain 10, 70, 197
Balmont, Konstantin 191, 193, 195, 201
Balthasar, Hans Urs von 64
Balzac, Honoré de 61

Bar Kokhba 75
Barth, Karl 63
Bassanio (*The Merchant of Venice*) 26–28, 34–35
Baubo 157
Bauman, Zygmunt 185, 187
Beckett, Samuel 138
Benjamin, Walter 14, 64, 173, 184, 194
Benn, Gottfried 99, 120
Bergman, Hugo 64, 67–68
Bernhard, Thomas xii
Besançon, Alain xi, 185
Białoszewski, Miron 137
Blavatsky, Helena 55
Bloom, Allan 25, 28, 32–33
Böll, Heinrich 116
Bonald, Louis Gabriel Ambroise de 68
Borowski, Tadeusz 115, 125, 135
Brentano, Margherita von 69
Brzękowski, Jan 139
Brzozowski, Stanisław 125
Buber, Martin 14, 67–68, 76
Bugaj, Jan. *See* Baczyński, Krzysztof Kamil
Burckhardt, Jacob 116
Burgess, Anthony 48, 52–53, 60
Bytnar, Jan ("Rudy") 126

Carter, Frederick 41–42, 55–56
Castro Rocha, João Cezar de 5, 18
Cavafy, C. P. 51–52
Céline, Louis-Ferdinand 110
Cézanne, Paul 61
Char, René 157
Charon 158
Christ. *See* Jesus Christ
Cincinnatus C. (*Invitation to a Beheading*) 173
Cioran, Emil 3, 34

Cohen, Geulah 64–65, 67–68
Connolly, the navigator 109
Copernicus, Nicolaus 77
Coriolanus 36
Cyrus 46
Czaykowski, Bogdan 135, 137
Czechowicz, Józef 129, 140–41
Czerniawski, Adam 139
Czerwiński, Marcin 130

Dale Scott, Peter 136
Danto, Arthur C. 160
David 77
Davis, Lawrence 136
Dawidowski, Maciej Aleksy ("Alek") 126
Debord, Guy 173
Deleuze, Gilles 42, 44–45, 48–49, 61
Descartes, René 32, 66
Deutch, Babette 140
Diné, Daniel 105
Dionysus 55
Döblin, Alfred vii–viii, x
Domenach, Jean-Marie 121
Don Juan 69, 154
Donne, John 152
Donoso Cortés, Juan 68
Dostoevsky, Fyodor 59, 61, 134
Dziekański, Robert 183

Earl of Gloucester (*King Lear*) 149–51
Edgar (*King Lear*) 149–51
Ehrlich, Ernst Ludwig 10
Eichmann, Adolf 95, 101, 113
Epictetus 145
Esau 9
Ezra (*Divorcing*) 68

Fedorov, Nikolai 194
Festus, Sextus Pompeius 175
Fichte, Johann Gottlieb 128
Fiedler, Arkady 171
Fiut, Aleksander 134
Flanner, Janet 110
Ford, Ford Madox 38
Foucault, Paul Michel 173–74
Four Winds 169
Franklin, Ruth 117
Frazer, James George 54

Freud, Sigmund 18, 54, 121–22
Frobenius, Ferdinand Georg 54
Fučík, Julius 89

Gadamer, Hans-Georg 68
Gajcy, Tadeusz (pen name Karol Topornicki) 129
Galilei, Galileo 49
Gamaliel 8
Garnett, Edward 38
Gawin, Darek 161–62
Gibbon, Edward 120
Gide, André 164
Giedroyc, Jerzy 134–35, 137, 139, 141
Gierek, Edward 125
Gilbert, Barry 161
Girard, René x, 5, 17–23, 35
Goebbels, Joseph 12, 66
Goethe, Christiana von 38
Goethe, Johann Wolfgang von 38
Gogol, Nikolai 157
Gold, J. R. 72–74, 76
Goldberg, Oskar 78
Gombrowicz, Witold 41, 101, 115, 157–60
Goodman, Mac 136
Gorecki, J. (real name Aleksander Kamiński) 126
Grand Inquisitor 56–57, 61
Greim, Robert von 111
Grochowiak, Stanisław 138
Guattari, Felix 61

Hadrian 76
Harnack, Adolf von 75–76
Harris, Arthur 111
Hegel, Georg Wilhelm Friedrich 149, 193
Heidegger, Martin 17, 29, 66, 144–45, 151, 156, 160, 168, 197, 201–5
Heine, Heinrich 87, 97
Henriquez, Mitch 184
Henry IV, King of England 34
Herakleitos 54
Herbert, Zbigniew 136–37
Herder, Johann Gottfried von 129
Hesiod 55
Hitler, Adolf 60, 66, 110, 118
Hobbes, Thomas 9, 22, 28
Hoffman, Paweł 86

INDEX OF PERSONS

Hölderlin, Johann Christian Friedrich 100
Horkheimer, Max x, 185
Hortmann, Wilhelm 27
Hotspur (*Henry IV, Part1*) 144
Huxley, Aldous 39

Inge, William Ralph 55
Isaac 64, 170
Iucundus, Lucius Caecilius 36
Iwaszkiewicz, Jarosław 125, 128–29, 135

Jacob 9
Jaffa, Harry V. 25, 28, 32–33
Jankélévitch, Vladimir 104–5
Jankowski, Dzidek (real first name Henryk) 162
Jaspers, Karl 13
Jastrun, Mieczysław 136
Jerome, St. 4
Jessica (*The Merchant of Venice*) 33
Jesus Christ 2, 4–7, 10–15, 19–21, 43–47, 57–58, 61, 71, 73–75, 144, 153, 158, 186, 197–200, 202, 204–5
Job 192
John of Patmos 43, 45–48, 55, 57, 61
John, the Evangelist, St. 43, 54
Johnson, Paul 4
Jonas, Hans 84, 185, 192–93
Judas Iscariot 44
Jünger, Ernst 63

Kafka, Franz 34, 166, 179, 199
Kalnins, Mara 41–42, 54, 56, 59
Kamieńska, Anna 130
Kant, Immanuel 49–50, 69, 118, 163
Karamazov Ivan 203
Keble, J. 37
Kirkoff, Milica 139
Kluge, Alexander 115
Kmita-Piorunowa, Aniela 124
Kojève, Alexandre 72, 205
Kołakowski, Leszek 8–9, 30, 105
König, Franz 10, 162
Koselleck, Reinhart 121
Kot (real name Konstanty Aleksander Jeleński) 139
Koteliansky, Samuel Solomonovich (pen name Kot) 56

Kozioł, Urszula 135
Kronos, 49
Kundera, Milan 60

Lafcadio (*The Vatican Cellars*) 164
Larkin, Philip 40
Lawrence, David Herbert x, 37–61
Lear, Jonathan 165–68, 170–71
Lear, King of Britain 149, 151
Lebovic, Nitzan 64–65, 68
Ledig, Gert 115
Lennon, John 20
Leśmian, Bolesław 153–54
Levi, Ben 63
Levi, Primo x, 93–97, 115, 189
Levinas, Emmanuel 152
Liiceanu, Gabriel 11
Linderman, Frank B. 165
Longfellow, H. W. 63
Lourie, Richard 136
Lustiger, Jean-Marie 11
Luther, Martin 182

Macbeth 61
Mackiewicz, Józef 91–93
Mansfield, Katherine 39
Marcel, Gabriel 108
Marcion 75–76, 78
Marcuse, Herbert 185
McCarthy, Mary 136
Meillassoux, Quentin 193–95, 205
Mentzel, Zbigniew 105
Merton, Thomas 135–36
Michalski, Krzysztof 143, 145–46, 148–49, 152–54, 156–64
Mickiewicz, Adam 171
Miłosz, Czesław 118, 128–29, 133–41
Mohler, Armin 63, 66, 78
Mombert, Alfred 105
Moses 12, 14, 27, 64, 70
Most, Glenn W. 202
Murray, Gilbert 55
Murry, John Middleton 39, 53

Nabokov, Vladimir 112, 173
Nancy, Jean-Luc 6
Nemesis 34
Nero 1

INDEX OF PERSONS

Nietzsche, Friedrich x, 9–10, 12–13, 22, 44, 48, 59, 143, 145–46, 149, 151, 155, 157, 160, 162–63, 165, 199, 201, 204–5
Noica, Constantin 11
Norwid, Cyprian Kamil 17, 129–30
Nossack, Hans Erich 115
Nowak, Piotr 185
Nowosielski, Jerzy 44, 185

Oman, John 41
Osiris 55
Overbeck, Franz 75

Pascal, Blaise 147
Paul of Tarsus, St. (Saul) x, 1–3, 5–14, 48, 64, 70–71, 73, 75, 189, 196–97, 199, 202–4
Pawlik, Robert 47
Pelagius 4–5
Pericles 174
Peter, St. 2
Peterson, Erik 46
Piętak, Stanisław 130–31
Pigoń, Stanisław 124
Piłsudski, Józef 171
Pius IX 68
Plato 4, 6, 54, 59–60, 167, 169
Plenty Coups 165–67, 169–71
Plotinus 55
Plutarch 55
Poe, Edgar Allan 23
Pompey 46
Portia (*The Merchant of Venice*) 34–35
Preen, Friedrich von 116
Przybyszewski, Stanisław 54, 125
Pseudo-Dionysius 158

Quintylian 36
Quinzio, Sergio 4, 32, 81, 84, 192, 205

Rafik, Y. 184
Rawls, John Bordley 28
Ricoeur, Paul 162
Rilke, Rainer Maria 100, 123–24, 154
Roby, Henry John 36
Rosanvallon, Pierre 163
Rosen, Pinchas (formerly Rosenblüth) 66
Rosenzweig, Franz 77

Roth, Joseph x, 81–90, 93–95, 97
Rozanov, Vasily (Rozanow, Wasilij) 43, 48, 56, 84, 191, 201–2, 205
Różewicz, Tadeusz 123–24, 135, 138, 152
Rudolph, Kurt 75
Russell, Bertrand 39, 59–60
Rymkiewicz, Jarosław Marek 111, 185, 188

Sabbatai Zevi 74
Sarah 8
Sartre, Jean-Paul 144
Saul. *See* Paul of Tarsus
Schelling, Friedrich Wilhelm Joseph 193, 195
Schivelbusch, Wolfgang 119–21
Schmitt, Carl viii, 64–68, 71, 79, 112–13, 165, 173, 186, 205
Scholem, Gershom 64
Schönberg, Arnold 106
Schulz, Bruno 79
Scottie, the flight engineer 109
Sebald, W. G. 60, 101–2, 106–7, 109–15, 117–19, 189
Sedakova, Olga 61
Shakespeare, William x, 25–27, 29, 33–36, 112, 134, 151
Shylock (*The Merchant of Venice*) 26–33, 35–36
Simic, Charles 112–13
Sitting Bull 170
Škirpa, Kazys 91
Słonimski, Antoni 32–33, 97, 135–36
Słowacki, Euzebiusz 125
Słowacki, Juliusz 124–25, 129
Snyder, Timothy 91, 93
Socrates 44, 153, 159
Solomon 77
Sophie (*Divorcing*) 68
Sparky, the bombardier 109
Spengler, Oswald 120
Stachura, Edward 125
Staff, Leopold 137–38
Stahl, Georg Ernst 50
Stalin, Joseph 130
Stanislaus II Augustus, King of Poland 86
Staś (*The Final Station*) 187
Stein, Charlotte von 38
Stendhal, Krister 12

INDEX OF PERSONS

Stern, James 112
Stern, Tania 112
Stirling, Brents 29, 33
Stirlitz (*Seventeen Moments of Spring*) 116
Strand, Mark 113
Strauss, Leo 64
Sullivan, Maureen 140
Szenwald, Lucjan 140
Szymborska, Wisława 109

Taubes, Jacob x, 2, 9–12, 14, 63–76, 78–79
Taubes, Susan (*primo voto* Feldman) 68–69
Terpstra, M. 78
Tevye, the Dairyman 29–31
Thomas, the Apostle 6
Thunders 169
Tillich, Paul 64
Tischner, Józef 162
Tocqueville, Alexis de 59
Tolstoy, Leo 88, 134
Torricelli, Evangelista 49
Tourgueneff, Ivan 158
Trzebiński, Andrzej 140–41
Trznadel, Jacek 130
Tsvetaeva, Marina 123
Tuwim, Julian 83, 156
Two Leggings 168

Vallega, Alejandro 162
Vallejo, César 74

Vaughan-Thomas, Wynford 109
Vonnegut, Kurt 114
Vujičić, Peter 139–40

Wat, Aleksander 134–35, 137, 141
Weekley, Ernest 39
Weekley, Frieda (née: von Richthofen) 38–39, 41
Wierzyński, Kazimierz 135
William (*Sons and Lovers*) 38
Wilson, Reuel K. 136, 139
Witkacy 125, 149
Wittgenstein, Ludwig 76, 143
Wojaczek, Rafał 125
Wolniewicz, Bogusław 162
Woolf, Leonard 56
Woolf, Virginia 56
Wordsworth, William 61
Woroszylski, Wiktor 103
Wyka, Kazimierz 129–30

Zabierowski, Stefan 124, 130
Zadek, Peter 27
Zagórski, Jerzy 124–26
Zarathustra 44, 143
Zawadzki, Tadeusz ("Zośka") 126
Zbytkower, Szmul Jakubowicz 86
Zieleńczyk, Adam 128
Zweig, Stefan 90
Zwolska Sell, Jadwiga 140

www.ingramcontent.com/pod-product-compliance
Lightning Source LLC
Chambersburg PA
CBHW021140230426
43667CB00005B/198